NIETZSCHE

GW00496613

NIETZSCHE

A FRENZIED LOOK

Robert John Ackermann

The University of Massachusetts Press

AMHERST

Copyright © 1990 by
The University of Massachusetts Press
All rights reserved
Printed in the United States of America
LC 90–31323
ISBN 0–87023–722–5 (cloth); 841–8 (paper)
Set in Sabon by Keystone Typesetting, Inc.
Printed and bound by Thomson Shore

Library of Congress Cataloging-in-Publication Data
Ackermann, Robert John, 1933–
Nietzsche : a frenzied look / Robert John Ackermann.
        p.   cm.
Includes bibliographical references.
ISBN 0–87023–722–5 (alk. paper)
ISBN 0–87023–841–8 (pbk.: alk. paper)
    1. Nietzsche, Friedrich Wilhelm, 1844–1900.
            I. Title.
    B3317.A25   1990   90–31323
    193—dc20   CIP

British Library Cataloguing in Publication data are available.

Quello però che davvero affascinava il dottore in ascolto, lo psichiatra Anselmo, era la lucidità della musica, un vero discorso, un eloquio proveniente dal senno e che per di più toccava il cuore; una musica che arrivava a spiegare le sfumature, il passaggio di sottili sentimenti, una bandiera di seta al sole, un damasco esposto al tramonto.

"Che stia spiegando il suo segreto? La storia della sua anima?" si domandò Anselmo. "Che ora stia aggiungendo, con piangente eloquenza: 'Perché, perché non mi capite?'"

—MARIO TOBINO

Contents

Preface

Nietzsche scholarship is often restricted to readings of single passages from his texts. The poetry, the prophecy, and the aphorisms seem to justify these disjointed points of view because of their apparently irreconcilable stylistic differences, but original thought grows like a biological organism, and it may molt or pass through stages while not altering a deeper identity. I try to give Nietzsche back the body of his thought, the body that unifies his work. I try to show how Nietzsche's thoughts develop and ramify from his early, concentrated vision of Greece before Socrates, a vision that Nietzsche never abandons and a vision that is the source of his shocking new tables of values. This structure makes the entire corpus coherent. My hope is that this skeletal reconstruction will bring the coherence of Nietzsche's thought into prominence. Nietzsche was more consistent than most of us, not less so, and this is quite compatible with his having been judged mad by everyday standards. When we seem on the edge of terminating human life, it's grotesque to point a finger at Nietzsche's Dionysian insights as though they were crazy by comparison to our own.

In Nietzsche's vision, Greek noble life before Socrates and Euripides, involving an awareness of Dionysian chaos through tragedy, was moving, profound, and superior to the superficial scientific optimism of modernity. It could be recovered in an age of nihilistic vacuity. Nietzsche's developmental trajectory depends on a slow philosophical maturation of his early conception of Greek noble life. Dionysian process is ultimately expressed in the clarified philosophical vision of the will to power, and the psychology of the noble is ultimately expressed in the clarified philosophical vision of the Eternal Return. The two major philosophical themes of

Nietzsche's mature philosophy are thus firmly rooted in Nietzsche's original vision. Further, Nietzsche's views of the structure of a good society, the place of women within it, as well as almost all of his mature views, are already present in his conception of early Greek society, a conception totally at odds with modern assumptions about social equality. Nietzsche is still shocking, as he meant to be, and his social vision, which provides a sharp challenge to other visions, is worth the effort to think through.

The frenzy in my treatment is designed to avoid placing Nietzsche on the bench of logical analysis in a manner that won't allow him any movement. Nietzsche forces intelligent confrontation in close readers, but the confrontation doesn't require ponderous scholarship. Nietzsche danced when he wrote, carrying an enormous personal scholarship with graceful ease. When one attempts to supply complete footnotes or to study the exact structure of his arguments, an inappropriate hermeneutical policy is invoked. The first reliable critical edition of Nietzsche's work has only recently become available in the edition of Colli and Montinari. I try to cite texts so that the reader can locate references easily in a variety of editions, any of which might be readily available. Although Nietzsche was always careful about the details of his texts, reaction to his views does not typically demand close textual accuracy so much as it demands concentrated reaction. In many cases, the variety of interpretations swamps the literal meaning of exact text with productive insights, and we will concentrate on active interpretation. Nietzsche thought that one shouldn't know more than one can digest and, in discussing older texts, he was an active interpreter of past authors, often relying on a few key citations to build his interpretations. A somewhat frenzied, paratactic look at Nietzsche seems in conformity with his own evaluations of others, and there are plenty of hints in his writing that he was looking for readers who would read as he did, by finding significance for contemporary life. I have tried to sketch Nietzsche in movement rather than attempt a postmortem examination. This does not comport with most contemporary philosophical exposition of past masters, but it seems especially apt in Nietzsche's case. If we can't approach Nietzsche this way, perhaps we can't approach him at all.

My reading of Nietzsche is personal, as should be yours. There are philosophers, and Wittgenstein and Kierkegaard are examples, who think that philosophical problems depend on the concrete situational placement of the individual philosopher. (By comparison, Plato, Aristotle, Descartes, Kant, and Hegel seem to have held that we all have the same philosophical problems.) Nietzsche's personal perspectivism raises expository problems. To work through Nietzsche in *our* locations means finding much of his personal baggage irrelevant. For example, his personal struggle with Wagner and the significance of Wagner's music, a struggle that follows a complicated and twisting path, is probably not very relevant to someone placed in the late twentieth century, for whom Wagner is but one of many past classical composers. The effort to find an intellectual reconstruction of the relationship between Nietzsche and Wagner does not speak to most of us at present with any existential force. I have tried to prise off the aspects of Nietzsche's thought most relevant to the rhythm of a contemporary engagement. Thus I am concerned not so much with what Nietzsche was saying about himself as with what he may have to say in the late twentieth century to his readers, or rather, what his texts may provoke in their readers. Other personal readings have emphasized an existential, self-development strain in Nietzsche's writings. Feminists and left-wing guerrillas have taken Nietzsche as a philosophical lodestar urging self-development as an expression of will to power. My reading is constrained by the observation that Nietzsche evaluated cultures, nations, and epochs in terms of their "highest" products, an evaluation that allows the misery of many not to be entered into the ledger, but one that counts only the items of greatest value. This seems to me to be wrong: and hence I am not a Nietzschean. Nietzsche remains a great philosopher because he is consistently disturbing, and perhaps most disturbing when he challenges others to prove that there are errors in his valuations. What he offers is a series of alternatives to solid ideological prejudices. It is not always easy to defend prejudice.

My classroom Nietzschean frenzies have been sobered by deflating criticisms from Frank Delaere, Cheryl Hughes, Alex Pienknagura, and Alan Schiffman. In addition to my gratitude for this help, I would like to acknowledge the friendship of Robert Paul Wolff, my competent lifeline to professional sanity, who was instrumental in developing background reflections concerning the philosophical significance of Marx and Freud. Leo Weinstein of Smith College gave the first draft a critical and penetrating examination and was willing to share with me his extraordinary insights into Nietzsche's texts. I am grateful to Provost Samuel F. Conti and the selectors involved for my year as a Faculty Fellow at the University of Massachusetts, providing the release time for the completion of this work.

Amherst, Massachusetts
June 1989

NIETZSCHE

Introduction

Friedrich Nietzsche, who was born in 1844 and died in 1900, is a philosopher whose productive career spanned about twenty years, followed by a final decade of silence. His productive decades were scarred by a variety of personal difficulties and physical ailments.[1] From 1869 to 1879 Nietzsche was professor of classical philology at Basel, having obtained his chair at an extremely early age on the basis of his promise as a philologist.[2] This period is marked by the publication of *The Birth of Tragedy*, a bold and philosophical treatment of Greek tragedy and its relationship to music whose daring and eccentricity, reflected in negative reviews, cost Nietzsche his career as a serious philologist. Nietzsche had published *The Untimely Meditations* and had begun to write books of aphorisms when he resigned his chair at Basel in 1879. His complex personal relationship with the composer Richard Wagner also began in the period when he was a professor at Basel. For the next decade, from 1879 to 1889, Nietzsche traveled and wrote, supported by a modest pension. This was a most productive period for him. *The Gay Science, Thus Spake Zarathustra, Beyond Good and Evil,* and *On the Genealogy of Morals,* as well as several other important titles, were published in this decade. Nietzsche's books were not well received nor widely read at the time of their original publication. In 1889, Nietzsche was thought by others to be mad, and he spent the last years of his life under institutional care, supervised by relatives and friends. During this period, it is not known that he spoke to anyone. His last public act was to embrace a draught horse that had just been severely beaten by its master. Nietzsche left extensive notes and drafts, versions of which have been collated by a series of editors into a

3

version of a book sometimes called *The Will to Power,* and the relationship of the unpublished to the published works constitutes a major interpretive problem. Nietzsche's is an outsider's biography, probably the most outside biography in the recognized mainstream of philosophy. Nietzsche's fame has been no doubt nourished by the existential price he paid for the expression of his thought.

Nietzsche's works are permeated with a knowledge of ancient Greek and Roman authors, as well as with an extensive knowledge of German literature, French literature, and the Bible. They are much more aphoristic and poetical than the works of other mainstream philosophers. For example, in *Thus Spake Zarathustra,* many of the lines contain allusions to Goethe's *Faust* or are parodies of lines from *Faust,* a fact that only a reader familiar with *Faust* in the original German, who was reading Nietzsche in German, could notice. Again, some of Nietzsche's observations depend on the sound of the German language. When Nietzsche observes in "Of the Virtues" (Part 2 of *Zarathustra*) that the word *just* sounds like *revenged* in the mouths of the virtuous, a claim that seems baffling in the English translation, he is relying on the fact that *gerecht (just)* sounds like *gerächt (revenged)* in German. It is nonetheless possible to approach Nietzsche's texts in a reasonable manner in translation.

According to the interpretation of Nietzsche to be offered here, Nietzsche's philosophy grows out of his early philological studies of the Greeks. His first transvaluation was that the standard European valuation of the Greeks could be completely changed. If the standard valuation depends on an Athenian golden age, preceded by preparation and followed by decay, and if that age is intrinsically linked to the philosophies of Socrates and Plato, then Nietzsche revalues by finding an earlier golden age in which Greek nobles had lived a completely different style of life that was degraded in the Athenian developments. Since little is known of these early Greek nobles, Nietzsche presents an artistic vision of what they might have been like, but he argues that such artistic visions are all that we can have in the way of assurances; the standard picture of Athenian greatness is also an artistic vision. Nietzsche's view of Athenian origins is not negative: it is the continued privileging of Athenian values that he wishes to challenge. Put roughly, Nietzsche believed that the European culture involving the standard valuation of the Greeks, a European culture that had once been powerful and progressive, had played itself out in his time, and that continued adherence to the values embedded in European history was now reactive and even deadly. New values and a new culture were necessary, and Nietzsche tried to locate such values in a philosophical reworking of his vision of early Greece.

Most of the major philosophers have been critics of their surroundings, but Nietzsche was a particularly virulent critic of his surroundings. He was not after revision but after liquidation. In bald summary, he considered the entire majority cultural tradition from Socrates to his time to have rested on values that unified and supported a logical and rational approach to knowledge as the acquisition of facts, as well as on a morality of calculation and retribution that was articulated in a synthesis of Greek and Christian ideas. Much of his writing is given over to isolating and attacking the value table underlying this cultural system, a system that had become completely rigid and life threatening by the nineteenth century. In agreement with many other philosophers, Nietzsche saw this system as embodying a set of dubious metaphysical principles. Where other philosophers have tried to alter or to negate these principles, Nietzsche wanted to root them out and start over again in a novel way. In this sense, Nietzsche's criticisms of his surroundings are intended to cut deeper than those of other nineteenth-century critics of prevailing metaphysical ideas. For example, Nietzsche did not try to save or purify the science of his time as a basis for a new social system, nor did he try to return to some set of religious values drawn from the post-Socratic epoch. Nietzsche saw himself surrounded by a played out nihilism, a total exhaustion of values that could not be restored. This nihilism doomed to extinction the age of humanity that had begun with the Socratic transformation of Hellenic values and that had developed into modern science.

New values and new forms of life were required, but Nietzsche's perspective on nihilism was derived from his reading of the pre-Socratic Greeks, and Nietzsche also knew that an exact return to the early Greek values was impossible. Christianity and science, in their nineteenth-century versions, depended on views of causation and time that permitted calculations of the past and future that could apparently assess the effects of the past on the present and could eliminate unwanted effects in the future. This was the basis for a silly science optimism. Nietzsche thought that the early Greeks had lived in full recognition of the fact that the universe was too unpredictable to allow for rational scientific planning and that one had to live in the moment, without the conceit of being able to accurately predict the future. But whereas the early Greeks had simply lived in tune with a different conception of the universe and had never completely worked out a self-consciously unified culture, a modern restoration of such a style of living had to be undertaken in recognition of the intervening era of science and humanity. Nietzsche, in short, needed to urge a value table like that of the early Greeks (as he conceived of them), but a value table that could be presented as a serious alternative to the value tables of nineteenth-century science and Christianity. Nietzsche's doctrines of will to power and the Eternal Return represent the philosophically purified value table of the early Greeks, a set of values that could be adopted now to transform life and to initiate a new culture, one that was powerful and life enhancing.

We have, in a sense, two Nietzsches to deal with, and pressing terminological problems. The first Nietzsche is content to attack the prevailing value tables of his time (and ours, since those values are still discernible), and the other Nietzsche is trying to produce progressive new value tables. The two Nietzsches are related, and both are essential to understanding the range of Nietzsche's writings, but the first Nietzsche could devastate value tables without the second Nietzsche succeeding in replacing the broken tables with new ones. Nietzsche did think it obvious that there is only one world, the one that we live in, pulsing with power, life, change, and decay. Humans have always created devices, linguistic, artistic, scientific, to deal with the world, devices that attempt intellectual stasis and attempt to arrest change by artificially creating identities over time. There is nothing intrinsically wrong with that, since humans must do so to create the cultural wombs in which they can tolerate existence. What *is* wrong is to make the artificial devices the test of life, rather than allowing life to test the devices. Nietzsche thought he could consider historical sequences, genealogies, by utilizing philological methods to study textual records of the past and that these genealogies could show how nihilism had arisen out of regressive valuations. This strategy of critique does not depend on his vision of the early Greeks. At the same time, the second Nietzsche uses his vision of early Greece to provide an alternative to the values embodied in post-Socratic science, art, history, morality, social and economic arrangements, and so on. Some of this is done before the philosophical table dependent on conceptions of will to power and the Eternal Return is in place. The second Nietzsche wants to root out the prevailing value table but he wants to put another in its place, one that is slow to develop and difficult to articulate. It is hard to read the second Nietzsche as though he isn't also a philosopher and metaphysician, even though he finds the received form of metaphysics to be repulsive.

Terminological problems press in on us in recognizing the two Nietzsches. There are Greeks and Greeks, the Greeks of the tradition, and the

Greeks of Nietzsche's revaluation. We will call the Greeks of Nietzsche's vision, the pre-Socratic Greek nobles in touch with Dionysian process, *Hellenes,* in order to mark this conceptual difference. There are also humans and humans, the Hellenes, the humans under the table of rationality stretching from Socrates to Nietzsche, and the new humans that would exist if Nietzsche's transvaluation of values were to become the basis of a new unified culture. Nietzsche at times apparently uses the term *Übermensch* to refer to those that would exist under the new valuation, or at least to refer to a kind of mythical "ideal type" anticipating those who would so live. This is a term that explicitly carries a connotation that such creatures would be superior to humans, or in some sense beyond them. There is no fluent English term available for translation of Übermensch, and so we will reluctantly use the German term, using *human* and *humanity* to refer to those living within the metaphysical table stretching from Socrates to Nietzsche. The Übermenschen, like the Hellenes, would have bodies grossly similar to those of humans, but they would presumably move, think, act, feel quite differently, if Nietzsche is correct.

Let's look at Nietzsche briefly from the standpoint of polemics and style. One can confront existing philosophical systems in two ways. The standard way is to confront a system with another system, that is, to rebut a system piece by piece, and to pose a new system supposedly demonstrably superior to the old system. Major philosophers in our tradition usually work in this fashion, through the patient rebuttal of previous views, and sometimes by constructing new, more comprehensive systems. Nietzsche's approach, nomad thought, consists of firing off a few critical arrows, hoping to hit a vital weak point in the system under attack. In the siege of a great walled city, to use a military metaphor, there are two workable strategies.[3] One is the method of brute force, system against system. An army is displayed before the walls, engines of destruction are employed, and the forces of the city are to be ground down under the constant pressure of the forces marshalled against them. It can work. The other method is to arrive unexpectedly and to fire a few arrows randomly into the city, and it might also work, especially from Nietzsche's perspective. If the defense of the city depends on the genius of one leader, a not implausible idea for Nietzsche, a random and unexpected arrow might just kill that one vital figure, subjecting the city to decay from within due to chaos in the wake of the loss of effective leadership. Nietzsche's method is just that, to fire off a few arrows in a sudden raid. He doesn't stay long before any one massive target, and he doesn't pause to assess the full consequences of his onslaught. For example, just one arrow, fired at Hegel.

Nietzsche observes that Hegel's notion of the overcoming servant in the master-slave dialectic is a final secular version of Christian preference for the weak and that Hegel's supposed argumentation is based on verbal and abstract moves that develop this prejudice, rather than grounding it. Why shouldn't this dialectic be written from the standpoint of the master? This is a poisonous little arrow that can seek out a vital spot in someone's Christianity, Hegelianism, or even Marxism. It's at the very least an annoying matter to think about and to attempt to rule out of court. The view to be defended here is that Nietzsche's importance lies directly in the sudden and explosive quality of these attacks, in the sudden pain of an arrow in a tender place. He simply does not fit smoothly into the philosophical tradition.

Nietzsche's attacks on philosophy, religion, and culture are developed in metaphors of the release of weight, of the sudden feeling of lightness and the ability to dance brought about by casting off the past. In attack, as we have noted, Nietzsche is content typically with a few barbs, an arrow or two. Typically, he makes no blanket judgments of other philosophers, but attempts to reduce particular doctrines to absurdity, to trace their roots to a dubious scale of values. At times, he even has good things to say about some of his targets, such as Christianity, as when he notes that the Christian doctrine of sin is "deeper" than post-Socratic scientific optimism. This scattered style is required for consistency with his objections to abstraction, since he will not fight abstractions with abstractions where he can avoid doing so.

Nietzsche knows that he is trapped in human language, a language deeply interwoven with dubious metaphysical assumptions, and that he must use its terms to attempt communication. He attempts, by indirection, to break the hold of this language while using it. He was too conscious a stylist to suppose that he could progress by inventing new language, as new language would still lie in the shadow of the old conceptual schemes. He was trying to gesture at ideas that could not be laid out in assertive language. Over a period of time, Nietzsche experimented with the aphorism and with various kinds of poetry as stylistic devices designed to liberate thought from the stranglehold of everyday concepts while not cutting ties to the resources of available language. He expected to appear as a buffoon to humans, and sometimes he encouraged that perception. A human, in the capture of nihilistic values, would have to find Nietzsche's prose unintelligible. Frequently Nietzsche must use the same word to do double duty, one duty for human use, and one for the alternative notion to be hinted at. This is the way that available language can provide a bridge to new valuations.

Nietzsche talks about culture and culture, truth and truth. If we put quotation marks around the human concepts, we can say that Nietzsche is nauseous before "culture" and "truth," but foreshadows the possibility of truth in a new culture of life. Nietzsche, as we will see; often uses quotation marks or other devices to mark such contrasts, but only after producing a text whose interpretive difficulties begin to suggest the existence of such a distinction. Many of the alleged contradictions in Nietzsche can be traced to this device of the double concept, and problems in interpretation can often be traced to failure to notice Nietzsche's double concepts.

The disappearance of the human involves other disappearing notions: rationality, authorship, and so on. Nietzsche does not present the disappearance of the (human) persons as coming before other disappearances, as may be done here for expository purposes, but he does connect these concepts by the fact that weight put on any of them under philosophical analysis causes them all to disappear, unsettling our seemingly settled daily language. As we cannot get outside our own language and our own perspective, the correspondence notion of truth must fail, especially correspondence to an abstract world of fixed ideas. Meaning is generated by metaphors that are imposed on the domain of experience, and quite different metaphorical schemes are possible. As there is no unified person (or mind) producing texts, rather texts that unify persons, texts cannot be determined to be true in terms of inner coherence or in terms of authorial intention. The latter fact removes at once the underpinnings of textual religion, and if correspondence and coherence tests of truth also fail, science is deprived of a secure epistemological basis. What remains is an ability to grasp texts in terms of interesting readings, an ability that can be supported by looking at the genealogical sequences of textual materials. Standard forms of hermeneutics, which attempt to link authors and opinions in texts, sifting the result for truth, cannot be brought into full play. The older notion of timeless truth gives way to short-term possibilities and the ability to seize these possibilities to increase will to power. Nietzsche's own texts are to be brought into this more flexible sense of hermeneutics. A given Nietzschean text may present the simultaneous presence and clash of opinions, all of which Nietzsche thinks must be considered. Rather than resolution or syntheses of these opinions, we may have to stand with their suspension. Understanding Nietzsche requires handling ambiguities and suspensions of opinion that are not found in more prosaic authors. Many of the alleged impenetrabilities in his texts can be traced to the application of an inappropriate hermeneutics brought to understand them and to the neglect of the possibility of the suspension of concepts.

The general interpretation of Nietzsche can be pulled in several directions. Many have tried to fit him into some one of the philosophical traditions. In order to do that, it is usually necessary to divide Nietzsche into parts, those parts that fit the tradition in question and those parts that are to be taken as irrelevant, vulgar, ironic, mad, or whatever. Others have tried to respond to his own claims that he stood at the end of a metaphysical tradition that had run its course and that he was proposing new philosophical interpretations and new values to ground those interpretations, although these values could be seen as reworked versions of values recognizable in history before the metaphysical tradition in question. Obviously, this second approach comes closer to Nietzsche's own evaluation of himself, but it also threatens to cleave Nietzsche into parts, the most relevant being a partial Nietzsche primarily interested only in language and in aesthetic questions. As aesthetics is only of secondary importance to the metaphysical tradition, this Nietzsche can prove exciting for literary criticism, but he is not employed to challenge scientific knowledge head on or to develop new images of social and political life.

Recently, some analytic philosophers have seen Nietzsche as a precursor. Danto, Schacht, and Nehamas have written from this standpoint. Abstractly stated, some of Nietzsche's opinions display a suspicion of metaphysics and of certain views about the self that are quite fashionable in current analytic opinion. It is also possible to consider Nietzsche as a guide to self-expression in a domain removed from the pressures of scientific knowledge. But the reliance of analytic philosophy on formal logic and factual objectivity is completely at odds with the basic thrust of Nietzsche's perspectivism, the latter being incompatible with any justification of modern science as having a privileged access to truth. Perhaps even more crucially, the optimism of analytic philosophers at the possibility of the progress of analysis is completely at odds with Nietzsche's pessimism. If these philosophers are correct, Nietzsche was a failure in his own terms.

Nietzsche is very difficult to knock into shape as an ideologue for someone else's movement. It has been claimed that Nietzsche could (or did) function as the philosopher of Nazism, but fascists require group submission to a leader, a submission not consistent with Nietzsche's nausea at politics and economics. One could also try to imagine Nietzsche reading *Mein Kampf* and grappling with its style, but not for very long. It is more interesting to consider the parallels between the lives of Jesus and Zarathustra, and to argue that Nietzsche was an unusual religious thinker.[4] For this purpose, the paradoxes of Christ's parables can be accepted as instructionally equivalent to Zarathustra's aphorisms, and

Nietzsche may seem to be urging a form of Christian pietism. Christian saints who are not judgmental concerning sin and value individual cases on their merits might be thought to approximate the psychological profile of the Übermensch. And this approach also tallies nicely with Nietzsche's attention to the solitary figure and to Nietzsche's minimal political observations. Nietzsche and Kierkegaard can be paired as offering stinging denunciations of official institutional Christianity and leaving open the necessity of new valuations. Both philosophers repudiate the Hegelian system, insisting that the individual is a surd that resists the system, and they decry any notion that their own philosophical positions can be proven true by logical argument. The major objections to this assimilation of Nietzsche to some form of religious apologetics can't really be mounted from internal textual evidence, although it is true that Kierkegaard chose Christian role models and that Nietzsche chose pagan role models, but they have to be largely located in the reaches of biography. Nietzsche is completely different from a philosopher like Kierkegaard in what he was interested in, in what he read, and in how he felt about his own work.

Attempts to make Nietzsche an existentialist philosopher make too much of the parallels noted between Nietzsche and Kierkegaard. Kaufmann and Jaspers have both attempted assimilation of Nietzsche as an affirmative philosopher in this way, and they can point to many passages that support this line of interpretation. Although *existential* can be pulled this way and that, covering Nietzsche with the term seems to accomplish little. Nietzsche is not a humanist, and he does not accept many of the assumptions about the modern world in terms of which existentialists deliberately define important human action as absurd. Nietzsche is definitely opposed to notions of withdrawal from the world that have been urged by some passive Christian existentialists. Above all, man is not the ultimate measure of things in Nietzsche's scheme; the ultimate measure is taken by Dionysian process, and progressive periods of human existence can withstand destruction only by means of a unified culture that is difficult to square with existentialism in its typical presentations. Nietzsche is sometimes presented as a precursor of phenomenology, as a philosopher who wished to set aside the cultural overlay of language for concentration on the things themselves. But in bracketing language as a vehicle of truth, Nietzsche found no things themselves that could sustain the certainties that phenomenologists have hunted for.

Nietzsche makes it clear that he thought that he was a singularity, that he had located and subjected to decisive critique the basic presuppositions of the entire Western philosophical tradition. Heidegger's important study of Nietzsche takes Nietzsche instead to be the last metaphysician, the ultimate subjective thinker, and announces that Nietzsche's termination of the metaphysical tradition has provided a space for the development and recovery of an analysis of Being, a concept that has been under erasure since Socrates. Heidegger then inserts himself into the role of the first thinker after metaphysics, adopting the rough time frame for the metaphysical era that Nietzsche had employed. More recently, and by means of a reaction to residual metaphysical elements in Heidegger's reading, certain French philosophers interested in the notion of a decentered, constructed self and in a conception of language that doesn't embody fixed meanings have utilized Nietzsche as an important point of conceptual origination. In particular, Foucault, Deleuze, and Derrida rely on Nietzschean themes. Horkheimer and Adorno, in *Dialectic of Enlightenment,* also concede to Nietzsche a position at the dead end of a nihilism that must be reached in any elaboration of Enlightenment reason.[5] They also trace a metaphysical tradition from Greek times to the present that has the approximate time frame suggested by Nietzsche and repeated by Heidegger, but a tradition that needs to be redeemed by a (Marxist) social and political Critical Theory. Critical Theory and recent French scholarship return to Nietzsche his oracular status, but the Nietzsche that results is aestheticized, and he functions once again as an ideologue in the philosophical campaigns of others. Perhaps it is time for exposition to begin.

Nietzsche's route rubs against the grain of deep-seated current attitudes about human nature and society, so much so that Nietzsche seems to many to be completely mad, his texts a jumble of inconsistent opinions, best excused by calling them playful.[6] Perhaps regarding Nietzsche as mad or trimming his sails to other purposes is an easier course than grappling with the full range of his thought. Here it will be argued that his thought is shocking, powerful, significant, and coherent. We will make an effort to interpret it in its own terms, exploring its coherence, and only after this has been done will we return to the question of a considered judgment of Nietzsche's place in contemporary thought. Even to say that is to announce in advance that we cannot exactly follow Nietzsche's path through to its end point. If we are changed by it, we will still be human, perhaps not sadder and wiser, but with new eyes and a higher, crazier perspective. Perhaps there should be more apology than gratitude to express to this lonely thinker if we do not think his critique through to his own conclusive and heroic silence.

1

Greece

Philology examines the textual ruins of the past that exist in the present, ruins that we can explore for our own advantages. Nietzsche thought that we shouldn't be passive before the past because it exists in the present. It must be interpreted, but it can provide suggestions of progressive values, especially to a mind that is already somewhat out of step with surrounding opinion. Nietzsche thought that conventional scholarship, in step with surrounding opinion, could only reproduce ideas that already prevailed. The residual grandeur of Greece forces on us the opinion that the Greeks accomplished something of great significance. Interpretations that fail to make the Greeks greater than their scholarly interpreters can't be right.

The field of Greek scholarship was dominated in Nietzsche's time by a conception of the Greeks as the most rational and aesthetically observational people of all time, responding to classical notions of form and moderation. In particular, the dominant picture of ancient Greece, which was due to Winckelmann, was based on the assumptions of Greek rationality and associated aesthetic forms.[1] The discovery of "other Greeks" is due in large measure to Nietzsche, who stressed irrational and intuitive aspects of Greek life that he used to account for the greatness of Greece.[2] Much of Nietzsche's conception was an artistic projection, since the role of color in Greek vision and the nature of Greek music, factors that are crucial to Nietzsche's conception, are scarcely apparent in the available texts. Nietzsche projected a point of view completely different from the views studied by his colleagues.[3] He knew that he couldn't prove his view on the evidence, and he didn't try for rational persuasion of the necessity of his view. What he did was to argue implicitly that all views with any relationship to available texts were equally interpretations. His view couldn't be refuted, and valuable lessons could be drawn from it. From the beginning, in talking about Greece, Nietzsche was also talking about the present.

Let us begin to look-at Nietzsche's central early account of his vision of Greece, *The Birth of Tragedy*. The first sentence of section 1 downgrades the importance of logical inference in comparison with vision as a touchstone of the past. Nietzsche is saying that his view is preferable in that it opens up an understanding of the Greeks useful for understanding the superficiality of our own lives, and that is why he adopts it. But the possibility of the deployment of Nietzsche's view accomplishes Nietzsche's purpose, which is to undercut the supposedly solid foundation of the prevailing view. Nietzsche's view can't be "rationally" demolished, since we can't go back to see how the Greeks "really were," and so the matter devolves to interpretation. Nietzsche avoids contradiction by *not* arguing that there is a solid logical foundation for his own view. Nietzsche threatened a certain settled and comfortable picture of Greek culture, and this fact is surely involved in the nasty attacks Nietzsche received from the philological establishment.

Nietzsche's view of Greek culture is, by his own analysis, of potential usefulness for all the Germans who could read his book. A dose of Hellenic tragic pessimism could sober what Nietzsche saw as the silly German optimism of his time. Nietzsche's view is thus, on his analysis, for everyone. On the other hand, the picture of Greece defended by his opponents drew a line between those who could grasp it, the refined "higher souls" of scholarship, and those who could not. Nietzsche would draw no distinction between intellectual and manual labor, partly because the Greek nobles of his vision did not come in two models.

✳ *The Birth of Tragedy* is divided into twenty-five sections, and these can be grouped under three basic themes. The first theme (sections 1–10) is the study of Greek tragedy as arising out of Apollinian and Dionysian forms of art. A major problem here is to see what the Apollinian and Dionysian are and how they are related in tragedy. The second theme (sections 11–15) is the destruction of the tragic outlook by Socratic optimism and rationality. It is here that Nietzsche clearly reverses the values of surrounding scholarship. Nietzsche sees Euripides and Socrates as destroying a superior Greek culture and as opening the era of the human. From Nietzsche's point of view, Euripides and Socrates were not Hellenic figures. If tragedy somehow arises from an opposition between Apollinian and Dionysian elements in Greek artistic life, it degenerates when this opposition is papered over by monological Socratic and Euripidean rational explanations of human action. The opposition between Socrates and Hellenic tragedy is as black and white as Nietzsche's distaste for intellectual abstraction will allow. There is no dialectical synthesis involved in the destruction of tragedy by Socrates and Euripides. This is also shown by the denial that a synthesis of Socrates and Dionysus can ground a healthy society, and the claim that the rationality introduced by Socrates is precisely what is now culminating in nihilism. The third theme (sections 16–25) is that hopes for a rebirth of something like Hellenic tragedy can be established on the basis of the nature of modern German music. In the concluding sections, the general nature of tragedy is reviewed.

Nietzsche's positive valuation of Wagner in the development of the third theme, supported by remarks in his preface to *Birth,* was something that he later repudiated, but this does not mean that the third theme can be forgotten. We can take it as an adumbration of the theme of the Eternal Return. There was authentic tragic vision in the time of the Hellenes, and it can return. That this theme is not abandoned, even if its attachment to Wagner is set aside, is clear in Nietzsche's later work, for example, at the end of aphorism 382 of *The Gay Science,* where the commencement of tragedy is associated with the arrival of Zarathustra. One can pick at the assertions in the first part on scholarly grounds, but scholarly quibbles with the first part are quite independent of the point of the last part. Tragedy might be commencing with Wagner or Zarathustra even if Nietzsche's account of Greek tragedy is illusory, whatever that might mean. It could also have been the case that the impact of Wagner on Nietzsche was essential to unlocking the ancient manuscripts. But to feel the movement of Nietzsche's thought, all three themes in *Birth* need to be retained.

What is the relationship of the Apollinian to the Dionysian? The indisputable fact is that they are *not* opposites and equals, despite appearances. The Dionysian is fundamental. The Apollinian is a mode of representation of the Dionysian that allows human beings to have a grasp of the Dionysian in a bearable or intelligible form. This was the case before the human era, and it can be the case again if the intimations of Dionysian process are not screened out by the filter of rationality. The Dionysian recognition that everything is transitory and that all seemingly fixed truths are illusions can only be hinted at, or indirectly represented, in Apollinian form. Tragedy is a particularly successful Apollinian presentation of Dionysus. Dionysus and Apollo cannot be separated in Hellenic tragedy, because the Dionysian is involved in all the Apollinian representations. We can contrast Apollo and Dionysus as gods, but then they are abstract fictions that are mediated in tragedy. The Apollinian is always produced ultimately by Dionysus. This is not a synthesis because the Dionysian does not disappear, it is not erased, and it is not altered, even if it can't be seen clearly, when tragedy is successfully achieved.

Music is the key Dionysian art. Improvised music comes as close to being Dionysian as anything we can experience. No preplanned intellectual structures or regular rhythms are involved, and performers should feel themselves in the grip of superior forces. Music improvisation, constantly in flux, should take unanticipated and challenging paths. Nietzsche, who loved to improvise at the piano, may have considered Greek music appropriately improvisational in thinking of it as Dionysian. The temporal aspect of music (but not regular rhythm) codes the Dionysian. Plastic arts, on the other hand, code the Apollinian, since they attempt to provide an atemporal vision that would arrest the flow of time. As art forms, the Dionysian and the Apollinian both grow out of life, i.e., out of Dionysian process. The Apollinian art form arises in dreams, and the Dionysian art form from spontaneous dancing and folk music. Dreams, in providing the originating display of the Apollinian, show that the Apollinian isn't cognitively rational until after the intervention of Socrates. Dreams indicate the possibility of a form of knowledge that simply contemplates the appearance of things.[4]

Nietzsche's remarks on the importance of music for philosophy, a minority view, remain important throughout his career, as Dionysus never wanders far away from Nietzsche's deepest insights into the nature of reality.[5] Dionysian art involves the body in intuitive response, as in dance. To some extent, we dream by ourselves, but we can lose our identity in dance or music or intoxication. Nietzsche felt the normal views of foundational individuality expressed by philosophers were illusory and was intrigued by the Dionysian as a means of indicating why these views might be false and superficial. Individuality is a construct doomed to eventual return to world process, a return that could be anticipated in losing oneself in a Dionysian performance.

Section 1 of *Birth* begins with general observations about the development of art as the occasionally fecund joining of Apollinian and Dionysian forms of art, a sufficient indication that the Greeks can still speak to us in the present. The Apollinian is recognizable in dreams and the Dionysian in intoxication. These are forms of physiological involvement, not phenomena to be contemplated by cool reason. Both are intrusions of an underlying Dionysian process into human lives, lives produced by the process, and they are intrusions that are not under the control of science or scholarship. Everything can appear in dreams, but as separate figures, as illusion, without which life would not be worth living. In Dionysian song or intoxication, the Apollinian illusion of individuality is stripped away. Dreams and intoxication involve everyone as an artist, and Nietzsche begins a persuasive deployment of his basic image of the one world of becoming and of his conviction that artistic production is a more basic activity than intellectual analysis.

Turning to Greek art in section 2, Nietzsche notes that these two Hellenic forms of art are suspended against one another in Hellenic tragedy, but not resolved. It was the peculiar Greek accomplishment to have *suspended* these joint products of Dionysian process, so that Dionysian power could reveal itself in a redemptive tension with Apollinian illusion. Joy and horror are simultaneously represented—especially in symbolism involving the whole body—in the Dionysian dithyramb. Nietzsche would himself later attempt to write such dithyrambs. The only thing missing in Hellenic tragedy is the hierarchy of actual social relationships, which arose in the world of action.

Section 3 traces Apollinian culture to its ultimate Dionysian foundations. The Olympian (Apollinian) gods carry the full weight of human contradictions. Like humans, they aren't just good, they're good and bad, everything all at once. These gods show us that the Hellenes recognized the full terror and horror of existence. In an important sense, their gods could still be rooted in amoral Dionysian foundations. Over time, the emergence of a more logically consistent Greek rationality tamed the gods, introducing a table of good and bad and ascribing only good to the gods. Christianity completed the process of evisceration. Dance, sexuality, horror were progressively banned from Christian worship as it developed into a rational theological form which lost all connection with Dionysian reality.

Nietzsche makes his point completely clear in section 4. The waking, rational state is more deceptive than the dream state with respect to the Dionysian ground of existence. Nightmares are filtered out of the waking state by rational tricks. This is reflected in art, where the most revealing art can be seen to be primitive and naive. There can be weak and strong Dionysian and Apollinian forms. Nietzsche sees the historical situation to have been one of increasingly more powerful Greek Apollinian forms having been developed to combat the threat of chaos posed by eastern Dionysian practices that repeatedly invaded Greece. Ultimately, the strong Doric Apollinian forms of art permitted a powerful suspension of Apollo and Dionysus in early tragedy.

Sections 5 and 6 back up in time to discuss this development in greater detail. Homer and Archilochus can be recognized as founders of Greek culture, the former having presented an Apollinian (dreamlike) account of Greek individual life in his epics and the latter having presented Dionysian aspects of life in his lyric poetry. Lyric poetry originated in a musical mode, this step being necessary to make a more Dionysian art form possible. It should be noticed that lyric poetry is Apollinian (as is all artistic representation), but it is more Dionysian than epic poetry. That lyric poetry was recognized as subjective shows that the potential loss of individuality to the Dionysian is at stake. When the lyricist speaks of self, a fiction is at stake, although there is a deeper self that is a temporary expression of the inarticulate Dionysian process that can overwhelm it again. The threat of loss of individuality, even the moment of loss, can be recognized by others, and this is why lyric poetry codes universal feelings and doesn't glorify the deeds of other individuals who could be named as distinct figures. The early folk song is a primitive union of Apollinian lyric and Dionysian melody, but it is almost impossible to describe.[6] That there is a paradox involved in trying to state in an Apollinian fashion what can only be experienced as Dionysian is shown by the peculiarly deep and unique place that music assumes among the arts. At this point, Nietzsche's alternative interpretation of the Hellenes has come into full view, and in a remarkably short and succinct analysis. The importance of music in representing Dionysian process has been introduced, and it has been linked directly to an aesthetic theory that provides an absorbing account of Hellenic tragedy.

The birth of tragedy is in music, as section 7 notes, and not in political or moral representations, because the temporality of music can directly represent Dionysian process without representing individuals except as limited and transitory. Music reminds us of important complexities, of pain and suffering that can't be satisfactorily elaborated in language. Tragedy arises in the musical expression of the chorus. When actors were added, the chorus did not at first interact with them, nor did it rationally analyze what was happening. In Hellenic tragedy the chorus is to staged action as the dreamer is to the dream image. Dream images can be shared by individuals, all of whom simply have the dream. Tragedy was literally a collective dream. Spectators merged with the chorus, which, speaking as one, could represent, as well as paradox allows, the Dionysian roots of the individually human. As in dreams, the dreamer could know that he or she was dreaming and yet will the dream to continue. Knowledge, presented here as dream vision, inhibits action, and the notion of individuality at the root of action has been placed in jeopardy. The dreamer is content with appearance as justification. The stage action (and early tragedy had none save for the presentations of the chorus) is simply the dream or vision of the chorus. Art is necessary as a way of handling, or of managing, Dionysian truth, so that action becomes ultimately possible. Apollinian justificatory deception is the foundation of human action—the delay of Dionysus so that an individual can seem to be something in a cultural setting.

The gradual introduction of actors and the downgrading and disappearance of the chorus is seen by Nietzsche as a process of degeneration, a leaching of the awful Dionysian vision. By the time actors give rational explanations, as in the plays of Euripides, the rational man or woman spectator evaluates the reasonings of the characters for their actions and stops feeling the suspensions that are embedded in significant art. And sharper, tougher reasoning can be found elsewhere, for example in philosophy, so that Euripides presents a theater that is already on the way to being mere entertainment. Nietzsche's account gives us a reason to privilege aesthetics as central to philosophy, because tragedy is a means of presenting reality. Theories of "identification" or "catharsis," presented as explanations of the effects of tragedy by later writers, are explanations of trivialized tragic forms.[7]

The man of culture is the desiccated remainder of the whole man, who had been appropriately represented earlier as satyr, as we learn in section 8. The physical design of the Greek theater was intended to make merging in a dream state with the chorus possible. People were not seated in view of each other, and they couldn't display themselves to one another. They were almost physically compelled to consider only what was happening on stage. Wagner planned to achieve a similar effect at Bayreuth through the plan of the theater, but Nietzsche later felt that Wagner's real motivations were otherwise.

In section 9, we return to a general discussion of the Apollinian and the Dionysian. Nietzsche's visual image suggests that the bright images of the Apollinian figures of later staged tragedy could only be intelligible when contrasted to a Dionysian darkness. Nietzsche accuses previous scholars of having noticed only the bright spots and not the darkness that gave them meaning. Their superficial conception of Greek cheerfulness is a result of this profound halving of the Greek legacy. Hellenic spectators knew the full horror of life, and their cheerfulness must be read in that context. Individuality must be paid for by suffering. Suffering is not a bad thing; it is what confers dignity on human beings. In the Hellenic view, evil is not equated with suffering—that was a later religious modification.[8]

Section 10 introduces the idea that Euripides killed Hellenic tragedy, quite at odds with the usual view that Euripides made a decisive advance. Of course it is true that Euripides made tragic drama much more like our own drama through the introduction of more characters and the suppression of the chorus, but Nietzsche reads this as an originating deflection toward nihilism and as a loss of awareness of Dionysian foundations. But Euripides was too puny to have done this himself against Dionysian power, which was the ground also of Euripides' efforts. Nietzsche expresses the problem by saying that tragedy must have committed suicide, Euripides being (strictly considered) guilty of murder only by circumstantial evidence. Nietzsche's opposition to humanist metaphysics requires this elimination of the foundational causal efficacy of the human actor, and the problem of agency will arise again in connection with the death of God. But we have reached the second theme, the negative evaluation of Euripides and Socrates, unexpectedly negative because it is at odds with the consensus evaluation of philosophical tradition.

Sections 11 through 15 discuss in detail the impact of Euripides and Socrates on early Hellenic culture. The pessimism associated with the possibility of recognizing Dionysian process is replaced by a superficial optimism. Actors on the stage now represent ordinary people and their actions, not dream images. This allows the audience to recognize itself in the characters on the stage, and changes profoundly the relationship between the audience and the events on stage. Drama now assumes a human form. Euripides presents a drama of the common person, recognizably human, who feels cheerful and comprehending in the face of an expected and calculable future. Christianity is initially more pessimistic than this when it encounters Greek humanism, since in its darker historical doctrines (sin, hell), it recognizes the complete superficiality of Euripidean notions. Section 11 shows Euripides to be a complicated figure. He feared his rational impulse, as opposed to his artistic feelings, but in conjunction with Socrates he worked out a rational conception of tragedy that replaced the older conception. Euripides felt superior to the audiences he set out to please, but he dissembled before them, attempting to make them feel that they were the judges of his own work. A peculiar deception is involved in any artistic production designed to please its audience. This decisive shift in authorial motivation was degeneration for Nietzsche, who felt that it foreshadowed the laws of an inevitably superficial mass art.

When Euripides removes the Dionysian from tragedy, rational explanation replaces Apollinian contemplation of the surface and recognizable human emotions replace Dionysian frenzy. As section 12 notes, the Dionysian and the Socratic become enemies, as the Socratic cuts against the complexity and profundity of the Dionysian. The Socratic, in short, is a truncated Apollinian artistic form. Socrates brings a morality and a worldview to bear that are endorsed by rationality. Beauty becomes a rational ideal; it replaces the complexity of life. To know what is good is to do it. Socratic drama is vain enough to suppose that it can project beauty onto the stage without the hideous, without the horrible, which disappear as that which has no value. Socratic arrogance was doomed to culminate in nihilism in the path of Dionysian assault.

Section 13 attempts to place Euripides and Socrates together. Socrates has everything wrong. Instinct should create. Consciousness is, at best, a critical tool. Socrates has this backward, taking the false abstractions of consciousness for creativity and downplaying the significance of the daimon's instinctive voice to that of criticism. The craziness of Socrates is exhibited in his cheerful attitude toward a willingly accepted death. Didn't he recognize the terror that awaited?

To understand sections 14 and 15, we need to distinguish *affirmation* and *optimism*. Affirmation is the stance of the Hellene who recognized the full range of existence and confronted it squarely. Optimism is a superficial stance in the face of Dionysian reality, a psychosis that is buoyed by the delusions of scientific rationality. Socrates is the prototype of theoretical, scientific man and of the shallow optimism of science and scholarship.[9] The extremely vicious characterization given in section 15, at least of the typical scientist or scholar, lays down a challenge that Nietzsche continues to develop throughout his writings.

Sections 16 through 25 develop the central place of music for Nietzsche's view of art, and, as we have already noted, Nietzsche has quite explicitly grounded Hellenic tragedy in the musical basis of lyric poetry. As music is felt, rather than seen, it is not so subject to the constraints of the rational filter. The German musical tradition is suggested as a possible location for the *rebirth* of tragedy. We don't have a chorus in the German tradition, so we don't have the same musical setting, but there is still the possibility of a German Apollinian form permitting a glimpse of the Dionysian. In section 16, we learn that Wagner and Schopenhauer have provided the musical and philosophical means of recognizing this situation. To Nietzsche, Wagner, in particular, seemed at this point to be providing an appropriate Apollinian crucible for the presentation of the Dionysian. Section 17 deals with the obvious problem that not all musical forms can reveal Dionysus. In imitating natural sounds or fitting artificial harmonic theories, music loses depth and complexity, just as Euripidean tragedy with specific characters is not able to present any longer an appearance of the suffering of Dionysus.

Sections 18 through 21 discuss various possible kinds of culture. The detailed text of these sections seems not to be entirely consistent, partly because Schopenhauer's observations are entangled with Nietzsche's emerging insights. Nietzsche is attempting to characterize the affirmative tragic culture he is looking for and to distinguish it from cultures that are superficial and empty. Apparent textual inconsistency refers to the fact that *Hellenic* doesn't seem to have a rigid reference throughout this passage; a double concept of Hellenic needs to be imposed on the text. At this point, Nietzsche does not yet have the double concept under stylistic control.

In section 18, Alexandrine culture, a culture based on the development of scientific ideas, must self-destruct when its slave class, becoming aware of itself, will avenge itself in a paroxysm of destruction. It is not the mere existence of the slave class that causes this situation, but the existence of the slave class within an optimistic scientific culture. Because Alexandrine culture recognizes no Dionysian foundation, it must crash without the possibility of recovery. Nietzsche is here anticipating much of the social criticism that he will bring to bear on his contemporaries in later works. Alexandrine music allows text to determine music, in the case of opera, allowing the libretto and its meaning to call the tune. Wagner's promise, noted in section 19, is that he can cap the German tradition of Bach and Beethoven with a dramatic suspension of text and music, reawakening the tension of tragedy. The musical history of Germany can thus be seen as recapitulating the developments leading to the suspension of the Apollinian and the Dionysian in Doric tragedy.

Sections 20 and 21 fine-tune the culture that is to be awakened. Nietzsche is attempting to make it completely clear that the appropriate model of Greece should be his model of Hellenic tragic culture and not the Greek culture familiar from the historicist accounts of his contemporaries. A culture of resignation, and here Nietzsche has in mind Schopenhauerian resignation derived from a picture of Buddhism that Schopenhauer projected, would all too quickly dissolve in Dionysian flux. An affirmative scientific culture would be trivial and would self-destruct in nihilism as its abstraction lost touch with the moment. What is needed is an affirmative, but profound, pessimistic, and flexible culture that stays in touch with Dionysus. Nietzsche makes a desperate effort to locate his vision in the conceptual space of his readers.

In section 22, Nietzsche returns to the question of tragedy as an aesthetic phenomenon, but now in the context of Wagner's possibilities. Moral interpretations of tragedy, for example Aristotle's, fail to grasp its Dionysian profundities. Life necessarily involves lies and deception; if morality would deny that, tragedy cannot. Tragedy can only be reborn with tragic listeners who can sense what it involves, not with critics who think too much about what they experience. If tragedy is talked about, if it is thought of as a moral tool, its real nature is concealed. When Hellenes responded to tragedy, they did not really understand it. Nietzsche feels that only now, with his higher perspective, can the nature of original tragedy be understood. Section 23 considers the relationship of myth to national culture. The destruction of Hellenic tragedy meant the end of one era of myth and its associated culture, but perhaps German culture can be reborn with the emergence of a new German form of tragedy.

In music, pleasure cannot be separated from the intrusion of disturbing discords. In their absence, music would be too simple to stimulate pleasure. The pleasure of the experience of tragedy, in a similar way, cannot be separated from the horror that it must contain if it is to reveal its true Dionysian roots. Aesthetic theories that deny these truths gain credibility only because they are repeated often enough amongst the simple-minded. Section 25 continues these observations of section 24 in a summary recognizing Dionysus as the foundation of everything; the greatness of tragedy is recognized again to lie in its revelation of the Dionysian in a specially adapted Apollinian form.

Before *Birth*, Nietzsche had written (but not completed or published) *Philosophy in the Tragic Age of the Greeks*, a work that is nicely complementary to *Birth*. Nietzsche's discussion of pre-Socratic notions of a universe in which everything originates from everything paves the way to his later process monism, and he resonates with a healthy philosophy of insight that depends on very little extensive rational discussion. In particular, Nietzsche is attracted to Heraclitus, who is a philosopher with a deep intuition for the flux of existence and a philosopher who didn't separate intuition and cognition so as to fall into the inanities of a purely rational discourse. For the pre-Socratics, to know good was also to know suffering, and they simply observed a Dionysian world without attempting to impose a rational order on it. In writing this early work, Nietzsche commented that he felt himself to be the last philosopher, the last human being, one able to converse only with himself.

Nietzsche later downplayed the significance of *Birth*, but much of his disapprobation is directed at its style. *Birth* had to be downgraded in view of Nietzsche's growing insistence that style and content were inseparable in unified cultural work. It is also clear that Nietzsche's later attitudes toward Wagner and Schopenhauer had shifted. Schopenhauer's pessimism seemed increasingly facile, and Wagner came to seem a self-glorifying romantic and not a truly driven Dionysian artist. Before his break with Wagner, Nietzsche argued that the very crudity of the German musical tradition (in comparison with the French and Italian traditions) might be the means of hearing the bass notes of the Dionysian. When Wagner turned out to be a weathervane, turning to catch intimations of praise and financial support, the German potential withered. The opposites Apollinian and Dionysian, crucial to artistic production in *Birth,* do not remain central to Nietzsche's ongoing discussions; rather it is the Dionysian ground of both forms of intoxication that assumes central stage in later discussions of art. By taking any of these features of *Birth* as central, it is easy to dismiss *Birth* as an early, youthful, enthusiastic work, as many commentators have done. To see Nietzsche's philosophical development from the rudimentary roots of *Birth,* we have to turn to other features.

In the last book that he published, *Twilight of the Idols,* there is an early section titled "The Problem of Socrates," in which the portrait of Socrates is just as negative as it had been in *Birth.* Socrates thought life, a transitory phenomenon, was an evil from which it was good to be free. Socrates is cited explicitly as anti-Hellene, and a scholarly reference points back to *Birth.* Socrates' plebeian origins and his ugliness are highlighted as ominous symptoms of a decadent attitude. His equation of reason with virtue and happiness is in *flat* contradiction to the instincts of the Hellenes. Socrates brought the cancer of dialectic, the ultimate expression of ressentiment, permitting endless self-defense against the opinions of others. Lucky Socrates! He appeared with this weapon just as decadence brought on by social change would permit it a place. The clash of instincts, brought about in cultural decline, was not to be resolved by healthy and integrated action but mastered by rational order. In warring against decadence, Socrates fought with a decadent weapon. Ultimately, and this is the only attitude compatible with the disease, Socrates wanted to die. If anything, the portrait of Socrates here is even more bitter than it was in *Birth.* The intervening discovery and development of ressentiment has allowed Nietzsche a generalization that brings Socrates under what had previously been thought a priestly and Semitic umbrella. Reason is an expression of ressentiment and consequently subversive of noble virtue. Although this incorporates ideas from Nietzsche's intervening genealogies, the place of Socrates remains the same. He stands at the divide between nobility and health, on the one hand, and reason and humanity, on the other. The trajectory of Nietzsche's criticisms of European nihilism continues to be charted against this lodestar.

In the next to last section of *Twilight of the Idols,* titled "What I Owe to the Ancients," Nietzsche makes a number of general remarks about his approach to the ancient world. Perhaps surprisingly, Nietzsche's overt references here are to the impact of Roman, rather than Greek, sources for his thought. Why these references to the Romans? Nietzsche reveals here that his *style* was modeled on a few Roman sources, Sallust and Horace in particular. By contrast, he reports that he did not *learn* much *from* the Greeks. To begin with, it's obvious that Nietzsche didn't learn from the Greeks except in a very selective way. He concerned himself only with what we have called the Hellenic period—a period whose philological basis was a set of fragmentary texts. This explains why Nietzsche immediately attacks Plato and the style of the Platonic dialogues in this passage, while praising Thucydides, whom he cites as an observer of life. Nietzsche (looking back over his career at this point) is aware that the Hellenes never unified their culture and that his task had been to transform Hellenic insights into a unified culture that could be presented in a persuasive style that might be instrumental in overcoming the terminal nihilism of the Socratic/Platonic project. Nietzsche would accomplish what the Hellenic philosophers had failed to do. Nietzsche had learned to write Hellenic vision in a style appropriate to his time, but learning to do so had involved developing stylistic resources that postdated the Hellenic period. Nietzsche then contrasts his Hellenes, the Greece of Dionysian instinct, with the world of scholars of Greece. His last words here close a circle begun with *Birth,* which Nietzsche describes as his first revaluation of all values. This vision stands opposed to the ressentiment of Christianity, as well as to the aseptic balance of the classical Greek scholars. What has happened is that the clash with Christianity has enlarged the critical significance of the original vision but has not changed its sources in excess and power. Dionysus remains the root figure, and Nietzsche describes himself, now the teacher of the eternal recurrence, as a disciple of the philosopher Dionysus.

A theory of Greek tragedy is not, of course, a total vision of Greece, but for Nietzsche it was the umbilical cord of that vision. Here the umbilical cord primarily nourishes an awareness of Dionysian flux, central to tragedy and essential to the total life of the early Hellenes. The Hellenes could be cheerful in spite of an awareness of Dionysian horror, indeed cheerful in a way constantly nourished by the awareness. Nietzsche's prophetic vision will philosophically purify Dionysian flux into will to power, while philosophically purifying Hellenic cheerfulness into an affirmation based on the Eternal Return. If will to power is Dionysian truth, the Return as presented in *Zarathustra* will permit a modern form of *affirmation* as the term is used in *Birth*.[10] Nietzsche's politics will also carry on the implicit structure of Hellenic society, taking only the transfigured nobles who could enter Hellenic tragic performance as the measure of society and placing women and slaves into supporting positions. There are no Nietzschean apologies for this, since the superiority of such an elite is proven in life by struggle between members of the elite that does not involve the violent suppression of other social layers. Hellenic nobles lived in the moment, accepting victory or defeat without rancor, forming alliances only to deal with pressing necessities, and living a healthy ethics and religion that did not involve guilt for the actions of the past or failures to achieve a divine standard of perfection. All that they accomplished was achieved without a state or a leveling bureaucracy. It is not the clash of the Apollinian and the Dionysian in art that retains Nietzsche's attention after *Birth*, but the figure of the Hellenic noble, a figure that becomes constantly reworked until Nietzsche can formulate visions of will to power and the Eternal Return that would allow the Hellenic noble to live again. Nietzsche wanted to be dangerous among the intellectual nobles of his time; he did not care whether science could give him cleaner teeth.

2

Style

Nietzsche's self-conscious development of an intensely personal style is reflected in the title of a section of *Ecce Homo,* "Why I Write Such Good Books." He ceaselessly experimented with his writing in an effort to increase its concentrated power, to fuse its content and form into an integrated movement of thought. In order to study Nietzsche's rhetoric and style, it is revealing to take a detailed look at the argumentative structure of the first untimely meditation. As one looks from the first untimely meditation to Nietzsche's later writings, certain pithy prose passages in the early text stand out as the kind of attack that is later coiled into the aphorisms. Nietzsche's later aphorisms are meant to avoid rational, scholarly discursive structure by spring-loading short passages with the destructive power of entire essays. Aphorisms work by suddenly jolting or piercing established opinion, causing a shift in thought, a shift that can then be assimilated more leisurely in terms of its implications. The proportion of treatment in the first untimely meditation lays the strategy of the later aphorisms open to inspection. At the beginning, density of expression requires close attention to each word, but the consequences are then developed more leisurely in a discursive examination. By the time of *The Gay Science,* Nietzsche discovers how to wind up his beginnings even tighter, and to let them fly alone as aphorisms, with the discursive development left to the acute and active reader.[1] *The Birth of Tragedy* had perhaps already convinced Nietzsche that attacking scholarship could never change the settled opinions of others. Attack, victory, consolidation; Nietzsche is learning to control committed writing in the first meditation, and here we can study its rhetorical anatomy.

There are twelve sections to Nietzsche's essay on Strauss. The first two sketch the image or ideal type of the cultural philistine, and Strauss is then inserted into this role.[2] At this stage, Nietzsche's writing is most condensed, most aphoristic. Strauss's ideas are discussed in sections 3 through 7, where Strauss is taken to exemplify the shallow optimism of German philistinism. Nietzsche finally attacks the idea that Strauss might be a good writer, no matter what the quality of his opinions. For Nietzsche, the notion that style and content could be separated is itself philistine. The discussion of Strauss's style culminates in a detailed examination of some of Strauss's specific sentences, showing that they will not bear the weight of grammatical and logical analysis and are ultimately shabby and confused. At this stage in the meditation, the writing becomes once again almost scholarly and discursive.

The first paragraph of the meditation begins with a sentence that seems to state a fact: public opinion is not interested in a discussion of evil and the perilous consequences (which may be difficult to discern) of a victorious war. Nietzsche is preparing for two movements of thought: a rejection of public opinion as being of any value, and a transvaluation of this particular public opinion. With respect to the latter, Nietzsche will not say that a victory can have aspects of a defeat; he will say that a victory can be a defeat, and this is not a dialectical synthesis. Nietzsche says that the value scheme of public opinion, in which victory is clearly a good thing, is the wrong value scheme to apply. Victory, for Nietzsche, cannot exist without being involved with evil and peril, and in noting that what the public has called a victory is actually a defeat, Nietzsche is not claiming that a victory must also be a defeat. What Nietzsche believes is that the public can't recognize a victory. The second half of the first sentence suggests that there are writers content to fawn on this public opinion, vying with one another to draw out the consequences of the victory for morality, for culture, and for art. Nietzsche despises those who lead and those who follow in such movements of thought. More independent thinkers should be prepared to discover that commonly accepted causal chains are mistaken and that what is commonly accepted as culture, art, or morality has no discernible relationship to the victories of nations at war. Nietzsche sets public opinion firmly to one side in the second sentence. A great victory is a great danger. Victory becomes defeat if it is wrongly evaluated on the basis of typical and current values. With just two sentences, Nietzsche has already joined issue with public opinion and with all those shapers of public opinion who lead by reflecting public values. He has also made precise his point of attack.

Nietzsche now ventures a psychological observation. Victories are harder for humans to endure than defeats. Victories are turned almost inevitably into defeats by wrong acts of interpretation. The error of interpretation is to assume that a military victory can be explained by the superior "culture" of the victorious side. It may be that culture has nothing to do with concurrent military superiority, varying in inexplicable ways with such superiority. Nietzsche will suggest that this is so, and that in fact the abstraction "culture" is such a mess, as was actual German culture when he was writing, that it couldn't be an actor in history and couldn't coherently be said to have any organized causal consequences.

The error or delusion in popular opinion is destructive, not because it is an error, as there are salutary and productive errors, but because it assists the creation of a deadening unity of thought. This unity of thought is not genuine; it is the illusory consequence of a superficial and rational construction. Victors are likely to attempt to utilize such construction to homogenize the thought of the home population so as to guarantee future success. The unruly German spirit, often correct in its impulses, may be homogenized to serve the *Reich,* to serve the state, or to serve the nation. Two aspects of this run against Nietzsche's grain. Nietzsche opposes such rationally imposed homogenization—like the uniform religious or philosophical codes of the past—because such abstraction, if successful, leads inevitably to decadence and stagnation. Further, such a view commits the error of supposing that we can learn from the past how to successfully address the future, as though there were historical laws that are valid over time. The theme that will occupy center stage in the second untimely meditation, that history should not be interpreted as a deadening weight on the present, is now quietly introduced.

Even this relatively simple reading of the first paragraph of the first section should make it evident that many of Nietzsche's later themes make an appearance here. Public and scholarly opinion have been attacked, a positive value (victory) has been transvalued, new psychological insights have been offered, causality has been questioned, decadence has been examined. And this is only a partial inventory. Further, this paragraph is a model of rigorous polemical writing. Nietzsche has found a precise point of attack, and he has opened space with a tactical movement that can now be relentlessly exploited. This paragraph is, itself, a partly wound aphorism; the thought, so to speak, has been fired out at us, and its destructive potential can now be more leisurely examined.

Nietzsche returns to the association of culture with victory. The fact is that the relationship between cultures and armies can vary over time, so that one victory by one army over another could be due to accident, luck, past but not present culture, a developing but not yet fully formed culture, differences in the anticipation of the possibilities of war, and even other possibilities. Readers are here invited to decouple their conception of culture from their conception of military might. Nietzsche doesn't share the view of culture that he asks the readers to isolate. He is driving the readers along established rails of thought to the destruction or deconstruction of the popular notion. The philistine decouples style and content but fuses victory and culture. Nietzsche will neither couple nor decouple either of these pairs in any automatic fashion. A victory allows a nation to preen itself and its culture in public through the ministration of tame intellectuals. Nietzsche does not hold that style and content are fused or not fused. The possibility must be examined afresh in each new case. Nietzsche is not a skeptic. Unity is better, and he values it positively. The Hellenes achieved it, but Nietzsche intends to show that the Germans haven't, no matter what they think of themselves. Just as a philistine writer can't fuse style and content, so a philistine nation can't fuse victory and culture. Nietzsche must hold out in favor of superior content that is not yet fused with a superior style, for he is struggling to find such a fusion. At this point, he is arguing that a nation can find itself not yet having integrated its potentialities for power into a coherent culture. Unlike the early Hellenic case of fusion, where nobles did their own fighting, the modern army is likely to fight in terms of an ideology that has almost nothing to do with the cultural impulses of the surrounding society, and the individual fighting soldier may be isolated completely from shifts in cultural opinion.

A confused nation writes badly. Its parts are not integrated in a manner that will allow its potential power to express itself. A victory for one side in a clash of nations cannot therefore automatically establish that the victorious side possesses a superior culture. Nietzsche's valuation of Germany takes the form of an independent and specific examination of its culture. He focuses on the ease with which philistine opinion, and its associated cobbling together of thought and style, is accepted within German intellectual circles. Victory is not complete if the defeated nation possesses a culture of any value. It would be wrong to overlook this in a mechanical tidying up of the victorious culture. Nietzsche suggests this is exactly the case in the Franco-Prussian War. French culture exists, and Germans should take note of what it has to offer. Now a small sentence is inserted that announces a crucial Nietzschean point, but suddenly and not as the continuation of an argument. Nietzsche attempts to completely sever culture and military apparatus. Martial success belongs solely to the body. Discipline (of the body), natural bravery (not calculated self-sacrifice), and endurance (of the body)—these are what determine military success. What of unity and obedience in the ranks? An alert opponent of this point could argue that coordination and strategy involve culture, at least a culture adequate to the requisite communication. Perhaps to defuse this thought, Nietzsche says quite carefully that the "refined" cultural layers are not involved in martial superiority. The culture of professors, insofar as it is opposed to army discipline on behalf of "higher" values, gives way to martial necessity in the heat of battle. If professorial culture is allowed afterward to claim a role in the victory, it may extirpate the crude German bodily feelings that did play the essential role.

What is being said here comes into better focus against the background of *The Birth of Tragedy*. The great early Greek military successes were there described as achieved in the context of a coherent "tragic" culture. Perhaps the victorious German army might have achieved, in its independent way, a primitive form of tragic culture that was responsible for its military success. This thought can't be advanced by Nietzsche in a straightforward manner, since the thought depends on the link between culture and victory that Nietzsche is undercutting in this passage. Nietzsche believes that tragic culture has consequences, but not that all "cultures" have consequences. After the demolition of clichés about culture, it will be possible for Nietzsche to dare more explicitly what he can only hint at here. In this passage, we encounter the body's importance for explanation in Nietzsche and its connection to an authentic sense of Dionysian process. We also confront Nietzsche's hostility to idealism and the eclectic "culture" associated with it. By running the popular sense of "culture" into self-destruction, as well as the associated cultural sense of "culture," Nietzsche can prepare the place where more coherent ideas can be deployed. Nietzsche suggests that German spirit, German bravery, could be turned against "culture" and that this might be the only hope for the creation of a genuine German culture.

Nietzsche is drawing a distinction between "culture" and "genuine culture," a clear case of a double concept that is sometimes marked only by intimation for the discerning reader. His efforts must now be directed in a variety of simultaneous directions because of the complexity involved at this point of his argument. Nietzsche is backing up again to his starting point, but with a new perspective. Public opinion and its leaders are not only complacent, they exude joy and jubilation at the consequences of their culture. German novelists and journalists are suddenly intruding into the ruminative "stray" hours of human beings, stamping out deviance of thought. Their readers are stunned into submission by the displayed uniformity of enlightened thought. False optimism can be traced to this manufactured culture. A relentless group self-awareness has appeared which allows citizens to recognize new classics at once. Taste is instantaneous; it does not require rumination. Nietzsche's bitter image is of a deformed people pluming themselves before a mirror. The more cultivated and learned (those more cultivated and learned than the journalists and novelists) are content to let this happen, agreeing that the culture in question is the ripest and fairest fruit of the age. The culture of the scholar and the journalists is identical, in fact, except for the superficial trappings of scholarly knowledge. In what concerns life, they are equally decadent. Could this apparently unified culture have defeated France? Unity emerges here as another double concept, the philistine version of agreement in opinion ringing hollow in comparison to the genuine unity of tragic vision.

A cautious *foreign observer* finds these matters easiest to notice. Is this Nietzsche himself? Nietzsche spent his adult life outside of Germany and did not regard himself as a German. He apparently invented a biography tracing himself from a Polish noble family in order to support his non-German self-image and his outside perspective on all things German. If the foreign observer isn't Nietzsche, such observations are possible only for someone who could escape the rigid conformity of popular opinion.

Nietzsche explicitly introduced a definition of *culture* as the *unity* of the expression of *life* of a people. This definition opposes the meaning of unity in popular opinion, although Nietzsche is working with deliberate ambiguities. Germany is described as a barbaric state because of the jumble of styles playing within its borders. *Culture* now goes into quotation marks with the correct definition of *culture* in hand. German "culture" in clothes, concerts, writing, whatever, is an unassimilated motley. Nietzsche's contrast of culture and barbarism is suited to calling up the distinction between Hellene and barbarian. The Übermensch will later be defined as someone who can act out of a true cultural unity, and Nietzsche anticipates here a Germany that is not ruled by a motley of incoherent ideas.

Cultural philistines operate with a form of false consciousness, in that they believe they possess culture, while in fact they are barbarians. A cultural philistine is someone who thinks that a philistine can have a little culture, or is someone who smudges the gap between culture and barbarism. Philistines accept that culture implies unity, but they give this a philistine reading, mistaking conformism for the structural unity of genuine culture. They thus take for culture precisely what isn't culture: a public consilience of opinion. Nietzsche's distaste for popular opinion again presses on the reader. A philistine should be embarrassed by comparison with genuine German thinkers of the past, seekers who looked for a German culture that they knew they hadn't found. The philistine reads them as sources for elements of philistine culture, turning them into atemporal monuments uttering timeless truths. Cultural philistines attempt to create a comfortable, unchanging world, an effort culminating in the Hegelian fixation of the real as the rational.

Philistine writers are ultimately cynical. They know that what they have to say is ultimately irrelevant entertainment, as long as they are allied with power. Nietzsche uses few lines from Vischer to expose the fact that philistine culture is ideological camouflage for social power. Philistine humor mocks those who are socially and economically disadvantaged. Whatever Nietzsche's preference for social hierarchy, he doesn't associate mockery of lower social layers with those in the higher layers of a superior society. Nobles measure their strength against one another; they do not demean their slaves.

As the track of Nietzsche's arrow has been laid down, sections 3 through 7 can proceed by a leisurely examination of Strauss's ideas. The vulgarity of Strauss's late opinions can be crudely characterized as an assumption of equality with greatness. One of the values that supports the power of Nietzsche's prose here is a sharp division of human beings into beasts of prey and barbarians, with little recognition of intermediaries. Strauss attempts, in the barbarian mode, to pick and choose ideas from the whole panoply of beliefs associated with modern faith in science. To do this, he appropriates and discusses whatever bits of literature, music, science appeal or do not appeal to his sensibilities. Nietzsche suggests that such disconnected beliefs are always collectively boring and their expression vulgar. Only small people take pleasure in the confirmation of their views by selection in the prose of cultural idols. Nietzsche is not interested in Strauss as a person here, but in the representative vulgarity of the views that Strauss happens to express. Strauss explicitly appeals to the consensual strength of an amorphous collection of those who share his views by use of the word *we*. This melange includes scholars, artists, office workers, soldiers, landed proprietors, and others. (Burst of laughter from Nietzsche.) Nietzsche has fun with the idea that what all of these people might agree to could be worth knowing. He is still laughing in section 7, where he notes that the humanistic concept of man embraces Strauss and all aborigines, making Strauss's opinion that we should live like men an abstraction without content.

Strauss's presumption of equality with greatness is captured in its full vulgarity in section 6. Optimism, Strauss notes, can be too shallow. Schopenhauer provides the cosmetic dash of pain and evil that is perfect for providing a tone of depth. How easily this shunts Schopenhauer and pessimism aside, a ridiculous move adequately exposed by Strauss's remark that it is only necessary to leaf through Schopenhauer's works to grasp their essentials.

Strauss tells his readers that he is telling them what they don't want to hear, a manifest absurdity if measured by the sales successes of his books. One cause of what Strauss takes to be his unpopularity, his rejection of Christianity, is quickly demolished. The rejection of simple Christianity disturbed the honest peasants who rioted against Strauss's academic appointment, but it cannot disturb Strauss's audience of philistines. They want a controlled and inoffensive substitute Christianity, one that tempers the violent judgmental core of early Christian belief.

Sections 8 through 12 shift the discussion from Strauss's opinions, a discussion of content, to a consideration of Strauss's style of writing. It is the lack of integration in Strauss's thought that permits form and content to be split in Nietzsche's discussion, a separation that is itself a critique. Nietzsche discusses the constructive development of good writing. A sound, unified overall plan must be crafted as the framework into which details are to be exactly fitted. The genuine craftsman trims away everything that is extraneous to his basic purpose. Philistine scholars and scientists write by stringing together individual items that they feel comfortable with, assuming that the assembled pieces will then make sense as a whole. Strauss writes as a philistine, his new faith being faith in science. He presents his faith as a motley of scientific ideas. A genuine new faith (like that to be presented in *Zarathustra*) must look coherently into the abyss that is Dionysian process. Nietzsche describes Strauss as a horticulturist decorating a summer home. This imagery is carefully chosen. A summer house (modern science) is something constructed out of an optimism that can withstand only the best weather. The horticulturist doesn't add anything essential; he camouflages and decorates. Strauss would refuse to be a philistine, but he chooses the curious route of wanting to be like almost everybody important, like Voltaire, Lessing, Goethe. The resulting blend of ideas automatically precisely convicts him of the status that he wishes to avoid.

Strauss confuses apparent simplicity of style with unity, missing completely the deceptive simplicity of genius. The great writer is playful and light, leaping about on high places where disaster is the consequence of a single misstep. Strauss's simplicity comes from poking about in a safe place. In abandoning writing on a theological topic that he could handle honestly and taking on the pretensions of a cultural spokesman, Strauss becomes a real buffoon. Philistine popularity is real buffoonery; later Nietzsche would reveal that a deliberate, deeper buffoonery might develop truths that would escape philistine comprehension.

Strauss's specific stylistic traits finally come under direct critical attention. Strauss attempts to find a style shaped by misleading philistine simplicities. For example, he is tempted by the manifest importance of metaphor and simile to try constantly for new metaphors and similes, but in doing so he confuses *new* and *modern*. Choosing metaphors from modern life, he fails to say anything that is actually productive or new. Comparing the world to a modern machine, for example, with pistons and circulating oil, doesn't by itself add anything to ancient metaphor in terms of understanding. Another idea of the philistine conception of style is that the didactic sentences should be long and abstract, the persuasive sentences, short and colorful. Strauss obliges right on cue and even experiments with sentences falling between these extremes. Mechanical construction cannot breathe life into Strauss's work. The ultimate problems with Strauss's style are subtly indicated by the fact that he can't be accurately translated into other languages, such as Latin, something that could be done if Strauss were making clear sense.

It's not at first clear that Nietzsche hasn't wandered off course slightly in the enthusiasm of his attack. The problem is how he can mean to say that style and content must be fused in good writing, while retaining the demand that good writing should be translatable into other languages. That Nietzsche thought that important ideas could be understood across vast temporal and linguistic distances is sufficiently shown by his interpretation of the Hellenes. Fusion means that concentration on style alone is impossible, because then style could be considered *apart* from its associated content, defeating any originating claim to achieved fusion. Where style can be considered alone, as in the case of Strauss, writing must be superficial in a pejorative sense. Where talk of style is necessarily talk about content, what is being said must always be in the focus of discussion, and successful style is transparent to its content. The style of Hellenic nobles had been precisely this for Nietzsche, although it had not been written into characterizing texts. At least at this point in his career,

Nietzsche cannot imagine a deconstructive play with genuine text, but looks for a style that, having caught one's attention, turns transparent to what is being said, leaving content to be clearly grasped by discerning later readers. A new style is required for Nietzsche's new value table, and he will shortly find the aphorism in his search. The structure of the aphorism, in conceptual slow motion, is lying before him in the first untimely meditation, and will be discussed in the next chapter. At this point in his career, Nietzsche is consciously concerned with a double concept of style. The negative moment is that of style as a filigree on top of borrowed ideas, leading to judgments that a writer has expressed some idea in a beautiful way, whereas the positive moment is the anticipation of a style that can fully embody healthy and progressive ideas. Strauss can't tell us anything in his style precisely because its exploitation tells us that he isn't anybody.

The last section of the meditation applies a nice final touch by examining single sentences from Strauss's work. Nietzsche notes that Strauss, conscious of the swamp of Hegelian expression, tries to find firm footing on dry land; he just never makes it. The brutal detail of Nietzsche's exercise is omitted in those English translations that, by omitting this section, avoid the subtleties of German grammar. This is an ironic confirmation of Nietzsche's remarks about the difficulty of translating Strauss.

The first of these single sentences from Strauss will be represented here as illustrative of Nietzsche's technique:

> Already as its power increased—the Roman Catholic Church recognized the desirability of collecting dictatorially its entire spiritual and worldly power in the hands of a pope who was recognized as infallible.

Nietzsche observes that this complicated sentence from Strauss is an assemblage of simpler sentences that cannot be fitted together so as to make clear the related temporal sequences. Just when did the Church effect this recognition and the transference of power? Before its power increased, or during the increase of power? And who is the dictator? The Church or the pope? Did the Church dictatorially transfer power, or was power somehow transferred to the pope, who was then a dictator? Actually, as Nietzsche points out, neither is correct, although papal infallibility in doctrine under certain circumstances suggests that the second reading is intended. The placement of the adverb, however, suggests the opposite, that power was collected dictatorially by the Church. Acting like a precise copy editor, Nietzsche blue-pencils the sentence as not saying anything clearly enough to be passed on to the typesetter. He performs a similar service for another sixty-nine examples. The first untimely meditation ends with the observation that this is *Nietzsche's* confession, the confession of an individual who knows that he is not in resonance with the thoughts of his time and cannot be sure of being heard.

Nietzsche's self-assessment concerning the care with which he constructed his works is sufficiently supported by a detailed look at this essay. The style of the first untimely meditation becomes terribly compressed in places, on its way to the aphorism. When aphorisms are collected in works, the relations between them are not important, rather the way in which each can hit its target. The works become barrages of arrows, any one of which can prove fatal. Rather than follow this development in detail, we will take a look at the work in which Nietzsche's mature fusion of style and content into the aphorism can be felt without qualification, *The Gay Science*. Clearly, the care exhibited in the first untimely meditation in terms of construction cannot be left to one side. A successful aphorism will be dependent on every single word involved in its construction.

The aphorism has been little studied, perhaps because of its violent compression and because it seems to represent the alternative to the privileged philosophical notion of system.[3] Aphorisms are threatening. They conjure up a sense of intellectual superiority on the side of the writer, and they may conceal a destructive force that can suddenly injure the reader as they are unraveled. A good aphorism, coiled and waiting, is actually detached from its author. What it implies may not even be known to the author, and may never be fully known by anyone.

A set of aphorisms will not have the structure of subordination to an overall architecture that had been Nietzsche's characterization of sound writing in the first untimely meditation. At the same time, aphorisms need not be merely carted together. Hippocrates, one of the first to use the aphorism, used aphorisms to link cure to diseases through diagnostic insights. Each aphorism can be used to cure a disease, but the diseases themselves can be organized (like the cures) around a complex web of relationships. Nietzsche, who at times viewed himself as a physician of sick times, used aphorisms to transvalue the superficial thought around him by suggestion of a sudden cure at a timely moment of impact.

The aphorism can't mirror much structure because it has so little itself. Therefore it can be applied over and over to changing circumstances. The aphorism is too finite to be true by itself; it's a device to open up the thoughts that are compressed within it in interaction with its surroundings. It pretends to a normal linguistic structure, but its content is a nonbelief, a knowing that something isn't so. A typical syntactic device is to reverse the normal sense of a biblical quotation or a line from literature. A rain of aphorisms is designed to produce chaos. Each, in a sense, produces a Hegelian explosion of negativity, but the sum is not a system of beliefs or of knowledge. The sum is the relentless destruction of the past, the possibility of novel affirmation of the future. Existing thought is not developed, but destroyed.

The title *The Gay Science* does not, as some commentators have thought, modify *science;* Nietzsche is proposing a newer, lighter transvaluation of ordinary science. He's after a Hellenic science, dealing with the appearance of the world as it is, and not seeking the abstractions and theoretical explanations of modern science. In the last paragraph of the Preface for the second edition, Nietzsche makes it clear that he is speaking with other free spirits who are *artists* in terms of a Hellenic valuation. He is proposing replacement of what science has become with gay science, a transvaluation of science into a higher, lighter, more resilient Apollinian form of poetic knowledge. *The Gay Science* is a translation of the technical name for the troubador poetry and song of certain wandering medieval poets in southern France. Rather than supposing that Nietzsche's epistemology is undergoing a shift, one can better suppose that experimentation with expression is at stake, Nietzsche's opinions developing into the space marked out as his expression becomes more poetic and more condensed.

In the Preface, Nietzsche identifies himself as a philosopher, one who is interested in overcoming the sickness of a fixation on (scientific) "truth." As artists, Nietzsche says, we must be "cheerful," and on that basis we must "forget." We must be like the Hellenes, remaining with the surface out of profundity and not generating theoretical explanations of the surface. Aphorism 12 states that science can serve the development of various sets of values (as a method), but it does not and cannot create value. The last segment of the Preface is a direct reprise of *Birth*.

Aphorism 46 appears to be straightforward praise of scientific certainty (Nietzsche is writing at a time before the great scientific revolutions were known), but Nietzsche is not opposed to what science does or how it can be used; he is opposed to its fixation as a body of truths. The general tone of this aphorism seems to belong to the historical observations that are common to Book 1 of *The Gay Science*. Once it was the case that life seemed ruled by necessity, so that fairy tales (i.e., dreams of alternative patterns of causality or the relaxation of causality) were the relaxation of the times, whereas now, when nihilism confronts us as a matter of rule, the promise of the necessities of science is our relaxation. In short, science is "fixed" because of its surroundings. It seems to offer the hope of cumulative control just when chaos is otherwise threatening. The *amazement* of the title of this aphorism need not be amazement at the "knowledge" that science produces, but merely amazement that the vagaries of history should have given it that role.

Aphorism 107 could hardly make it clearer that "science" is not being praised in any simple fashion. Science is explicitly said to realize general untruth and mendaciousness. Art is required to make the discoveries of science bearable. Art is the good will toward appearance that helps to cancel the nausea that science would produce with its hoarding of "facts." The gay science, which is really an art form, chooses the value of gaiety, looking at human existence from a medium height from which perspective both human seriousness and human folly are visible. This is the new attitude that replaces the more serious calls to unified culture that had characterized *Birth,* as well as the first two meditations of *Untimely Meditations.*

In aphorism 123, the modern dominant stand of science is related to a monomania to know everything. This passion is not widely recognized. The Church has publicly praised science, but privately considered it second rate, not connected to passion. The ancient world saw science as subservient to virtue. Nietzsche's judgment that science wants to be more than mere means is offered as a statement about the peculiarity of modern times. Aphorism 124 describes us as having left the land and being in an open sea that may appear calm at the moment, but that can suddenly roar and rage. Here "we" free spirits are experiencing nihilism and the potential of Dionysian forces. Notice the subjunctive mood of the last sentence. Land had only seemed to offer more freedom, but that was an illusion. The fixed ground of science (see aphorism 56) could be swept away or buried by a raging storm. These passages should be sufficient to indicate that Nietzsche's attitudes toward "science" and "art" and their division, expressed earlier in *Birth,* remain in place.[4]

The text of *The Gay Science,* in its final version, and not considering the prefaces, consists in nearly four hundred aphorisms sandwiched between two sets of poems or songs. A division of the aphorisms into books is also indicated, and it is true that within the books, related themes seem to occur. For example, Book 2 contains most of the aphorisms concerning women and concerning art. It would be possible to produce a brief exposition of this material only if Nietzsche's aphorisms (and poems) were a complete failure. Later in his career, when Nietzsche realizes that his aphorisms are not being understood, he writes an entire monograph as an introduction to a single short aphorism.[5] The complete expository task of the interpretation of the aphorisms is, simply put, impossible.

We will barely begin the illustration of this fact with a consideration of aphorism 56 of Book 1. A basic aspect of the structure of this aphorism that must be noticed is the transvaluation implied by the last sentence. Up to the last sentence, Nietzsche has been discussing what others are doing, projecting the suffering of yet others. To this, he opposes the projection of his own happiness (not the suffering of others). This is clearly how the gay science differs from science, and to notice that, the "break" announced between what precedes and the last sentence must be heard by the reader. But the last sentence does not state a transvaluation; it announces it by means of a Nietzschean paradox. *They project others' suffering: I project my happiness.* This is thought-provoking provided that suffering and happiness are opposed concepts, as they are in majority discourse. Thus the paradox is aimed at exploding everyday thought. In Nietzsche's own valuation, of course, suffering is not a negativity since it is intrinsically involved with the path to self-transcendence and (real) happiness. Real suffering is personal suffering; it begins as internal suffering. This is the suffering (not that of others) that needs to be overcome. Affirmative happiness represents the overcoming of negative (personal) suffering. The actual transvaluation of suffering is from an external matter to an internal matter (happily) provoking self-transcendence. We see here how the discursive structure of *Untimely Meditations* has been compressed into a sentence. A paradox is utilized to provoke a transvaluation. The first task of interpretation is to recognize the dramatic impact intended by the last line and to provide an account of it. Now let us look at the last line.

Where has Nietzsche painted his happiness? Others have put the sufferings of others in the public domain; Nietzsche has done this with his happiness. Nietzsche's painting is clearly not in his imagination. He also suggests that happiness can approach from the outside, that is, that it is involved in something that overwhelms us. Ultimately, Nietzsche will do without the nihilistic phenomenology of inside and outside, which he utilizes here somewhat paradoxically as a clue to his actual intentions. Who are Nietzsche's friends, referred to in the last line? It might seem tempting to think biographically, perhaps of Schopenhauer, or of Wagner. In producing works of art, they also painted on the wall, producing works requiring interpretation. But Nietzsche's call for action is not very compatible with Schopenhauerian resignation. Further, the sense of the whole aphorism is that young Europeans are being addressed. Chronologically, this would leave Wagner and Schopenhauer out of consideration.[6] Figuratively, given Nietzsche's use of youth as a stage where self-transcendence is possible, they might be included, although by this point Nietzsche's biography shows gathering doubts about both of these predecessor father figures. The phrase "Pardon me, my friends . . ." seems best taken as a rhetorical flourish designed to request the quiet reflective attention of young European free spirits, to indicate to them that Nietzsche is doing something different, something distinct.

What comes before the last line is all of one piece. Nietzsche is describing "young Europeans." They feel a craving for action (naturally associated with the body) but satisfy it in their social context by projecting a suffering toward whose elimination they can direct action. Nietzsche is not saying that there isn't suffering. He's saying that it is turned into a monster, wildly exaggerated, in order to make action a necessity. The craving to do something produces the recognition of suffering. That's Nietzsche's analysis, even if from the perspective of those who will eliminate suffering, it is the suffering that produces the action. True suffering, incidentally, is not projected elsewhere; it is a stimulus that causes authentic distress and provides the source of self-transcendence. False feelings of distress can be internalized because action can't conquer the illusory distress that the young Europeans project. Nietzsche is saying that the goal of eliminating external suffering can't be satisfied, because it is based on a causal delusion. Activists need others and other others, so that if one monster is conquered, another will be found to take its place. The craving for action can't be based on a cycle that terminates in rest. The true craving for action terminates in affirmation, something not having a basis in others. Self-realization takes the peculiar form it does in Europe because of the falsity of the dominant European scale of values. The phenomenology of the young is described as a craving, a response to a tickle or to a spur, indicating that it is not a genuine feeling for Nietzsche, but a distorted form of self-realization. Reigning values call for the quickest possible elimination of suffering as something that is bad or evil. People can't live with their boredom; they sense its inconsequentiality. (That boredom is not really all bad was already noted in aphorism 42, lending support to the idea that the current totally negative valuation of boredom is in error.) The combination, for the young Europeans, is explosive. They respond by acting too quickly. A deeper insight might lead to a recognition of genuine distress in the face of the full terror of Dionysus. That the inventions of the young could be more refined alludes to the fact that this deeper articulation is possible, but it would still remain (like Nietzsche's paintings) an illusion. As it is, the illusion of distress doesn't fill the world with real distress, just with the illusion of distress.[7] These feelings are projected out, leaving the mess on the inside unexamined. Perhaps Nietzsche speaks to "friends" because he recognizes the valid feelings concealed in their urge for change, suggesting that boredom be conquered instead in the affirmative culture he is trying to adumbrate.

Nothing is inaccessible to the whole sensing body for Nietzsche. It is always a mistake to postulate a "true" world to which we have access only through a special rational faculty. This error might be ascribed to Plato, to Kant, and to all the major philosophers in between them.[8] The apparent world *is* the true world for Nietzsche, and the true world is the apparent world all over again. The Dionysian is not a manifestation of the universe; it *is* the universe, and access to it through rationality is limited. The Apollinian, in treating appearance as appearance, does not deceive. It forms part of the Dionysian, like the foam on top is part of a wave.

Our purpose here is not to settle the question of whether Nietzsche is at his best or his worst as an aphorist, nor to attempt to decipher the full range of the aphorisms, but instead to note the structural place of the aphoristic works, *The Gay Science* here representing the sustained use of the device of the aphorism in the development of Nietzsche's thought. Who can fail to understand Nietzsche's vanity concerning his aphorisms? He was conscious that he was not arguing, but was attempting to be lethal against argument. A Nietzschean arrow, striking home, was designed to deal the death blow to entire systems of thought: science, Christianity, and the classical conception of Greece among them. If Nietzsche took deliberate chances and sometimes wild aim, he was hardly after small game.

3

Prophecy

Thus Spake Zarathustra, possibly Nietzsche's most famous work, stands as a singularity in the body of his writing. The vision of the Hellenes is fused with the style of the aphorism in Nietzsche's sustained mature efforts other than *Zarathustra*. *Zarathustra* is the only work to have a narrative structure featuring a central actor. It is the only work that presents a sustained discussion of the Übermensch. It is the work in which the Eternal Return is presented in a clear visual image. Because of this, many commentators have concluded that *Zarathustra* is of secondary importance to the interpretation of Nietzsche and that its points of view need to be retrospectively interpreted through later discussions of will to power.

Perhaps *Zarathustra* should be approached as a nineteenth-century Hellenic tragedy, as an Apollinian illusion in which the central figure is presented as a god who will allow Dionysian process to become bearable to Germans who recognize the fraudulent nature of Wagner's efforts. *Zarathustra* contains the poems, the songs, and, implicitly, the music appropriate to such a project. Zarathustra has his eyes on the unpredictable future while he experiences the present. *Zarathustra* fuses a view of tragedy with a purified Hellenic awareness of Dionysian process. If the aphorisms are arrows of destruction, *Zarathustra* can be read as an Apollinian tragic construction appropriate to an era that has experienced Socratic optimism; it would not have to be written twice. On this reading, *Zarathustra* presents an appearance that continues the second Nietzsche's absorption in his Hellenic vision, and it is the full expression of the artistic alternative to a philosophical expression of the table of values announced in *Birth*.

Zarathustra, clearly intended to refer to the seventh-century B.C. Persian religious figure, is carefully chosen for a variety of reasons involving parallels with Nietzsche's own thought. Zarathustra also saw good and evil as unalterably opposed but yet interrelated, interpreting the world as the battleground between good and evil, with the outcome of the battle uncertain. The Persian prophet was not a god, but a human being with deep feelings for forces underlying human existence. Both Nietzsche and Zarathustra insisted that untimely truth telling was a supreme virtue, no matter what the personal cost, and Nietzsche's perception of himself as a nomadic warrior may well have been partially derived from Zarathustra's biography.

But Zarathustra and Nietzsche are not the same, in that Nietzsche explicitly and consciously recognizes the necessity of moving beyond good and evil, even if one playful reading of the Eternal Return makes Nietzsche into Zarathustra's return. This effect is heightened by the observation that almost all the references to time and places in *Zarathustra* parallel events in Nietzsche's life. The doctrine of the Eternal Return is central to *Zarathustra,* as are the concepts of the Übermensch and of will to power, but these important doctrines are explicitly referred to on only a few occasions in the text, and the Eternal Return doesn't appear at all in explicit form until late in Part 3.

The subtitle of *Zarathustra* is "A Book for All and for None." Let us try to find a crude relationship between this subtitle and the major themes. *Zarathustra* is divided into four parts of approximately equal length, and each of these parts is further subdivided into about twenty short sketches. In Part 1, Zarathustra appears and literally gives lectures or sermons to his disciples. These lectures are basically on various practical matters. In Part 2, Zarathustra combine periods of withdrawal and solitude with lectures or sermons about religion and philosophy. In Part 3, Zarathustra retreats from human companionship (but remembers his disciples), and at this point the doctrine of Eternal Return presents itself. In Part 4, Zarathustra meets some humans who are beginning to show evolutionary signs of becoming Übermenschen and talks with them in his cave, while indicating that he has finally transcended pity, the last vestige of the old morality. Looking at these four parts, one can see that the key doctrines of Eternal Return and will to power appear explicitly only in Part 3. Parts 1 and 2 do deal with the concept of the Übermensch. This structure suggests that Zarathustra turns from being a teacher (as did Nietzsche) when his reflections force him into truths that are not communicable. To put it in modern terms, the doctrine of the Übermensch, the possibility of the Übermensch, can be stated, while the other central doctrines must be realized privately by the individual, not being statable in the public language—so that Zarathustra (or Nietzsche) could only be making sense to someone who had already traveled this road of thinking. Over the period of development in *Zarathustra*, Zarathustra's audience shrinks from *all* to *none*. The significance of the subtitle seems to reflect this fact. *No one* can learn the doctrine of Eternal Return by simply reading *Zarathustra*. At the same time, anyone can see that certain of Zarathustra's criticisms of society are legitimate. Thus the significance of the subtitle is not that only a few can understand the book, which many commentators have supposed, but is that the book is an appeal to anyone to travel a road of thought that none seems capable of pursuing very far and whose end is not available to discourse.

Who is Nietzsche's Zarathustra? The parallels already noted seem to make it clear that Zarathustra is (also) Nietzsche himself, tracing his own trajectory into madness and solitude, or at least that Zarathustra is what Nietzsche wanted to become. Many commentators have assumed that Zarathustra is more than Nietzsche and functions as an ideal for Nietzsche, who himself appears in the guise of the magician or sorcerer whom Zarathustra meets in the fifth episode of Part 4 and who announces that he is collapsing under the weight of having wanted to achieve greatness. There's no problem with this, especially since Nietzsche, who often pitied or despised others, did not consistently conquer pity in his own life, save possibly near its end. In this episode, on one level, Nietzsche is talking to himself. It's a dreary fact that commentators seem often fated to try to locate one figure as Nietzsche in a corpus whose author warned that there are no integral selves and whose author explicitly engaged in reflection with himself from different perspectives.

Other commentators see the text as Nietzsche's commentary on Zarathustra's failures, thus postulating *Zarathustra* as a metacommentary by Nietzsche on Zarathustra's ideas, which represent only an early stage of Nietzsche's development. What is quite interesting in this connection is that the text of *Zarathustra* is just that, a text. Zarathustra's personality is never developed, and it is pointless to look beyond the text for clues to Zarathustra's nature. Portions of the text represent rather a clash of ideas, and we should be prepared for a kind of atemporal diary of Zarathustra's (or Nietzsche's) ideas in various stages of development, the ideas coming into collision in the way that they do in any active thinker. *Zarathustra* is not the statement of a completed system, but a signpost on a tragic route of thought.

The first three parts of *Zarathustra* seem to have exhausted Nietzsche's original intention and were published together. Part 3 ends with a hymn to eternity that sounds like it could be the end of the text. Yet Part 4 was added later, and we have a serial production reminiscent of that of the composition of *The Gay Science*, where an originally conceived conclusion also winds up contained within additional material. The fourth part could well be a discovery of lines of thought latent in the first three parts, a development of their implications, and this is a view quite consistent with Nietzsche's studied reworking of other texts. Such a view would be suggested by a structural reading in which the four parts are each taken to illustrate one of the four major tropes of figurative language: irony, metaphor, metonymy, and synecdoche.[1] Nietzsche would have had to have sensed this gap, the gap outstanding with only three tropes represented, and then have written Part 4 to fill it. A more likely interpretation in the absence of any explicit reference in Nietzsche to such a tropology is the suggestion that Part 4 anticipates some of the doctrines of *Beyond Good and Evil* and *Genealogy*, describing some of the developments from the human that are implicit in the doctrine of the Übermensch coupled with the Eternal Return.

Nietzsche's prophetic mode here is intended to break with previous philosophy and even with the conceptual aspects of the aphoristic period. If the aphorism is an invitation to thought, Zarathustra attempts, out of the divine appearance of his existence, to convince by tragic poetic parable. Images such as the height of Zarathustra's cave, his descent to conversations with others (at a lower perspectival level), need to be viewed as imagery conjuring up a Nietzschean image of transcendence that is appropriately religious and ordinary. Both Plato and Zarathustra describe caves and emergence from them, but this pretty well exhausts the parallelism. Truth is grounded outside the cave (at a higher level) in Plato's imagery, but inside the cave (at a high terrestrial level) in Zarathustra's imagery. Human beings are inside Plato's cave but outside Zarathustra's, save for the few who are invited into the cave in Part 4. Zarathustra reluctantly leaves his cave and is glad to return, the outside world being hostile and empty. Plato's philosopher leaves the cave to seek truth and only reluctantly returns to it. These negations seem more a consequence of transvaluations than of parody. Zarathustra's cave connotes a prophetic loneliness and a highest possible perspective; more significance than that is difficult to discern. The imagery here, as elsewhere, seems to be driven primarily by the exigencies of Nietzsche's own development, rather than by parody of the explicit imagery used by other philosophers.

The text of Part 1 of *Zarathustra* begins with a prologue that explains that Zarathustra deals with individuals or disciples, rather than with crowds. In the opening scenes, we can learn why Zarathustra will avoid crowds, since crowds follow the rails laid down by received opinion. Zarathustra leaves home at the age of thirty (like Christ), but he doesn't preach. Instead, he seeks solitude on the mountains and lives alone there in his cave for ten years. He then decides to return to people. Zarathustra first meets an old hermit and is astonished that he does not know that God is dead. Coming to a town, Zarathustra finds the townspeople assembled in the town square in order to watch a tightrope walker. Zarathustra gives a lecture on the Übermensch, the person who has cast off repugnance of the body in an evolved form that rejects reason, justice, and all concepts founded in current philosophy. The assembly laughs at Zarathustra's foolishness. Zarathustra contrasts the Übermensch with *ultimate men,* an obvious reference to democratic or social man organizing societal existence according to rational principles. The assembly prefers ultimate men. At this point, the tightrope walker appears and begins to traverse the rope rather slowly, in an obvious parallel to man's inching along the rope between animal and Übermensch. Another man then appears, looking like a buffoon, and, after verbally attacking the tightrope walker, he leaps over him. The tightrope walker falls to the earth, where Zarathustra comforts him. The fallen man says that he knew that the Devil would trip him up, and that he's going to Hell. Zarathustra convinces him that there is no Devil and no Hell. The fallen man replies that in that case he is no more than an animal. (How often has this charge been laid against philosophies of a material or biological grounding?) Zarathustra says "not so"—in making danger a calling, the man had lived appropriately to his end. Zarathustra will honor him by burying him. The dying man's hand moves to suggest that he wants to thank Zarathustra.

What is the meaning of this extraordinary episode? Clues are scattered through the work. See, for example, the remarks in the fourth paragraph of "Of Old and New Law Tables" in Part 3: "There are diverse paths and ways to overcoming; just look to it! But only a buffoon thinks 'man can be jumped over.'" In *Ecce Homo,* at the end of the last paragraph of the section on *Zarathustra,* Nietzsche says that Zarathustra overtook him. From the Prologue, section 9, we learn that Zarathustra (Nietzsche) will leap over the hesitating and the indolent, an optimism that deserts him by Part 3. The only way to put these remarks (and others) into one coherent image is to take this scene as Nietzsche's compressed biography. Zarathustra is the mature Nietzsche (at least in his best moments) who is learning that his ideas transcend discourse; that he has no current auditors. In a dreamlike sequence, he sees his former self, the author of *Birth*, attempting self-transcendence while making cautious advances, all the time hoping for approval from the crowd. The buffoon, also Nietzsche, but appearing as the free spirit, leaps over the hesitating scholar, who falls to his death (the crowd no longer caring about the scholar). Embittered, Zarathustra recognizes the buffoon as a careless optimist, and in a voyage of discovery with the townspeople, and later with his own disciples, he finally learns to abandon pity. The earlier forms are redeemed in the figure of Zarathustra. This scene alone should make it convincingly clear that no one figure in *Zarathustra* represents Nietzsche.

In section 10 of the Prologue, we encounter a remarkable image, that of the eagle and the serpent. No one can miss the importance of this odd pair of creatures. In many ancient mythologies, these animals often occur as locked in important struggles. In *Zarathustra*, right from the start, there is a break with this tradition. The snake and the eagle are inseparable, but at peace, and they function as patient and attentive interlocutors of Zarathustra. In the religion of the historical Zarathustra, light, represented by an eagle, and dark, represented by a dragon, are in conflict. Nietzsche must have known this from his sources. The Greeks and Romans took the eagle as the bird of Zeus or Jupiter. The eagle was a solar symbol, having slipped the bounds of gravity and flown close to the sun. The snake often has a connection to wisdom or to learning. Eating snakes, in some cultures, helps one achieve wisdom or learning. Zarathustra's snake is positive, but the other snakes that he encounters, often representing conventional wisdom, are malign and repulsive. Reconciled with the eagle, and having the higher perspective of the eagle, Zarathustra's snake is good. Zarathustra rejoices in what humans see as evil, transvaluing it. He also transvalues what they see as good. In the shepherd episode to come, the shepherd is transformed by spitting out the head of the snake, a symbol of the hierarchical rationality of learning and conventional morality. Zarathustra's two animals, in the context of these other images, show that good and evil must be transcended, but that both are necessary.

In the speech titled "On the Three Metamorphoses," we meet a remarkable set of creatures. First there is the steady, earth-bound camel, burdened with the past, then there is the lion, who fights destructively as a leaping free spirit. The lion feels no weight of tradition, and opposes an "I will" to the "thou shalt" of the past. Finally, the child, playful and innocent, is an affirmative creature capable of finding new values everywhere. This tripartite sequence obviously codes Nietzsche's own development, but there are a variety of interpretive possibilities. A typical version of Nietzsche's career, in which he moves from classical scholar to gay scientist to prophet of the Eternal Return, is often based on this passage. This scheme, of course, is manifestly consistent with the biographical suggestions of the earlier scene in which the tightrope walker plunges to his death. It is suggested here that Nietzsche's career follows this trajectory without supposing that his basic values are reoriented in a scientific phase, but only that the means and emphasis of expression alter as basic values were developed. In this imagery, the child, not conscious of a past, is exploring everything anew, without prejudice. The child, achieving the simplicity of action of the Hellenic noble, expresses the open orientation to the future that had permeated the picture of the Hellenes in *Birth*.

The title "On the Afterworldly" suggests a discussion of those who postulate another world to explain events in this world. This section could even refer back to Nietzsche's discussion in *Birth* of aesthetic deities as abstractions. It now seems to Nietzsche that his earlier projection of a god (Dionysus) contemplating a universe was his own illusion. Transcending himself in thought, he has banished this demon as a convenient fiction for discussing process. Or the section could refer back to Nietzsche's Christian and scientific origins. We have the same problem that we had with the last section. Several interpretive schemes seem compatible with the text. The first interpretation suggested doesn't involve giving up Dionysus, but simply refining interpretation, and is probably preferable given the larger context. Nietzsche, the convalescent here, says that those who believe in heaven and hell cause suffering in him by the projection of such objects of belief. This remark expresses Nietzsche's antitranscendentalism: there are only humans, animals, things in this world. At this point, the Übermensch has to be developed out of the human, as a creature in this world, mutating within the process that is this world. The convalescent, one who is getting better, will return in a later section.

The "leap" next referred to could be a reference to Kierkegaard's religious philosophy, but it also recalls the buffoon in the original scene, whose leap caused the death of the tightrope walker. Weariness attempts to steal what must be won. The "ultimate walls" here is, probably, a reference to death (the death of individuals). Only the body exists, and an attempt to penetrate beyond death into another world is mere projection. Seeming to get the head through is a philosophical illusion. Christians want to project the whole body into heaven, but there is only one body, and it has to remain here.

The ego is the most wonderful of things. Although contradictory and confusing, it is the source of all that we can call knowledge and value as an aspect of the body. Its attempts to escape the body cripple it. Now Nietzsche announces that this insight should lead to the formation of a new will, one that brings desire and the body into coincidence. The sick and dying have despised the body with the body's own creations. In wanting to escape, to avoid work, they created an "automatic heaven." They despised the very source of their own creations. Zarathustra understands the sick because he is himself recovering from sickness. (He will shed this attitude in Part 4.) He has learned that the sick must recover by repairing or improving their own bodies. The mistake is to want to leave these bodies rather than make them healthy. The healthy body doesn't wish to leave itself; it reaches an understanding of its place on earth and doesn't need to project fantasies.

In "Of the Despisers of the Body," Nietzsche offers some advice to despisers of the body—try to leave it—that should shut them up. The body is a multiplicity, a contradiction. The body performs I; it is what I is. It doesn't posit a false abstraction. The spirit is part of the body; the body contains it. Self, not I, is the center of the person, creating the "I" as a projection invented for its own purposes. Ego can carry out the deeper commands of self. Those who attempt to control self with ego turn this around and make the self sick. The self then wants to perish. But ego can't create. Only the body can do that. System thinkers are thus static thinkers and cannot be bridges to the Übermensch. We need a transcendence of the body, not of the spirit. At the same time, the Übermensch can't be achieved by a conceptual definition and an act of will. It must be discovered by a voyage of feeling, undertaken by the body, in which the resolution of inner contradictions is gradually traced out.

This passage of *Zarathustra* can be read as a critique of existentialist "leaps," as we have seen. It can also be read as a critique of Hegel. Rather than making body (self) a posit of absolute spirit, Nietzsche says that the ego is a projection of body, with the consequence that only development of the body, rather than development of the spirit, could improve human beings. Systems of thought are only loops created for some special service to self; nothing more. This is, of course, not a very interesting differential critique of Hegel, since it would apply to all idealisms and doesn't recognize any version of Hegelianism that sees spirit as immanent to this world, requiring only elaboration to be discerned. This passage can also be seen as an anticipation of certain doctrines of Freud. Typically, selves are not unified, but appear as the locus of warring impulses. The ego, and all conscious thought, is a deceptive projection of the body. Biological Freudianism gets a foothold here as does Lacan's variant, in which the "I" that speaks can never be identical with the person, but is an actor who plays a role for the person who cannot speak.[2] One sees that a little poetry can have rather complicated and provocative consequences.

In Part 2, his doctrines having been misunderstood and rejected, Zarathustra returns to the mountains and to his cave. We have a long series of solitary reflections on human beings and on Zarathustra's relationship to them. Near the end of Part 2, after sections titled "On Great Events" and "The Soothsayer," of uncertain biographical significance, Zarathustra does reappear in human society in the section "On Redemption." The reflections of Part 2 seem to have changed Zarathustra's perceptions of human beings—they are even more misshapen and nauseating than he had earlier thought—heightening the necessity for the Übermensch. It has to be noted that the preaching of the Übermensch in Part 1 has not succeeded, and Zarathustra is beginning to realize that he must simply become the Übermensch, must live the possibility.

In "On Scholars," a thumbnail sketch of Nietzsche's scholarly past is presented. Nietzsche has left the house of scholarship; that means that he is no longer regarded by scholars as a scholar and does not think of himself any longer as a scholar.[3] Zarathustra and Nietzsche collapse into one here, Nietzsche using his personal knowledge of the scholarly life to evaluate it.[4] The sheep are those who would follow the dictates of the scholars. Children know better, because they know less. Nietzsche has left the scholars with an angry gesture. They sit indoors, away from life (which they observe through the windows, without experiencing it directly), and attack little problems with well-worn conventional restrictions. In a nutcracking image, Nietzsche suggests that scholars crack one nut after another, making no real progress and never achieving a higher perspective. Scholarly virtue is deadening; it kills everything, reducing it to dust. Scholars poison while protecting themselves, and they don't mind playing with loaded dice. Above all, their industry and cleverness are directed solely to the trivial.

Nietzsche's reference to living above scholars when he lived among them probably refers to his early elevation to a professorship at Basel, an occurrence that no doubt triggered grudges and envy. It also refers to the fact that he always saw more from his height, animating *Birth* with a philosophical perspective that his colleagues could not grasp but whose pretensions they recognized and attacked. Subsequently, he has been ignored. His early works were like resounding footsteps, going somewhere that other scholars didn't want to listen to and couldn't deal with.

They therefore created false ceilings of wood, earth, and filth to deaden his footsteps—so they couldn't hear them or hear them clearly. This is a complex image. "Filth," "wood," and "earth" probably refer to the intemperate early reviews of *Birth*, which did not take careful note of the direction of Nietzsche's footsteps.

Scholars work to strengthen the boundaries of their domain—not allowing outside influences to creep in. The scholars here are restricting, narrowing their domains, particularly by eliminating any stimuli from a higher source. They can only tolerate sounds of movements like their own, movements that take place at the same level. The lowered height of the false ceiling is more comfortable for them. Nietzsche can be more clearly heard outside the house of scholarship after these alterations have been accomplished. Meanwhile, the scholars stay in their rooms, in a controlled and controllable environment. The term "false ceiling" also suggests that the restrictions are not real, but are phony. One might take the false ceilings of earth to suggest that the scholars are buried, dead, in coffins. The feeling here is right, but this reading breaks the image of the house of scholarship, which is clearly above ground. The false ceilings are simply human, all too human. Scholars are content to shield themselves from reality with a very human valuation. This cuts against the coffin image as well, but is quite compatible with the first reading of "dirt." "False ceilings," like those barriers inserted physically into houses in order to deaden upstairs sounds, is a metaphor for scholarly deafness. Nietzsche therefore walks on his own mistakes, not on the limits of the thoughts of scholars. This very nicely marks the "break" between Nietzsche and other scholars. Nietzsche's admission of error is not a loss of stature. His errors are higher than scholarly truths, more daring, more false, more progressive, and more affirmative. His errors comprehend the opinions of scholars, while only incomprehension can be returned. The phrase about justice goes back to earlier passages, especially section 6 of the second untimely meditation, to be discussed in the next chapter. If Nietzsche is accused of not being just, he will turn to the meaning of *justice*—which in its healthy form incorporates an inequality.[5]

Zarathustra is told in "On Redemption" that he should heal cripples in order to persuade everyone to believe in his doctrines. What happens then is significant against the background of the New Testament. Christ heals the sick but Zarathustra wants to transcend the human. He is not interested in healing the sick, who would still be driven by ressentiment. Zarathustra refuses the role of physician. He sees humans as misshapen against the vision of the Übermensch. Human genius is the cancerous growth of one human modality. The past is no better—i.e., these humans are not the degenerate consequences of an earlier and better human form, as they are in the myth of the Garden of Eden. The sight of the human would be completely nauseous if the vision of the Übermensch were not there to provide an imaged mutation. One notes that the imagery suggests that the Übermensch will be produced by the discovery of a better body, not by the development of theoretical power. Human fragments have been noted in Zarathustra's survey of existing human bodies that are over-developed in comparison to the rest of these bodies. These can suggest fragments of the future whole.

Now we have a crucial passage on the will and on ressentiment. The problem for Zarathustra is to overcome ressentiment or pity for what has happened in the past, in order to find a purely positive affirmation. Human willing could not escape the trap of pity and ressentiment. We can't do anything about what has happened. For a human, this is a source of frustration. The Übermensch must learn to affirm everything—redeeming the past by willing that it be what it was (or is), and putting energy into a transformed future. Punishment is the human response to the wrongs of the past, based on ressentiment cashed as resentment that wrongdoers seem insufficiently punished for their bad deeds. The will of the Übermensch sees the past in the present as fragments—to be put together in the future, in something higher than mere assemblage.

Why isn't this notion of redemption Hegelian? It nearly dissolves the weight of the past, allowing it to appear in the present as fragments to be affirmed. But what happens to these fragments? Are they changed in a forward-looking synthesis that is the material counterpart to idealist progress? In Hegelian history, *synthesis* means the retention of some common features of the thesis and antithesis that force the synthesis, while these features are transformed in the context of the new features that arise in the synthesis. In Hegel's historical progression, for example, heathen-ism (Hellenism, in particular) and Christianity are synthesized, the best features of both appearing (although transformed, still recognizable) in the synthesis. Everything past is good and bad, but the good is retained as synthesis proceeds. An optimistic view of history results. By contrast, Nietzsche sees heathenism and Christianity as unalterably opposed. The nihilism that is the consequence of Christianity is nothing; it is worthless, and it will completely disappear in any process of historical redemption. In Nietzsche's biological metaphor, the good (superior) forms of will to power either conquer other forms or decay and die out. The fragments in the present may be assembled in this process, but at the expense of other, rival fragments. The fragment metaphor, and all talk of mutation, is not Hegelian. Current nihilism doesn't "contain" absolute knowledge; either it will terminate human life or it must be overcome and replaced by vigorous new values.

Clearly, Nietzsche's history is moved by eminent individuals representing the direction of overcoming. This is again a biological metaphor. If they cannot breed, their superior possibilities will be swamped by the reactionary quality of the larger population. Particularly in the area of art and philosophy, which he takes to drive the process of overcoming, Nietzsche is an elitist. The elite individual who doesn't further overcoming, because of not being heard, is a terrifying prospect for Nietzsche. By contrast, Hegel's historical movements can be seen as the realization (more and more perfect) of already existent ideas in time. Hence the Übermensch simply will or will not occur; but Zarathustra cannot be content with Hegelian resignation.

We now encounter a passage that contains rather aphoristic rebuttals of other philosophies of history in this new setting. The quoted judgment that everything that passes away deserves to pass away seems a reference to the value optimism of Hegelianism in history. By contrast, Nietzsche's affirmative stand is not a judgment from a human perspective based on the disappearance of things but is an affirmation of whatever comes in the Dionysian flux. The second quotation, referring to a moral order based on justice and punishment, suggests the moral transcendentalism of a philosopher like Kant. By contrast, Nietzsche's universe contains no intrinsic moral structure. The third quotation, to the effect that no deed is annihilated and that existence is an eternal recurrence of deed and guilt, suggests the cosmic fatalism of Schopenhauer. Although closest to Nietzsche's own view, this also rests on the illusion of a transcendental principle. Rather than will a void, we should will the Übermensch, a new creature that could arise on earth. Nietzsche makes an effort to provide a biologically grounded affirmative history in which values are removed from the universe and placed into human perspectives projected onto the universe and in which we are free to affirm what happens as progressive, affirming it without regret. Regret is invariably involved with a transcendental retention of certain features of the past.

This discourse is now broken off when Zarathustra realizes something—perhaps that he is about to try to say what cannot be said—to say what the Übermensch would be like. Zarathustra has been talking to his disciples at this point (those who might be able to understand him), and the hunchback then asks why he speaks differently to his disciples. Zarathustra offers the reply that one might as well speak to a hunchback in a hunchbacked way. Then the hunchback makes a shrewd thrust. Why does Zarathustra's discourse to his disciples differ from his own reflections? Zarathustra realizes (as we do reading the text) that he has said something that starts up wrong thoughts, and he regrets his inability to keep silent. Now he does keep silence, in the sense that this paragraph does not end with anything that Zarathustra says. Zarathustra is alone in his realization of the possibility of the Übermensch.

There is an interesting transvaluation in the first section of "On Human Prudence." At the edge of a precipice, one is tempted to look down and to put one's hands up for balance. Zarathustra is looking up, but wants to reach down (to man). Pity still plays a role in his thinking. Zarathustra is, as it will turn out, still too human to take the step to the Übermensch.

In "The Stillest Hour," Zarathustra must return to his cave; the human remnants prevent him from commanding the Übermensch in spite of the fact that he stands on the edge of this in his thought. These sections attempt a dramatic buildup to the culminating insights of Part 3 and are meant to retrace the difficulties that Nietzsche had in working through his own vision to its loneliest consequences. "My stillest hour" refers to the thought that is both most quiet and most compelling. It speaks without a human voice (Dionysus?), urging Zarathustra to leave humanity, to break with humanity, to speak the doctrine of the Übermensch as clearly as possible. The voice urges Zarathustra to take a step backward, to become as a child without the crippling effects of pride. Without this backward step, the path to the Übermensch is blocked. The human inside must be completely shattered in order for the Übermensch to appear. This completes the significance of the child image that had been introduced in the Prologue.

Part 3 of *Zarathustra* introduces the key themes of the mature reworking of Nietzsche's vision, especially the theme of the Eternal Return. "Of the Vision and the Riddle" is a pivotal section in this respect. Zarathustra can tell his vision as a riddle only, and chooses to do so for mariners, who have already dared to venture beyond what is knowable. Perhaps the meaning can be guessed, but it cannot be rationally calculated or methodologically secured. The dwarf on Zarathustra's back while Zarathustra strode a solitary path upward was half mole, a creature of earth bound by gravity. The dwarf utters the philosophy of equality, pressing Zarathustra toward "normal" thought. The dwarf represents the entire weight of historical tradition, at least that part that remains. Zarathustra, suddenly, confronts the dwarf in an existential moment: "You or I." This verbal courage produces a physical change, not a leap of thought. When Zarathustra acquires the courage to assert himself, the dwarf leaps—off his back. They find themselves conscious only of the present moment, with a straight path behind and in front, although they cannot see much more than that these paths are attached to the present moment and are present in the present moments.

The one infinite straight path is contrasted by the dwarf to a crooked or circular path, which the dwarf suggests is the actual path of time. Zarathustra says that the dwarf is wrong, unmistakably. Nietzsche would have wanted to repudiate the Christian view that a straight, finite past implies a creator and the Christian view that singular events will arise in the future that have never been seen before. The dwarf's view rules out these possibilities, but, as a scientific hypothesis, it has depressing consequences. Zarathustra suggests that an infinite past must have already produced all the possible dice throws of chance. In thinking through the consequences, it would seem that there must be exact repetition and recurrence, a thought that condemns one to an inactive stupor of pessimism. This moment can occur only in exactly this way, and in saying that what could have happened has happened and that this moment draws the future to it, the Eternal Return allows for only one actual history of the world. There are no opportunities to undo what we are doing or what we have done. We shouldn't look for alternative histories; possibility is conflated into the display of the necessity of all options within this world, the only one. We have to affirm what happens, good and bad together. The Eternal Return involves two reactions; one of pessimistic reason, the other of an active affirmation.

Nietzsche has found the only location for value in a world that admits of no transcendental possibilities. Eternal Return doesn't imply determinism; it urges us to live present moments that we can look back on without wishing that we had done otherwise. Denying the body will cause resentment. Our behavior now and our treatment of the past must be transformed. The Eternal Return is the only nontranscendental eternal verity. Immediately there is a remembrance of a dog howling. Commentators have noted that Nietzsche's father died from a fall and that Nietzsche was attracted to the scene by the sounds of a barking dog. More accurately, the fall was followed by madness and death. Could Nietzsche be worrying here that he would meet the same end? Quite the reverse. The doctrine of the Eternal Return produces the release of therapy. Nothing in the doctrine forces the pessimistic conclusion that sons must die like their fathers. Rather, in recollecting the moment exactly as it was in the present, the moment is redeemed, is accepted, in conformity with the doctrine. It could not have been otherwise. Nietzsche now accepts this, as he can now accept his onrushing madness.

Then a young shepherd appears who is being bitten inside the throat (mortally?) by a snake. This is surely a vision of Nietzsche himself as a young professor, being choked by the knowledge represented in the snake symbol. Biting the snake is an *action* of the body, one that kills the paralysis of wisdom and allows the body freedom to feel once again. Biting off the head of the snake eliminates the symbol of rational structure, leaving a snake like Nietzsche's positive coiled snake that flies with his eagle, a form of knowledge without a privileged point. This is the vision of Zarathustra, the most solitary man, but in actuality the remembrance by Nietzsche of his own past. The transformed, laughing shepherd is the author of *Zarathustra* and the image of the new affirmation.

More is learned about the snake episode in "The Convalescent." The language suggests that the Eternal Return allows for the recurrence of types over time, especially the recurrence of the prophet of the Übermensch. Zarathustra and Nietzsche are one under this sign. The episode with the snake is mentioned again as though it had happened to Zarathustra. Here we learn that it was knowledge choking the shepherd because of the disgust at man that knowledge ultimately causes. Instead of rationality, it is real knowledge that provokes real disgust. Wickedness is, in fact, a strength. Spitting away rational knowledge allows one to move beyond good and evil. But the little man must also recur. Disgust seizes the convalescent once again at this realization that permanent progress seems impossible.

His animals urge that Zarathustra learn to sing (not talk), but Zarathustra is sunk in a deep wordless pessimism that he may return eternally without consequence. Because Zarathustra is only spoken *to* in this passage, it is not at all clear what his final views are concerning the Eternal Return, or whether they could be articulated. We will return to assess the Eternal Return against the full textual possibilities below. By the end of Part 3, Zarathustra has laid aside the pessimism he shows here as a form of the old error of resenting the past (as well as what may come in the future). Part 3 ends with an affirmation of the future, of eternity, but in conformance with the Eternal Return.

As with Nietzsche's reworking of the original ending of *The Gay Science*, the final version of *Zarathustra* contains new material in a Part 4 that follows "The Seven Seals," the hymn to eternity that concluded the original version of *Zarathustra*. These additional materials seem to have been added after the first versions had seemed incomprehensible to read-ers, in the hopes of facilitating communication, at least to Nietzsche's close friends.

The important image of a great noon appears in this material, although it is adumbrated by earlier passages in "On Virtue that Makes Small," "On Passing By," "On the Three Evils," and "On Old and New Tablets." These references are anticipatory and occur typically at the end of sec-tions, without elaboration. In Part 4, the Great Noon is assumed to be an already familiar image.

The Great Noon marks the moment of greatest transition, and as such is a transvaluation of midnight, the normal point of transition from one day to another.[6] The Great Noon is not taken to be recurrent even though it is the important transitional point to the Übermensch. It is as though there could not have been an Übermensch before. In the Great Noon, every-thing is southern, bucolic, peaceful. There are no shadows; as Nietzsche has placed his image it is physically graphic. The absence of shadows means that neither the past nor the future is intruding into the present; there is only the now. By contrast, Christian and scientific points of transition receive significance from what is projected on either side by a transcendental scheme. There is also a suggestion of ancient Hellenic festivals here, familiar to Nietzsche through his studies, in which the normal division of the real world and the underworld was broken at noon, when gods and men could walk freely together. The Great Noon is the moment of realization that Zarathustra must move to the Übermensch and cannot rely on his preaching to effect self-transcendence in others.

The early sections of Part 4 are concerned primarily with various "higher men" who recognize Zarathustra and have partially accepted his teachings. They have climbed (partly) to Zarathustra's cave, but Zara-thustra is not pleased with all this, although he invites the higher men to his cave. (His displeasure is clearly shown in his speech in "The Wel-come.") After noon, in the late afternoon, Zarathustra climbs to his cave to find the "higher men" already present. Zarathustra gives them a lecture. The dwarf (tradition) is on all their backs, and the mob appears within them. They are not Übermenschen. They speak only of their human selves. Zarathustra, at the last supper, gives them his history (again) and a tongue-lashing, and then leaves the cave. The magician's song brings truth into view, suggesting that Zarathustra is "only a poet," something ob-viously depressing to Zarathustra. Shortly thereafter, in Zarathustra's absence, a new religion is founded, based on the ass. The worshippers suggest that Zarathustra himself could become an ass. But, after this exchange, the ugliest man is ready to say "yes" to life—looking to its coming round again—and expressing the psychological release entailed by the Eternal Return. Now, at the midnight hour, strange things occur that are very little commented on in the literature. One rather straightforward reading would be that Zarathustra is finished at midnight, another cycle then beginning. This is compatible only with the deepest pessimism about the actual arrival and permanence of the Übermensch, the cycle leading only from prophet to prophet. But what other reading is there? A possible clue is provided by "Night Song" in Part 2 and by section 7 of the discussion of *Zarathustra* in *Ecce Homo*. At night we are alone. We can only hear. Night calls for silence. The pure vision of theory is precluded, and silence codes the inadequacy of discourse to represent tragic awareness. What light there is (exclusive of moonlight) must come (figuratively) from within. At night, Zarathustra no longer gives, can no longer give, out of pity. This is his final accomplishment in realizing the figure of the Übermensch. At night, the Dionysian process can be heard (as music can be heard) and can be glimpsed in dreaming. The suffering of Zarathustra fades into the cosmic suffering of Dionysus, and tragedy begins again. At one stroke, we have a presentiment of the absence of a coherent notion of a society of Übermenschen, as well as a presentiment of Nietzsche's last years of total silence.

The Übermensch makes no sustained explicit appearance in Nietzsche's works before *Zarathustra*, where the Übermensch appears, beginning to preach what will become will to power and the Eternal Return. But the concept of the Übermensch is not without antecedents in the earlier work. One way to express this would be to say that the Übermensch represents the solution to the problem of how Hellenic nobles lived, unencumbered by history and a morality of ressentiment. Hellenic nobles would not have recognized themselves as Übermenschen, since the recognition of the possibility of the Übermensch depends on its production on the terrain of nihilism. The vision of *Zarathustra* is not a vision of the future course of history; it is rather a tragic vision of how a disciple of Dionysus could live, a vision that must be presented in a frenzied tragic mode that avoids the constipated prose of scholarship.[7] If the aphorism is the arrow fired by the nomadic warrior, the Übermensch represents his redemptive dream back in camp.

4

History

Nietzsche's interest in history derives from his philological studies and from the vision of the Hellenes presented in *Birth*. From the beginning, Nietzsche felt that the past should only be exploited to aid the present. The past, as such, is not accessible to us. Its remains may confront us in the present, but we are free to use these to enhance life. By contrast, the standard attitudes toward history work as fixatives, establishing a tradition that must be respected or sketching a picture of constant human progress. *Birth* was appropriate history; it read the Greeks so as to show Germany how to return to Dionysian process.

The second untimely meditation can be seen as a form of philosophical attack against various criticisms of Nietzsche's historical practice. Hegelian historians were interested in understanding other cultures as the progressive unfolding of various ideas, hoping to achieve a systematic integration of historical detail by organizing details around ideas. Historicist critics of Hegel had insisted that insufficient detail could be accommodated within such a scheme for a sufficiently rich understanding of history. Each period had to be understood in itself through the presentation of all the relevant detail. Other historians argued for understanding through motivation, so that we come to understand other periods in the same way that we understand other human beings, through imaginative projection. The nineteenth century is often regarded as the century in which German scholars created a new science of history, all the approaches cited being capable of a "scientific" defense. Once again, Nietzsche stands virtually alone, opposed to this onslaught. Nietzsche denies the pretensions of other historians to have achieved scientific understanding. Historical understanding for Nietzsche proceeds out from the perspective of the historian, whose values can be jogged by strange texts, but whose perspective can't be made universal by methodology. The second untimely meditation produces a general argument that useful history, rather than objective history, is the only kind worth having, thus expressing Nietzsche's growing awareness that he must leave his education behind. He stands alone, and he must develop his own perspective without reliance on others.

Nietzsche is not concentrated this time on a victim or representative as he was when in the first untimely meditation he focused on Strauss. Eduard von Hartmann is mentioned and attacked, but not with the same concentration or sustained attention. Nietzsche attacks all false postures and debts toward the past and sharpens his active disencumbrance of the remains of the past in the present. The imagery of *Zarathustra* confirms the idea that the weight of the past must be cast off and that the past must only be affirmed.

The second untimely meditation is organized as though Nietzsche wanted to take one strand from the first untimely meditation and from *Birth* and to discuss it in depth, that strand being the decadence of any "objective" history. To make sure that this point is not missed, Nietzsche discusses all kinds of history, in order to ascertain their potential value for life. Arrows are fired, so to speak, at all the targets. The annoying problem is that human life can't do without history, and Nietzsche's problem here is thus to find ways of minimizing the damage to life that is caused by the impact of history. Before we start a consideration of the meditation, the title is worth looking at closely. Expanding the conjunction of the title, we get "On the Uses of History for Life, and on the Disadvantages of History for Life." History can be advantageous or disadvantageous. This will be true for all the varieties of history. As we can't do *without* history, the task is to seek its most advantageous form, and that is the explicit topic of the meditation. If history is here taken as providing an inescapable problem, Nietzsche has not yet fully left the house of scholarship, and he is still attempting to find a readership.

The first paragraph of this untimely meditation lays out the single theme to be pursued, grounded in a quotation from Goethe. Goethe's stature is used, once again, to force the attention of the conventional reader to the topic at hand. But who is being addressed? Who does the *we* of the first paragraph include? Clearly not everybody. The idler in the garden of knowledge (the scientist, and especially the scientific historian) is excluded. Idlers do not recognize the import of humbler truths as they regard themselves as above such matters. Idlers would think vulgar any appeal to what is useful for life. History is for Nietzsche only valuable insofar as it is useful, only insofar as it serves life, something that will involve the affirmation of base and evil actions. *We* includes those who *can* anticipate the necessity of the affirmative construction of a German culture to include elements beneath the notice of scientific history.

The first sentence of the second paragraph reveals that the necessity of the usefulness of history has tormented Nietzsche. He will revenge himself on it by turning it over to the public. Nietzsche knows that he will be told that he fails to grasp the greatness of the new German historiography, but he proposes (tongue in cheek) that perhaps he will be instructed in a better expression. This is, then, a test of the supposed virtues of public discussion, and Nietzsche's quiet reversal of values here is obvious. The disutility of public discussion, the democratic and scientific ideologue's source of truth, will be demonstrated by its manifest failure to resolve the problem of the necessity of history.

Why is this meditation untimely? Because, like the examination of the potential for defeat in victory examined in the first, it is saying that something is injurious that everyone else takes to be a glorious achievement. Nietzsche sees himself out of step, moving in the wrong time. This relatively precise sense of *untimely* is not always noted. Truth is only taken to be untimely by public opinion. Truth is always timely because it is always unwelcome.

Now for another Nietzschean paradox. The paradox here is that a hypertrophied virtue can be worse for us (less useful to life) than a vice, or even a hypertrophied vice. Goethe's approval means that it must be all right to let Nietzsche speak to this. The addressee subtly shifts as Nietzsche writes. Sometimes he's speaking more or less to everyone, as here, using Goethe's authority to legitimate what he's saying (journalism turned against the journalists), and sometimes he's only addressing those who can feel the intimations of a genuine German culture. Nietzsche attributes his ability to be untimely to his study of Hellenic culture, which had produced a different perspective on the Hellenes than that utilized by his scientific contemporaries.

In section 1, the essential difference between human and animal life is noted. History provides the division, as animals do not labor under conscious constraints from the past. This comparison appears elsewhere, even grazing cattle are used as an image, such as in Kant's essay on history from a cosmopolitan standpoint. Kant seems to have intended a different point, stressing human reason as legitimating a higher status for man. Kant suggests man's physical weakness triggers rational superiority, a form of secularized theology. Nietzsche makes the life of the animal seem more desirable, tracing the alleged superiority of humans to a curse based on memory, rather than to an advantage based on reason. For the Christian philosopher, reason overcomes our animal nature, while for Nietzsche, excessive reason is to be rejected, so that we become more like animals in our relationship to time. The animal, contained wholly in the present, cannot dissemble. It can only appear as it is. Humans, with the illusion of a past, draw a distinction between what appears to others and what is inside. Nietzsche will shortly trace human decadence to the ability to create a "subjective," inaccessible interior, the place where science and history can be illusorily protected from the ravages of time.

That history is necessary to some extent is shown by the fact that complete forgetting and death are synonymous. Happiness is forgetting, i.e., happiness is a temporal experience of life as unhistorical. As in *Birth*, knowledge conflicts with action. Action involves forgetting, distorting, lying, setting aside the impositions of science, and happiness is an action. Nietzsche defines the happy person as someone who acts in a certain way. That's the meaning of the idea that happiness is spread out over time, unlike a transitory "feeling" of happiness. The historical and the unhistorical are both necessary for healthy human life (individual or social), but the appropriate mixture of the two is relative to plastic power, adaptability, and an existing state of happiness. The actor, in setting the past aside and *doing* something, is not "just," is never judicious, is not rational, and is not moral. Nietzsche's appropriation by the existentialist tradition has a point of contact with this observation.

The suprahistorical vantage point on history is now defined as a perspective that realizes only this relationship of knowledge and action. Its only use is to note the inverse relationship between knowledge and action. The suprahistorical vantage point is paralyzing. It counsels the abandonment of action, impossible for continuing human life, in favor of a detached survey of historical fact. Suppose you ask people if they would like to relive the last decade or more of their lives. They will answer in the negative. Those who don't want to relive because they want to improve, want to achieve the unrealized goals of the past, are historical. They only look at the past to attempt better control of the future. Others who say *no* may not be evaluating the past—they may simply see no point, or no possibility, of reliving the past. (An adumbration of the Eternal Return occurs.) The suprahistorical viewpoint causes nausea. There is too much; nothing can be screened out by forgetting, by valuating. Everything is different, but also the same. Because of the nausea, the suprahistorical point of view is not the point of view of the historian; the scientist evaluates through the application of laws.

What does the expression "pure science" mean at the end of section 1? Literally, a useless pile of facts that is not in the service of life. It can be "knowledge," but only at the expense of having nothing to say for life. Nietzsche's hermeneutics of commitment are inescapable, and here the commitment is to useful history.

The second section proposes an analytic distinction between three kinds of history: monumental, antiquarian, and critical. These types of history are not sharply distinguishable, but they pertain to three aspects of human beings; striving and acting, preserving and revering, and suffering and wanting redemption. Thus there are three distinguishable uses of history for life, each of which can take a decadent, negative, scientific form.

Monumental history acknowledges the fundamental role of "great men," "great actors," knowledge of whose roles in history can be useful at the present time. This conception of history is meant to be opposed to Hegelian history, which stresses the process of developing ideas. The content of monumental history is in error—it minimizes the distance between the great person and ordinary people, for example, but its lesson is useful. It can offer the promise of self-transcendence and betterment, spoken of earlier as the aspect of history that the suprahistorical perspective can't find. Monumental history is rejected by those who would subsist in a cocoon of caution, not wanting to take chances with their lives.

The following statements are very complex and need to be looked at again against the Eternal Return. Nietzsche begins by saying that the notion that an exact repetition of the past is possible depends on "smoothing," "abstracting," unless one accepts the (Pythagorean) idea that the very same event could recur, in all of its detail. Nietzsche is obviously well aware that many of the Greeks accepted a notion of cyclical time, and he will urge a version of cyclical time as life-preserving against the teleological history of Christianity. But is he approving of astrology, or is he simply saying that the Pythagorean version of cyclical history is the one form of monumental history that doesn't require the falsity of abstraction? Probably the latter. After observing that causes must be simplified to obtain (monumental) history, he asserts that if cause and effect, historical cause and effect, were really understood, the dice game of chance would be seen never to produce exactly the same events. This suggests that a true understanding of the universe as Dionysian precludes the truth of the Pythagorean account, since the historical strands of cause and effect that are traced in it are illusory. Their repetition would be the repetition of a simplifying picture. If this is so, Nietzsche doesn't accept the Pythagorean account except as a special form of monumental historical illusion. Some commentators have interpreted the later doctrine of the Eternal Return as though it were the same as the Pythagorean doctrine mentioned here. If this interpretation is accepted, then this passage must be interpreted differently. *Birth*, of course, presents a defensible monumental history. Nietzsche notes that either illusion or a monumentalized past may trigger action. The disadvantages of monumental history come from its misemployment. By making monuments classics and worshipping them, historians may prevent appropriate action in the present by demanding that it conform to standards abstracted from the past. The rogue historian will let the dead bury the living. *Birth* willed that the living should bury the dead. The constant theme urges casting off the dead weight of the past.

Preserving and revering gave rise in section 3 to antiquarian history, which is necessary for sustained community life. The talent of an antiquarian historian lies in wanting to preserve whatever was good in the past. Antiquarian history can help to make a wretched life tolerable. But antiquarian attitudes become decadent when they collect and preserve without considering implications for current life. Nietzsche's limited approval of a form of antiquarian history recognizes that historical progress requires bold acts but the simultaneous destruction and preservation of the past. If all knowledge of Hellenic culture were impossible because its traces had been erased, the possibility of the rebirth of tragedy would have been seriously compromised. Nietzsche's integration of the traces of Hellenic culture is antiquarian, but it is placed in the service of a renewal of Hellenic culture that does not depend on more accurate Hellenic scholarship. The possibility of monumental history itself depends on the conserving aspects of antiquarian history.

Critical history is, in some sense, the opposite of antiquarian history in that it tears down and redefines the past in search of its redemption. And, in fact, destroying everything is as disadvantageous to life as preserving everything. On the other hand, in locating the unjust origins of present practices, it can "correct" the impressions of monumental or antiquarian history. Critical history "deadens" events, freeing us from the confines of past and present.

Monumental history includes explanation through narrative projection into the actions of great individuals; antiquarian history includes the efforts of historicists; and critical history includes the perception of history as a redemptive process involving the unfolding of ideas into ever more adequate forms. Nietzsche has surveyed the major historical schools of his time, including variants and fissional forms, and has done it lightly, but the list is obviously incomplete, since Nietzsche's own views as a practicing historian must lie outside these strictures. Nietzsche now addresses the question of whether specific versions of history, tailored to specific nations at specific points in time, but kept so minimal that serious negative effects can be avoided, can be useful to life, like small medicinal doses of poison.

The services history can render to life have been examined in the first three sections of the meditation, and Nietzsche now points out in section 4 that every nation requires a certain knowledge of the past, some mix of the three kinds of history, depending on the nation's goals, energies, and needs at a certain point in time. This set of flexible and useful relationships is ruined when history is made uniformly into a science. Historical science disconnects history from life. Hegel (or certain Hegelians) is probably the target, in that Hegelian history attempted to subsume everything worth knowing into a historical system. This loses the lightness of impact that history should have to advantage life and violates the stricture against the weight of the past. Scientific history is directed by the modern subjective goal of mastery by intellectual system. This subjectivity is a new human condition that may not have existed before the nineteenth century.[1] Genuine culture does not separate "inside" and "outside." Genuine culture is always visible; it shines through. Nietzsche thinks *culture* has come to mean what is stored up "inside," in subjective consciousness, and that it is a mishmash or jumble of stuff that is illicitly protected as an illusion by its decoupling from action. This includes a historical sense that can't affect action. If we take these observations back to the first untimely meditation, to the fifth paragraph of section 1, where culture is defined as *unity of the expressions of life of a people,* we begin to see (partly) what *unity* means. Culture, on Nietzsche's definition, must be expressed; there can be no legitimate split between "inside" and "outside." This, of course, does not yet show what gives the expressions a unity, so we are still unable to solve the problem of what a unified culture would be like, except by looking at the model offered by Nietzsche's vision of Hellenic tragic culture.

We then learn that a genuine culture will be rather simple, by comparison to what ours packs in. The historical should not weigh on us very heavily; it didn't weigh heavily on the Hellenes. The Hellenes knew that *educated* (cultured) and *historically educated* (knowing as much as possible about the past) were not the same. Greek advances were made by throwing away the past. We find that hard to grasp, because it runs counter to the received wisdom of our scientific outlook. Nietzsche directs these remarks especially to the Germans, notorious for "inner" cultivation. Germany's Protestant religious inwardness is Nietzsche's target. Nietzsche will later call it a sickness.

Section 5 deals with the weakening of the personality entailed by the excess of history. The first paragraph lists a variety of ways in which history is dangerous to life, and the first one is then extensively developed. The weakened personality cannot use the historical information that overwhelms it. Even wars and revolutions can cause a stir for only a moment. Wars are described, and examined as aesthetic delicacies, as mere entertainment. The weakened personality retreats into the "inside," and only a role is exhibited to others. People no longer express themselves, although they would if they were healthy.[2] In context it is clear that Nietzsche's notion of self-expression requires a unified cultural context, otherwise the expression would have no impact. Nietzsche is hardly arguing that there is a natural human being whose self-expression would be significant. The rather obscure remarks about the "identical" bourgeois coat are Nietzsche's way of commenting on the crowds or masses of outwardly indistinguishable people who appeared in the large nineteenth-century European cities, a population divided primarily by illusions of distinct personality.[3] Nietzsche's unified culture does not include equality, clearly, but features a hierarchy in which superior types will be visible as leaders by the manner of their expression and even of their experience.

Suddenly we encounter praise of unrestricted philosophy, here taken to be equivalent to the Stoic conception that inner conviction should be wedded to outer expression as a personal statement. Nietzsche, in a sense, anticipates the degeneration of philosophy into a specialized discipline and finds it a reprehensible shift.[4]

In a series of dense sentences toward the end of section 5, Nietzsche first asserts that history can only be borne by strong personalities. A weak person will be either destroyed or dominated by the weight of history. In an image reminiscent of the strong suspension of Apollinian and Dionysian elements in tragedy, Nietzsche proposes that only strength can reduce history to the small role that it should play in our lives. Otherwise, timidity before history turns one into an actor playing a role and results in what we have already learned is philistinism, the supposition that we are similar to, and the equals of, the great figures of the past. The weak person has no principle of selection and winds up supposing that any choice of role from the past is defensible. An image of the eunuch captures this. To the eunuch, because all women are unapproachable, they are interchangeable. To the scholar, all historical facts are equally valuable, and none of them is usable. Genuine history is manly, active; it poses a challenge to be overcome with strength.[5] The cultivated scholarly eunuch looks past the significance of the historical and asks for facts about the author. By implication, Nietzschean hermeneutics looks to the significance of the text, not to the relationship between text and author. In scholarship, critique piles upon critique, with no consequences for action. What is needed is a sense of history that can unseal this hermetic vault.

Section 6 discusses the putative defense of the scholar: that "objective" history is more "just" than Nietzsche's project. But in Nietzsche's version, justice is closely coupled to judging. Justice (the virtue) is the necessary accompaniment of sound judging. Disregarding himself and laying magnanimity to one side, the judge attempts an active assessment of the situation fully prepared to overturn existing convention or to change the egoistical boundaries of possession. True judges will not treat all things equally; some things are more important than others. The truth wanted in judging leads to change of opinion, and consequently, to action. Judgment is not the abstract opinion, hedged in with uncertainty and dithering, of the scholar; it's a propaedeutic to action. The just God of the Old Testament is a perfectly coherent conception. He is the active judge who is after truth. Nietzsche accepts the idea of the importance of justice and then characterizes it so that it is important. His definition has the consequence of not separating an "inside" and an "outside." The just person acts on tested opinion; truth is sought in order to overturn existing boundaries and existing judgments, in order to motivate affirmative change. As usual, Nietzsche feels that those who only "appear" just are received well by public opinion—for the reason that these "just" persons do not threaten ordinary opinion or the status quo.

Nietzsche sees tolerance becoming magnanimity becoming justice as a scale of attitudes, where magnanimity involves a pity that tempers judgment. Overcoming the temptation to pity is crucial in the step to the Übermensch. That history is not a science; that justice and objectivity are not coincident; and that history is a matter of judgment (action): all these are interrelated in Nietzsche's point of view. When scientific historians find laws, they have to be trivial.[6] Nietzsche thus assimilates the writing of history to an art form, and he must do so, given his distinction between art and science. Genuine history is always the product of one person imposing will onto the material, judging the past in Nietzsche's sense of judging. In Birth, Nietzsche already provided his own example of a judgment that settles the significance of the past in the light of legitimate current needs.

What the artistic moment can add to historical judgment, as noted in section 7, is a vision or purpose for the future. The fate of objectivity is traced for Christianity. The ecumenical movement has evenhandedly reduced a synthesizing Christianity to vacuousness.[7] The constructive moment will wither if it is exposed to scholarship—and Nietzsche now advances his own generalization that growth to healthy maturity requires a period of protective development, a period of illusion. To stick with a new theory may require an "irrational" conviction that it will succeed, ultimately, in providing a much superior explanation of data as yet to be gathered. This is analogous to the factor of judgment that makes relevant history. Nietzsche wrote in ignorance of the revolutions that were to come in the development of science.[8] Ultimately, we will have to return to the science/art dichotomy that he employs to see whether it will withstand a current evaluation, that is, whether it is still life-enhancing. Clearly, creative scientific theorizing is in fact so difficult to separate from artistic creation and from transvaluation that Nietzsche's judgments must be modified. He is perhaps only on target for the typical scientific career. The fledgling scientist must put the rails of past practice to one side and attack the opinions of the past, if creative contributions to the illusions of theory are to be fashioned.

An undercurrent of fear gives a subtle ironic twilight self-awareness to scientific culture, as noted in section 8. This is expressed as the belief that humans earlier were children and that we are now at an advanced stage of life. A single human life can't really grasp the whole panorama, or scope, of human history, so this attitude must have a source that is not in fact, and Nietzsche traces it to a secular remnant of Christian belief. People now give their obeisance to scholars, to experts, as it was once given to the clergy. Historical thought says we are the "heirs" of ancient culture—but can't this mean that we should seek the right model of ancient cultures in order to transform our own, that there is a rich legacy that we simply haven't appropriated to our benefit? Far from showing progress, history may trace degeneration, starting as early as Socrates.

A more aggressive style is announced by the Hegelians, who see us in the grip of implacable world development and redescribe latecomer fulfillment of earlier tendencies as a completion of world history. This is an inversion of veneration of the ancients and the view that history is degeneration from a golden age, and it is just as unsatisfactory. The miserable conditions of the present could hardly be the fulfillment of history. Any ability to judge history is lost in these mechanical evaluations. Followers of the Hegelian historical religion must simply say, passively, "yes"—to whatever happens. This is not affirmation, and the "yea-sayers" who are described in *Zarathustra* are clearly a portrait of these Hegelians.

The start of section 9 plays with the notion of being firstborn, which was introduced at the end of section 8. Can there be a way of living that would make us firstborn? In one sense, we *are* firstborn. We are the first human beings whose lives are dominated by a conscious awareness of history. This situation tends to immobilize us in a feeling of helplessness, as though what we can do now is largely or completely determined by the past. An ironic stance to history is possible, but it can slide easily into cynicism. If Strauss had represented a shallow, superficial, rational optimism, Hartmann is now introduced to represent a shallow, superficial accommodating pessimism or cynicism of a sort that stands in the way of grounding an affirmative culture.

Eduard von Hartmann (1842–1906), a philosopher of marginal current importance, was a major philosopher in the eyes of Nietzsche's contemporaries. His highly successful *Philosophy of the Unconscious* appeared in 1868 and formed part of collected works that run to thirteen volumes. The sheer success of this book must have infuriated Nietzsche. It ran through seven editions in an incredibly short time, and in a few years, over a thousand studies of Hartmann's philosophy of the unconscious had been published.[9] As an epistemologist, he was a nominal Kantian, but he denied that the noumenal realm was unknowable, thus erasing the skeptical and critical bite of Kant's investigations. This sketch of Hartmann's career may be sufficient to indicate that Nietzsche's negative judgment of his eclectic and superficial philosophical outlook was correct. One can easily imagine Nietzsche goaded into a fury by the mere appearance of such philistine essay titles as "The Comforts of Pessimism," or the presumptuous "My Relationship with Schopenhauer." These titles sufficiently express assumptions similar to those that Nietzsche had exposed in the work of Strauss. Nietzsche looks at Hartmann as, at best, a philosophical parodist, one whose silly clarities allow notice of the problems standing in the way of truly affirmative cultural beginnings.

Much of Hartmann's philosophy seems a bizarre caricature of Nietzsche's, and Hartmann's publications may even have goaded Nietzsche into clarification of some of his own views. For example, at the start of the *Philosophy of the Unconscious*, Hartmann argues that will is universal. He attempts to support this by examples such as the purposive movements of decapitated animals. Hartmann suggests that willing in humans can also be unconscious, concealed under the integrated movements of intentional action. The conscious system is superior, however, in that it can employ the unconscious system, dominating it for its own purposes. Because of this fact, the conscious human system is the culmination of the development of living systems. In Hartmann's scheme of things, only conscious intentions can have an influence on world events. Nietzsche turns this nearly around, arguing that unconscious actions shape world history in an unnoticed fashion that is terribly important to historical movement. By the time actions are undertaken on conscious grounds, they are typically in the service of a conservative maintenance of values, values that are losing their consilience with the direction of Dionysian process. Hartmann, in Nietzsche's view, had missed everything of importance. When Hartmann finally replied to Nietzsche's attacks, it was with little awareness of their corrosive force.[10]

Section 10 opens with an attack on the educational system, which Nietzsche knew only too well, as the guardian of the weight of history. Nietzsche sees the educational system as assuming that "the educated man" is the sole appropriate product of the system. This passage (and others) causes Nietzsche to turn up at times in books and articles calling for educational reform, calling for an education permitting free development of the individual. But Nietzsche is calling for the inculcation of a tough and consistent culture, not "freedom of opinion" for the student. The first step to reform is to teach the realization that there is no German culture. When youth is unchained from the existing "culture," it will create a new culture by employing the unhistorical and the suprahistorical against the historical. What is called for is not a form of self-enjoyment, or of self-satisfaction, but a severe self-transcending. The Hellenes are again cited as examples of those who could control chaos through a sufficiently light regard for the past. The Hellenes did not allow themselves to be swamped by oriental imports, as the Germans had been disoriented by taking in surrounding cultures. In line with the analysis of *Birth*, the Hellenes developed Apollinian forms strong enough to oppose corrosive Dionysian impulses and create Hellenic tragedy. The Germans (here German *youth*) are called on to achieve this again. They are to cast off the weight of false imports and fashion what they have available to them into a true German culture. Nietzsche is describing the same project that had occupied him with respect to German's future in *Birth* and the first untimely meditation, but now his target has narrowed to awakening the enthusiasm of the young.

The appeal of youth to Nietzsche is undoubtedly related to his feeling that the Hellenes were young, at least in the sense that their history was not sufficiently worked out so as to constitute a burden heavy enough to prevent lightness of movement. Among the Germans, Nietzsche's first appeals had fallen on deaf ears among the scholars, rigidly set in their attitudes and opinions. Youth seemed the logical possibility for the emergence of free spirits who could cast off the past and create the unified German culture that had already been adumbrated in *Birth* and the first untimely meditation.

From this point on in Nietzsche's career, as optimism about Germany slides inescapably into pessimism, the topic of history largely disappears, except for some residual jibes at German historiography. This first essay on the topic of scientific history does not lead to a sustained study of scientific historiography. One reason is obvious. Nietzsche is concerned to cast off the weight of history and to live as a Hellene, without a coercive past. *Zarathustra*'s vision is of the past completely shaken off, permitting total freedom of movement, as we have already seen. The problem is to see how Nietzsche can move from the necessity of history in the second untimely meditation to its elimination. If the human is suspended in the untimely meditation between the necessity of history and the necessity of minimizing history, Nietzsche comes to attack this suspension, reducing the necessity of knowing the detail of history to zero. However much the suspension of Dionysus and Apollo is permanently unresolved, dissonant, fruitful, the necessity for suspension between detailed artistic visions is finally removed in the philosophy of the future.

One key to this movement in Nietzsche's thought is his gradual recognition of a scholarly presupposition of *Birth* and the *Untimely Meditations*, namely that humans are inescapably arrayed into nations. It is really nations that require history as a coercive force for managing their citizens; the individual does not need history except as a dutiful citizen, and the Übermensch does not need history because the Übermensch is not a citizen. *Nation* becomes a double concept. The Hellenes, with a (nearly) unified and yet deep culture, were a nation. Modern nations are artificial collectivities that appeal only to the name. Nietzsche works out the implicit content of the second untimely meditation, that history is in the service of the free individual. In *The Gay Science*, Nietzsche notes that his contemporaries are without culture and that socialist analyses of free societies of equals produce outright contradictions. *Birth* really talks of individuals, but Nietzsche is bound early in his career to the press of history on the scholar and the philologist, and he writes under the constraints of that concern. He confuses man and society when he insists on the necessity of memory, arguing that the cessation of memory is death, rather than the creation of life. The nation without a memory will die, but the necessity of narrative memory does not carry over to the individual. Later, Nietzsche will observe that morality with a memory is a morality of ressentiment and will note that this morality must also be dissolved. Will to power and the Eternal Return will signpost a way of life not dependent upon the cultures of nations, or their history, permitting the philosophically transformed Übermensch to live as a true individual.

5

Transvaluation

The peculiar dangers of Nietzsche scholarship now press in on any sensible form of exposition. Nietzsche's aphoristic works present a complex crisscrossing treatment of the transvaluations we have already noted, as well as many others. There is simply no sensible way to survey this complex material; it would be like doing Paris in two hours. Many of the topics that seem suddenly to appear in Nietzsche's work are not easy to trace to Nietzsche's original confrontation of his Hellenic tragic vision with what he took to be the nihilistic vestiges of Christian and scientific value tables, although it always seems possible to tease out a developmental strand from this originating confrontation for any particular aphorism. The problem is that the route from origin to aphorism is often quite different for adjacent aphorisms. This defeats a general interpretive plan. We will proceed by looking at the way in which themes from *Birth* and the first two untimely meditations grow organically into the variegated complexity of some selected topics in Book 1 of *The Gay Science*. We will then see how the development of the philosophically inspired notion of genealogy permits Nietzsche a control of history that allows him to project a philosophy of the future. In the following three chapters, we shall then look closely at Nietzsche's treatment of the genealogy of morals, the nature of society, and the status of women, in three even more concentrated selections from the lines of development that reach into Nietzsche's later works. These three specific topics will all involve the essential use of the Hellenic tragic value table as a touchstone for the transvaluation of contemporary society.

As we move from *Birth* to Book 1 of *The Gay Science*, we encounter many transvaluations beyond those of rationality, science, victory, culture, and history—those that we have already noticed. For example, aphorism 4 of Book 1 of *The Gay Science* transvalues good and evil, aphorism 14, friendship and love, and aphorism 43, the relative importance of what is said in comparison to what is not said. In aphorism 14, avarice and love are taken as completely different in common opinion. But perhaps they are both expressions of the desire (or instinct) to possess. Possessive love, especially possessive sexual love, is actually, Nietzsche suggests, rather disgusting. Glorification of love in this form must have resulted from the impact on our language of lower types, who fantasized about possession that they desired but couldn't have. Eros has been able to afford to laugh at those who didn't worship possession, namely the nobler types, because the latter have been so few in number that they could be laughed at by those who could not understand their situation. Friendship that is not possessive, a mutual thirst for a higher ideal, is to be more highly valued than love. In this aphorism, we have a transvaluation of Christian love and friendship. The higher ideal, which friends can share, decouples the notion of possession from a crippling rivalry in the personal relationship. An aphorism like this one is linked both to Nietzsche's past and to Nietzsche's future. His friendship with Wagner in the service of the new tragedy and the new German culture, developed in *Birth*, is circumspectly defended. The Hellenic ideal of male friendship between nobles is also defended. But at the same time, we have an adumbration of the savage onslaught of mass envy, controlled by priestly ressentiment, which Nietzsche comes to see as having shattered this ideal historically.

The true phenomenology of happiness escapes utilitarian calculation, which looks for the best compromise solution, not the highest pleasure. Aphorism 21 discusses the significance of *good*. *Good,* it should be noted, is grammatically attached to individuals, but is actually good only for the surrounding society. A virtue (as generally regarded) is typically ruinous to the individual who has it, as it calls for the regimentation or elimination of instinct. Virtues are praised generally for their instrumental value, but this is a trick offensive to Nietzsche's sense of argumentative taste. To inculcate virtue, a great lie must be told, and it must be pretended that virtue is to private advantage. For example, industriousness, which makes one pinched and boring, is praised publicly as the path to wealth. Once it's an ingrained habit, it doesn't matter. Whether or not the industrious obtain wealth is of no real significance. The point of all this is that current morality is actually contradictory. "You should sacrifice yourself" would be its honest expression, but then it would be hard to inculcate as an "inner" compulsion. That pleasure or virtue could be inculcated by itself seems incomprehensible anyway to the Dionysian vision. Nietzsche relentlessly argues for the necessity of the full suspension of pleasure and displeasure, virtue and vice, against one another.

The aphorisms of *The Gay Science* deepen Nietzsche's treatment of the body as transcending a superficial division between the "inside" and the "outside," symptomatic of modern "culture." Hellenic tragic action depended on bodily unity and the smooth expression of culture, rather than on its concealment in mental superiority. Aphorism 11 expresses this concern as a critique of interior rational thought that is supposed to control the irrational impulses of the body, a view insidiously introduced by Socrates and Plato. Instinct is said in aphorism 11 to be more preserving, more deeply rooted in Dionysian process, than is reason. Reason (consciousness) is so poorly developed, such a thin aspect of total life, that it is a danger, a cancer. One can make it the essence of the human only if one ignores its history, its possible development—and this error is deeply rooted in philosophy. Whatever is of value in consciousness will need to be made instinctive if it is to survive. The potential fixation of consciousness as additional instinct may actually be a ruse of instinct, although with the attendant struggle and pain that must be associated with such a process. Too much reason is a danger. Its only legitimate purpose is to shake up grooved instincts, not to dominate life. Nietzsche's view of social hierarchy might seem to permit reason to dominate human life, as nobles dominated tragic society. But Nietzsche's highest types exhibit a harmony that shows this to be wrong, to be forced by our modern notion of domination as control. Nietzsche's Hellenes do not exhibit a harmony achieved by the control of reason, rather they exhibit an organic harmony, in that their mellow use of rationality only briefly and occasionally affects the path of action suggested by instinct. Further, Nietzsche's nobles do not control their societies by force, but, at least partly, by a charismatic example that is recognized to be unattainable by the slave layers of society.

Other new themes in *The Gay Science* are also an elaboration of *Birth*'s contempt for the primacy of reason. Utilitarianism receives an explicit discussion in aphorism 3, where Nietzsche notes that the democratic thrust is to reduce everything to personal, calculable advantage. From this point of view, nobles must surreptitiously calculate or they are fools. Common nature reveals itself to be unbearably dull. Nobler natures are at their best, are noblest, when reason pauses. The higher type acts out of a value standard that is more flexible than the one that utilitarianism would impose. Nietzsche is very careful here to preserve his perspectivism. Utilitarianism is not false; it is boring (which is worse), and it preserves only a single perspective. The viewpoint of the noble can't be captured within the perspective of the calculator. Nietzsche almost instinctively hits upon one of the most serious objections to utilitarianism that has been subsequently developed in the literature—the incommensurability of different utility tables. The critique of utilitarianism is derived here from a confrontation of its outlook with the Hellenic tragic vision. Nietzsche does not, for example, pursue internal inconsistencies within utilitarianism.

The historicity of virtue is developed in various aphorisms of Book 1 of *The Gay Science*. This theme rests on the observations in *Birth* regarding the difference between Hellenic tragic values and Socratic (modern) rational morality. Subsequent works develop this extensively, but the roots of the later discussion can be found in aphorisms 4, 31, and 48. Aphorism 4 starts with a transvaluation. Evil helps to preserve a species when it takes the form of new or forbidden thought. "Evil" thinkers are so called because they are following new value tables, sometimes (as in Nietzsche's case) value tables that are exhumed and revivified versions of what had been forgotten. Progress in history always comes from outrageous acts, from outrageous and wicked thoughts. In fact, *good* and *evil* need constant revision. In England, among the utilitarians, "good" means (by definition) "what preserves the species." The utilitarians mean by "good" what preserves the species as it is, on the current valuation, in the current situation. But preservation comes over time. What will preserve the species may at present be destructive and not at all understood. Utilitarians fix the present and are hence inherently reactive. People currently called "evil" in conjunction with utilitarian tables, or at least a currently unrecognizable subset of such people, will actually turn out to be preservers. Thus utilitarian valuation is trivial. Nietzsche, of course, refers to himself in all this. He has dug up the past and revivified it, and he's considered "evil" for what he has done. The great transvaluation of "good" and "evil" is to come, but this passage sketches out the defense of the transvaluation in terms of a sense of historical flux.

Hunting was once common, as aphorism 31 notes, but it is now as rare as the leisure activity of current nobles, and its status has completely changed. Current hunting (excluding poaching by the poor) has no utilitarian status. But buying and selling, now central utilitarian activities, might also become exotic under historical change. Even politics, pursued actively by the leisure class, might become vulgar. This aphorism, emphasizing the historicity of social structure in an imaginative setting, is a subjunctive thought experiment of a kind that is relatively infrequent among the aphorisms. It shows Nietzsche's awareness of the corrosion of social structure by Dionysian flux and provides another point of attack for his conjecture that utilitarianism is hopelessly mired in a contingent and temporary vision of society.

Not only is social structure a historically contingent matter, but aphorism 48 suggests that feelings are historically contingent as well. Misery and pain are now avoided; they aren't experienced with any intensity or discrimination. Pain is pushed back; people don't want to talk about it. Pessimistic philosophies (as opposed to deeper philosophies of affirmation) may be coherent only at such a historical conjuncture. The pessimist considers the contemplation of "painful" general ideas to be real suffering. The only recipe for this misery is real misery. Real misery also heightens, and then develops, compensating happiness, and can produce a joyous, affirmative attitude. At this point, Nietzsche is achieving a historical perspective from which his differences from Schopenhauer and Wagner are finding articulation, while at the same time the sweep of historical shifts in valuation is attaining the scale of the concentrated studies to come.

Nietzsche's psychological studies have an origin in the perspective on our psychological nature that is opened up by its contrast to the Hellenes. Aphorisms 13, 18, and 40 are central examples of this accelerating interest. Aphorism 13 notes that benefiting others and hurting them are two ways of using power over others. We hurt people to get them to recognize our power, since people look for sources for their pain. The fact that we may sacrifice ourselves does not affect the nature of these actions. Hurting people, which involves a recognition of questionable power and a need to show it (intentional hurting being at stake), may be less agreeable than benefiting others, but it depends on our temperament. Proud natures may only wish to struggle with near equals; hence knights (and nobles generally) are courteous to one another because they are equal enough to demand mutual recognition. This earned recognition, of course, can't be artificially extended without producing absurd results.

As aphorism 18 notes, we have lost a feeling for the pride felt by the Hellenes, because the requisite social distances have disappeared. We have the doctrine of equality without actual equality, but the conflation of social distance means that we can all see one another, and we can all imagine being in one another's places. The ancient noble couldn't see the slave, and when he could, he found the slave contemptible. When we see our slaves, the sight arouses pity rather than contempt; our historical position thus denies us the opportunity to understand Hellenic pride.

Nietzsche's phenomenology of life doesn't allow class consciousness to arise. Nietzsche's view of contemporary society lacks the class fractures of Marxian theory. Social mixing and nihilism are hand in glove for Nietzsche; to eliminate both, some form of social upheaval is required.

The relationships of soldiers and leaders are compared in aphorism 40 to those of workers and employers. Submission, or its degree, are not at all to be correlated with pain. Rather, pain is correlated with the nature of the dominant side, its charisma or lack of charisma. Leaders can be noble, fascinating. They can simply decide to act without justifying their actions to others. Others may experience their behavior as transcendentally beautiful. Modern employers and leaders are shabby human beings; they calculate, and they give reasons for their actions. There is nothing to admire here, no source of wonder. This has ramifications for slavery. The slave need not be as unhappy as a modern worker if the slave is ruled by someone noble, someone the slave cannot aspire to be. The modern employer seems as human as his employees and therefore seems to be someone who dominates through chance. This can give rise to workers' desire to help chance, to extend chance, producing the downfall of employers. The pungency of such passages places Nietzsche into the space of modern political dialogue with just a few strokes of the pen.

All our developmental examples so far have been adaptations of the clash of Nietzsche's vision of Hellenic Greece with his vision of his contemporaries. But Nietzsche has at least one change to ring on the question of historical scholarship. Nietzsche draws a useful and fruitful distinction between microhistories of events that are not observable to human beings, and macrohistories of events that are accessible to human perspectives. Events can unfold in a microhistory, shaping and being shaped by Dionysian process, but escape the macrohistorical perspectives contemporary to them. *Birth* contains the seeds of this idea in its conception that the *significance* of Hellenic culture could not have been accessible to the Hellenes, but became accessible much later, after the experience of the development of rationalism and the nihilism that terminates this tradition. Aphorisms 8 and 9 develop this theme.

Aphorism 8 suggests that there are realms of human qualities that follow their own lines of development. These realms, which could be described as nonconscious, or not accessible to current recognition by consciousness, are independent. They develop as they please. Like the nonutilitarian designs on the scales of reptiles, they could be seen by a microscope, but an appropriate microscope isn't necessarily invented until long after this development has made substantial progress. Suppose one tries to convince others, captured by normal morality, of the existence of a new realm not within their control. They will simply imperialize with their already accepted valuation, trivializing the new as a realm of virtues that could be described with the vocabulary and the virtues we already have.

What can't be noticed at one time may develop quietly and then erupt, shattering or altering existing structures. This is explored in aphorism 9. A history written as pure description is useless. It can only describe what can be seen from its perspective. We need to trace developments, to guess at what's coming, in a way that "scientific" history misses completely. Often we can't grasp the significance of what is happening until it has laid down lines of influence. That hidden centers are acting beyond our awareness is an adumbration of the doctrine of will to power to be developed later, and it is also a form of psychoanalytic presentiment, that much of the activity within ourselves is not accessible to conscious monitoring. We can see this position growing out of the criticism of Hartmann in the second untimely meditation and providing a coherent view as to why scientific history is short-sighted and trivial.

Nietzsche's perspectivism, to be consistent, implies that we must achieve perspectives on ourselves by studying the natural world.[1] To suppose that we should begin with what is obvious to us is to ensure philosophical disaster; it is to begin with the greatest illusions. Nietzsche, throughout *The Gay Science*, is looking for a higher perspective from which the questions of who humans are, what their potential is, and so on, can receive a less restricted answer than either self-knowledge or science, both captured by current valuations can provide. Far from being a pile of disconnected aperçus, the transvaluational aphorisms are all arrows drawn from the same quiver, but they are directed at divergent targets.

In order to explore a unified transvaluation of the Western metaphysical tradition, Nietzsche needed to find a way of dealing with history lightly enough to slip the moorings of the Socratic value table and its extensions in favor of a restored and affirmative Hellenic value table of values. His extraordinarily fecund mind developed an appropriately light form of history in the genealogy. A genealogy is simply a sketch sufficient to illustrate the history of values in transition from affirmation to negation. It isn't a scientific history, tied down to dates and facts. Nietzsche makes much of etymology in constructing genealogies, since etymology can be traced by philologists even when precise historical dates are not possible or necessary. As words shift in meaning, shifts in values can be traced independently of detailed history. If the Übermensch escapes history, the genealogy is the light history necessary to complete the critical project of transvaluation.

The section of *Twilight of the Idols* titled "How the 'True World' Finally Became a Fable" is illustrative of genealogy, being a highly compressed example of its type. Originally, sages and philosophers simply expressed their existence in the world without an epistemic consciousness. This could be established philosophically by the statements of early sages and philosophers—who spoke of themselves. The true world of personal experience moves on to become an elusive "true world" of ideas, unattainable except by a special elite. Theories are no longer expressed as the personal statements (truths) of their authors, but they are expressed as universal, abstract knowledge. In terms of the new valuation of science, the true worlds of theory (constructed by avoiding the apparent contradictions of the old true world), are contrasted to the old "true world," which is then downgraded to a world of mere appearance. The worlds of theory, constructed on the basis of the Christian and scientific value tables, are regarded by scholars as true, and the world in which we live is judged and downgraded to mere appearance. The apparent world in this valuation is a selection from the original, true, Dionysian world by means of a valuation derived from the constructed and abstract worlds of Christian morality and science; thus the *apparent* world in terms of the new valuation is *not* the same as the *true* world in terms of the old valuation, and the old true world has disappeared.[2] Hence nihilism. This compressed genealogy could hardly be a better example of the type.

The concept of genealogy, which brings the need to minimize history under conceptual control, allows Nietzsche to undertake transvaluation, not in the mode of the nomadic warrior, armed with barbed aphorisms, nor in the mode of Zarathustrian prophecy, but in the mode of the (pre-Socratic) philosopher. *Beyond Good and Evil* announces the philosophers of the future, not ones who produce systems, but ones who remain riddles, who speak of their own experiences. These philosophers can grasp the slide into nihilism of the Socratic table by tracing its genealogical decline. The aphorisms, no longer mere arrows, open up somewhat to philosophical reflection that follows the threads of etymology. Let us take a closer look at *Beyond Good and Evil*, starting with aphorism 6 of Part 1, titled "On the Prejudices of Philosophers." In the first sentence of aphorism 6, Nietzsche argues that a value table or morality is always the root of philosophy. Philosophy creates the world in its own image, and then gains "knowledge" through investigating its own creation. Nietzsche is simply asserting that this approach is revealing (as no other approach could possibly be) of what is actually at stake in the exposition and defense of any particular philosophy.

Nietzsche can accept that each philosophy has a moral, or valuational, perspective at root and drives to establish this perspective as its motive force, and yet his view does not lapse into relativism, provided that values or moralities can be definitely sorted out. Reactive moralities will be terminated by Dionysian process, just as the master Platonic value system is ending in nihilism. The comparative superiority of the valuation of the Hellenic tragic vision is its conformity with process, and hence its avoidance of a reactive, projective fixity. This deflects the question of validity to Dionysian process—whose existence is not to be proven, but to be shown. If Nietzsche is correct, his view would explain why the famous epistemologies of philosophical history don't cancel one another: they are always alternative schemes. As value systems, they can't be shown true or false by comparison to a neutral, adjudicating world. Nietzsche indicates that they are all at an equivalent altitude from his higher perspective.

Nietzsche says that every important philosophy so far has been a personal confession or memoir of its author. It would be too easy to see this as an attack on all the supposedly great philosophical systems of the past. *Zarathustra* has been written, and Nietzsche is not merely attacking bad philosophical systems here. *Great* is used here without irony. Anything worth calling a philosophy, and generally recognized as a philosophy, is the expression of its author. Nietzsche is no exception. And of course Nietzsche has not forgotten that the meaning of these memoirs is not coincident with authorial intention. *Zarathustra* is an explicit memoir, written with this in mind. Nietzsche is therefore simply generalizing about philosophy: a philosophy is a personal memoir. *Zarathustra* is a self-conscious instance of the pure type. Other philosophies have tried to conceal their basis. The philosopher does not produce his text; the philosopher is the means by which the text comes to be written. Its involuntary aspects are caused by the drives compelling expression in a philosophy, and the philosopher does not originate, and does not fully control, the process, unless the philosophy is an unbearably superficial display of rigid rationality. "It" controls the process of thought and *not* the conscious Ego. Because of this, the aspects of the actual memoir of record are often unavailable to the author and must be read by the philologist/philosopher/reader. This is why the author's memoir can be unnoticed and must be located by the reader. What about *Zarathustra*? Didn't Nietzsche think that he was in control of the writing? Well, obviously not. Zarathustra doesn't speak his own message, by his own admission, and it is part of the Nietzschean hermeneutics that all important texts can never be given a complete reading, since they always retain as yet unnoticed aspects. This hermeneutics is folded back into the text of *Zarathustra*.[3] For example, the hurdy-gurdy song of Zarathustra's animals in Part 4 of *Zarathustra* quite explicitly does not notice everything about Zarathustra's message, and Zarathustra cannot say what it is that they have not noticed.

The morality or value table of an author is *not* the germ of life of a philosophy, but the drive to realize such a table is the life of the philosophy. This is required, because the table itself is abstract and dead. In other words, philosophy is not the abstract explication of a value table, strictly speaking, but the achievement of the table, driven by the deeper drives of will emanating from Dionysian process. This is true whether the intention be *moral* or *immoral*. The use of both terms in this sentence invites us to notice that what is moral on one table may be immoral on another, what is "good" in Christianity or Platonism may be transvalued in Nietzsche's philosophy. Nonetheless some morality is at stake in every philosophy.

The second sentence of aphorism 6 suggests a methodology for interpreting philosophical texts. The reading of the most obscure and abstruse philosophical claims should be reduced to the root moral intention to make it clear what these claims are expressing. The apparent order of importance may then be reversed, the abstruse claims being recognizable as concealed versions of the grounding values.

In the third sentence, Nietzsche gives us an example. "Knowledge," which may seem fundamental, is typically the expression of underlying values, especially those expressing a reluctance to experience flux. Epistemology is typically waffle; it has nothing to do with Dionysian process (the world)—it only interprets underlying attitudes that have already been projected into features of the world.

Let us consider Nietzsche's phrase in the fourth sentence, "Anyone who considers the basic drives. . . ." What are the basic drives? Nietzsche sees them as including an enterprising spirit, foolhardiness, vengefulness, craftiness, rapacity, and the lust to rule, although this is not a complete list, because our vocabulary won't do to describe or separate these drives.[4] The basic grammar of this sentence suggests that those who consider the basic drives will discover that all of them have done philosophy (i.e., have driven philosophical production). They have driven philosophy as inspiring demons. The *kobold* image is this. Accidents in mines and other underground places are caused (in some German folklore) by kobolds, unseen (although potentially visible) creatures. Any of these drives can do philosophy, and in doing so each will represent itself as the master drive, i.e., the ultimate purpose of existence and the master of the other drives. With this passage, we encounter a basic aspect of the perspective called *will to power*. A person has no center, no ego, in reality. A person is a collection of drives, each one in contention for mastery over the others, and what seems to be sweet reason is the result of these ongoing struggles.

Nietzsche's model is somewhat different from Freud's, essentially because of the emerging doctrine of the will to power. A person always contains many conflicting drives, or at least potentially conflicting drives, that are not subject to an easy resolution by any notion of logic. But, as the presence of civilization makes Freud permanently pessimistic about happiness, Nietzsche's failure to consider society points in a different direction. Here conflict does not arise between person and society; it comes from below. The clash of lower power centers for supremacy introduces a conflict that does not depend on a clash between individual desires and social constraints. Nietzsche thought that the conflict could be brought fully to the surface, and at least shown to exist. In a pessimistic mood, Nietzsche thought that the conflict was ungovernable in the long run and that Dionysian chaos would always reclaim it. The destruction of the individual, rather than partial reclamation of the individual for social purposes, is the only resolution of this analysis. In an optimistic mood, the superior human could be thought capable of forcing unity of style onto the cauldron of drives (although permanent efforts of feeling would be required to sustain this unity), and such a person might achieve a form of accommodation with this world (and society) in a sustained mood of affirmation. In *Beyond Good and Evil*, the mood is optimistic.

The last section of aphorism 6 gives a psychological observation for the discerning. Suppose the above analysis in aphorism 6 were to be wrong, and that the drive to knowledge was actually a basic drive. Examples of this supposed possibility are given by scientists. They pile up knowledge, but in doing this, they're hardly human; they're robotized. Only part of their existence, and none of their feelings, is involved. They function like clocks; deeper drives aren't involved. Wind them up, set the time, and they will tick away. Their deeper drives, Nietzsche suggests, will always surface somewhere other than in their displayed scientific work.[5] It is a matter of indifference where the scientific "machine" is placed—it will proceed to grind out facts.[6] Only a value placement can bring this mechanism on line, but the value placement is not a factor inside the mechanism.

The genealogy of religion is discussed in aphorism 58 of *Beyond Good and Evil*. Religion doesn't have to be nihilistic; its drives don't have to be attached to the defense of an abstract metaphysical creation. Serious religion is not concerned with superficial topics. Modern religion and modern science ignore this possibility, staying with trivialities, by an unnoticed choice of values. Aphorism 58 explores the arrival of nihilism and anticipates the twentieth-century discovery of secularization and the debates concerning its significance. The Enlightenment philosophical version of modern history is that modern science has destroyed the credibility of religion, inevitably making the world more secular and lessening the hold of religion on those who grasp the principles of science. This is interpreted as progress. Now it would be expected that Nietzsche couldn't accept this version of an epistemological victory since the relevant epistemologies can't conflict over neutral data, but merely express deeper value commitments. Nietzsche's account couples the existence and disappearance of religion to class structure in society, the existence of religion with depth requiring a leisure class that accepts a value table quite at odds with the value table of democratic man. Nietzsche's economic theory is simply that where everybody is essentially involved in the economic structure, where there is no noble class freed from economic concerns by the labor of slaves, economic concentration dissolves the religious instinct for profundity.

The first sentence of aphorism 58 of *Beyond Good and Evil* suggests that genuine religion requires leisure. This leisure is not guilty; it recognizes that work disgraces, and makes us meaner, coarser, without in any way ennobling.[7] "Half-leisure" turns its energies to something other than work; something that may ennoble us. Like our own, any society that involves everyone in the economic process will inevitably be secular.[8] The impact of scientific beliefs, it is suggested, is a consequence, rather than a cause, of this situation.

The new secular person can accept religious customs, but only at a distance. The commitments of the new secular person are to pleasure, nation, family, and newspapers. Religion disappears as being either too trivial or too demanding. All of this carries over to the scholar.[9] But scholars, historians, philosophers, who explicitly manage to include religion in their work, still fail to grasp its seriousness. Religious insight is not commensurable with the life of a scholar or with *tolerance* toward religion. Because of naïvete, the scholar treats the religious man (the prophet?) as beneath him; but nothing could be beneath the scholar. The existence of the scholar is too superficial for such a metaphor to carry any meaning. An age tormented by religious insight/awe/terror might well envy such pleasant tunnel vision as the form of escape possessed by the scholar.

Aphorism 58 is an opportunity to develop further an issue that has been raised before and will be discussed more extensively below. Compared to his historical treatment of morality, Nietzsche's treatment of social and political themes verges on being unhistorical—the same vision of Hellenic society is always applied as the touchstone. The remnants of theology in the various religious seminars of the German university are a riddle for the psychologist, Nietzsche notes, and while that is certainly true, they are also a riddle for the social theorist. Surely they can't be explained without reference to the ideological function of religion in the nineteenth century, that is, the ideological function of eviscerated religion, but Nietzsche doesn't have such connections in view. In shifting from social analysis to psychological analysis, Nietzsche slides away from serious problems. In the original shift from Hellenic tragic society to democratic society, a social shift was used to explain a shift in morality, but Nietzsche doesn't utilize such a social shift in any obvious way to raise the possibility of the transcendence of democratic society. Nietzsche speaks vaguely of being the prophet of a period of wars, conflicts, and so on, and he knows that a shift in the structure of society is required for a genuine extramoral society, but the individualistic concept of the Übermensch is made to carry the weight. Here a shift in individual psychology will cause social change rather than the reverse. Nietzsche's views thus seem to exhibit a curious asymmetry. The shift from the Hellenic tragic vision is carried by social theory, so as to avoid talk of individuals who can stand up to Dionysus, but the renewal of tragic culture isn't carried by a social theory. Nietzsche is reduced to saying that we may be on the threshold of a change and to describing the moral table after the change, without providing an account of how the change could actually take place. Perhaps he believed simply that the Dionysian process would bring it about but that the details couldn't be foreseen.

Aphorism 189 of *Beyond Good and Evil* is a remarkable anticipation of later forms of cultural criticism. If we couple this with aphorism 58, we see that leisure becomes transvalued into play or pleasure of a very special form in an industrial society, a form so trivial and boring that it redirects us to what we call "work." "Work" is hardly satisfying, but a Sunday hedged by blue laws and restrictions designed to make it religious is perhaps even more intolerable. Sunday involves an abstention that can sharpen and focus powerful drives back onto the necessity for action, action that here takes the form of "work" because there are no acceptable alternatives. The revenge of the body in the face of this kind of stringent control can take unanticipated directions. The last paragraph of the aphorism suggests that Christian delimitation and exclusion of profane love may have, in terms of this mechanism, purified and sharpened profane love, turning a relatively undifferentiated sexual drive into a specific romantic form. The paradox here is that Christianity itself produced the form of love apparently most in conflict with its own ideal of love through the mechanism of denial, the consequences of which it had not understood nor anticipated.

Nietzsche begins aphorism 204 of *Beyond Good and Evil* by noting why he believes he is entitled to speak against the silence surrounding the suppression of philosophy to a position of lower rank. Science, not philosophy, now seems to get to the bottom of things. Once again, the emergence of this valuation is tied to the democratic order, or to democratic disorder, as it would be seen on an aristocratic valuation. Science will also repudiate all masters—an allusion to philosophy's former place as queen of the sciences and to theology's dominance when it was taken to provide the true account of the world. Science will now play master. Since real philosophy *is* mastery for Nietzsche, a way of increasing will to power that is stressed in many of the aphorisms, this is expressed by saying that science now wishes to play the role of philosophy.

Nietzsche's autobiographical remarks center around the threat that a whiff of real philosophy poses to the scientific scholar, but also around the opportunity provided for skepticism about philosophy when it is presented as a series of refuted systems. An attachment to one philosopher, broken off, often leaves contempt for all philosophy in its place. The original philosopher, having "refuted" all the others, leaves no space for philosophy when he or she is then repudiated. Nietzsche does not draw this conclusion in his own case, presumably because he considers himself to have been a philologist-scholar and his own philosopher throughout his career. Schopenhauer's repudiation of Hegel, however, has played this role for many German scholars. Schopenhauer's war on the historical sense in Hegel ruined what was of value in Hegel's system for many of his students. To do this, Schopenhauer had to strike certain dogmatic attitudes that are indicative of a philosophy of intellectual poverty. This is symptomatic of the new "scientific" philosopher—a creature who adapts to scientism in academic life in order to pursue success, but who loses any conception of what philosophy really is about. Such a philosophy can only be pitied. It could hardly dominate, for it isn't really a philosophy at all. The images of aphorism 204 of *Beyond Good and Evil* are picked up again in aphorism 211. Perhaps to become a philosopher one must first of all work through all lower perspectives, especially those of science. The task of philosophy is not that of a chameleonlike ability to adopt any perspective; the task is to create values, i.e., to transcend old values and to create new ones. Nietsche's critique of Kant and Hegel is precisely that they only attempt to lay out and synthesize existing perspectives.[10]

Aphorism 217 discusses a specific transvaluation. The new virtue is forgetting; the old virtue is never forgetting in the application of morality. Morality may force one (under the old morality) to remain friends with someone whom one has injured. But Nietzsche has a remarkable insight into a major problem of ethics. If (as a human) I consider myself good, and I injure someone (make a mistake in my treatment of another), either I have to confront the fact that I am not as good as I thought, or I must reduce the victim to someone who deserved what happened to him. Hence the instinctive slander or detraction that seems to issue forth in such situations. This is a very common pattern of behavior, which many people never notice and which has been announced as a "discovery" in twentieth-century moral philosophy. Nietzsche may have been the first to notice it. Nietzsche's parody of a beatitude follows: Blessed are the forgetful, they get over (forget) their stupidities without utilizing this form of revenge against others. At this point, Nietzsche is close to the repudiation of the necessity of memory that had concerned him in the second untimely meditation.

6

Morality

We are so used to splitting fact from value and discussing their relationship that we may read Nietzsche as merely inverting a known epistemological structure. Nietzsche's inversion invites relativism if we take values
to be freely chosen as personal preferences. For Nietzsche, values and life
are interwoven in that values are integral to any mode of interaction with
the surrounding world. A detached, objective posture is already dead and
is of value only to those who can pawn it off onto others as a controlling
vision. Which mode of interaction at any given time will increase will to
power, will increase strength and unity of action, is hardly a subjective
matter. If Nietzsche's use of values makes transvaluation the only strategy
for a philosophical warrior, this can still miss the shock of Nietzsche's
recognition that *values* could be located in the heart of *any* presumed fact,
a recognition that undercuts the universality of fact, even where the values
recognized are not merely private pleasures.[1]

Nietzsche's values are not to be confused with internal, subjective
preferences. When Nietzsche inverted fact and value, he thought he was
providing a real and stable test for human perspectives. During the nineteenth century, the concept of value was involved in a variety of conceptual wars, especially in Germany. Aesthetic and moral values were gradually distinguished, and arguments about their relative importance were
resolved in philosophy by making moral value closer to fact and by gradually turning aesthetic values into subjective preferences. In this movement
Nietzsche is in the minority and maintains the centrality of (objective)
aesthetic values over the importance of both moral values and facts, a
transvaluation that is pursued later by Heidegger and Gadamer in a

movement of thought that can be grounded in Nietzsche's opinions.[2] At the same time, moral and aesthetic values are gradually distinguished as values from the original locus of value discussion, the sense of economic value or worth. The use value and the exchange value of anything involved in economic transactions is not a subjective matter as the science of economics is developed. No matter if the exchange value of a commodity can be distinguished from the actual market price of a commodity, as a true value from a momentary value that may be influenced by such matters as temporary shortages, it is a theoretically objective quantity. Nietzsche's values are still related to these objective economic roots in that they are capable of objective assessment in terms of their impact on our interactions with the surrounding world. At the moment in which he wrote, Nietzsche thought that the nihilism of the table of good and bad could be decisively demonstrated and was even open to inspection once the affirmative possibilities of the alternative table of good and bad were recognized. The Nietzsche of individual liberation who is utilized by various social and educational movements can be identified as a construction based on confusing modern subjective valuation with Nietzsche's more objective notion of values.

If transvaluation shows that value tables inconsistent with those now adopted are possible, genealogy shows that there is a history to value tables, a turning of will from the use of values to the self-destructive protection of values. This is seen most clearly in the case of the development of the moral code associated with the table of good and evil, a code that wishes to present itself as binding and universal, but that in fact expresses the historical conquest of a leveling ressentiment. The exposure of the limited perspective and prejudicial value structure of this morality was Nietzsche's major explicit expression of his deepest transvaluation, an expression culminating in the sustained studies of *On the Genealogy of Morals*.

Genealogy begins, of course, in *Birth*. If Socrates, Plato, and Euripides mark the entrance of the value table of good and evil, they also mark the possibility of its transvaluation. The later parts of *Beyond Good and Evil* intensify the movement of thought that provides the backbone of *Genealogy*. Aphorism 186 of Part 5 introduces what may seem a new idea—and an idea to be developed extensively in the *Genealogy*. This is an idea that is not foreign to the instinct of a philologist. If we want to study morality, Nietzsche notes, the first task is an assemblage of the relevant texts of morality. Philosophers assume too quickly that they know what morality is, and they then attempt to give it a rational foundation. All philosophy has occurred in the modern era; an assemblage of actual texts would show moralities so divergent that the project of providing rational foundations for all morality would be obviously ridiculous. The relativism, the clash of the attempts, is an offense to linguistic taste; there can be no question of science here. The basis of linguistic perception provides the aesthetic grounding for Nietzsche's vision of compelling genealogy—a history that convinces, but not by rational argument grounded in facts.

Section 1 of the Preface of *Genealogy* repeats an idea of *The Gay Science*—that we understand ourselves least well, especially our present experience. This reverses the structure of Cartesian philosophy, which starts from a supposedly secure reflective self-knowledge. The significance of what we take for granted will be most difficult to realize; it requires the adoption of another perspective. Section 2 tells us that philosophers must take up their relatively poor ideas and develop them over and over into some form of interwoven coherence. Nietzsche explicitly notes the developmental scheme we have worked with here—that disconnected insights of the aphoristic works will here be joined into a coherent attack on current morality. Nietzsche is not searching for the origins of our concepts, rather for the first visible instances and circumstances of what later became our concepts. We simply take it for granted that what is called "good" is better than what is called "evil." What is needed is knowledge of the actual domain of morality, how it has evolved and changed, and above all, a resolution of the crucial question as to whether it can be currently justified.

This preface, so apparently clear in its style and content—what does it mean? The last sentences, noting that Nietzsche's writing will not be readable until *rumination* is recovered, is surely an expression of despair. Nietzsche has come to realize that his contemporaries do not understand him. The first sentence of section 7 explicitly says that Nietzsche feels alone. In section 8, the difficulties with *Zarathustra* and the major aphoristic works are recognized. *Ecce Homo*, in retrospectively commenting on *Genealogy*, reveals that *Genealogy* is a primer for readers of the aphorisms, more precisely, for *future* readers of the aphorisms. *Genealogy* is a signpost to reading Nietzsche's aphorisms for any free spirit who may happen to find it later. All three essays in *Genealogy* end with a caesura; they invite a continuation. These essays discuss morality, religion, and aesthetics, the three ancient roots of philosophy.

In the first essay on morality, Nietzsche notes (sections 1–3) that although he is not attracted to the English (utilitarian) accounts of morality and its history, he is intrigued by the utilitarian movement of thought, which contains an implicit moment of anti-Christian suspicion. Nietzsche notes in section 2 that the utilitarian "history" of morality is nothing but a total projection from the present moment of the received utilitarian notions of "utility," "habit," and so on, as though the current valuation could provide the only possible explanatory categories. Utilitarians must assume that nonnobles in Hellenic times considered what they did for nobles "good." Nietzsche finds this to be psychologically impossible. The nonnobles could not have adopted the noble value table. The nobles must have created the relevant values from their own perspective. Slave calculation came later and involved a different sense of "good." The utilitarians, in short, cannot learn from history.

Nietzsche now explains in sections 4 and 5 how his genealogical method permits restoration of the Hellenic origin of values. "Good" and "bad" are opposites that can be correlated to the difference between "noble" and "common." What nobles did they considered descriptively "good," and what nonnobles did was descriptively "bad," since it was the nobles who articulated values, but this *fundamental* insight is hard to achieve now because of the screening of democratic prejudice. The clue to grasping this example lies in the etymology of the relevant words.

A new system of valuation is the product of priestly construction, or so Nietzsche suggests in sections 6 through 8. Those belonging to the caste of priests think themselves superior to the rest of the population due to their dietary restrictions and other life-constricting prohibitions, and these become the basis of a distinction between the priests and the rest of the appropriate population. The priests take over the word "good" and its positive valuation, but under this second division of society, the complement "bad" now includes members of the nobility who are not priests. In short, two valuations, that of the noble and that of the priest, come into direct conflict as society fragments into classes. If the noble (knightly-aristocratic) class and the priestly class can't resolve their differences, their two valuations come into revengeful conflict. Priests are dangerous in such a conflict because of their hatred, which they can't release into a healthy physical form, and their hatred turns into a permanent desire for vengeance. Of all the priestly castes, the Jewish priests have had the greatest impact. As a small nation of limited military power, Jews have even functioned collectively as a priestly caste.[3] They inverted the original noble valuation in a religious construction that they then exported to lower layers of other societies. What the nobles had called "bad" becomes "good" in this transvaluation, and what the nobles had called "good" becomes "evil." This is not a simple inversion because of the connotations of "evil," which are vengeful rather than discriminatory. The sinister connotations of "evil" are the expression of priestly revenge. This new valuation was then assimilated and enlarged in official Christianity. The "good" of the Christian revaluation grew into a sublimated and important notion of "Christian love." Only this, Nietzsche notes, could allow one to swallow the paradox of God on the Cross. When we go back, we see why the early Christians had to emphasize the paradoxical nature of their claims. They existed as a minority in a larger community that had other values. Although they did not confront Hellenic values directly, they confronted other systems of values, and in the Roman Empire Christian morality ran into the legacy of a rationalism with which it was ultimately compatible, but with which it had to struggle before synthesis was achieved. When the Christian valuation becomes a majority valuation, the paradoxes seem to be little more than abstract verbal tricks, and they receive dubious theological explanations. The preservation of the text, however, is incontrovertible evidence of the original situation.

Everything now shows the signs of a complete victory of the Christian valuation, as section 9 notes. The Church, which had seemed the center for spreading the disease, has lost its place of importance. But there is a little Nietzschean paradox here; the sheer crudeness and rigidity of the institutional Church allows the revenge of Dionysus upon the fixation of Christian belief. The Church is actually the hope for the birth of free spirits, who can feel its nihilistic insignificance. Precisely at this point, the "free spirit" who has followed the argument is to begin to ruminate, forced to contemplate the silence of Nietzsche—who cannot speak his message in the existing language of values.

The valuation of nobles is affirmative (What *I* do is good), but that of the slave and of priestly revolt is negative (What *they* do is evil). Slave morality depends on a division between inside and outside. The noble valuation can openly accept the existence of slaves, but concentrates fierce action on competition with equals. Failure, for nobles, is a consequence of weakness or inflexibility. Resentment is discharged immediately and then forgotten. Slave morality demands uniform moral compliance on the inside. Hence, for example, the great *thou shalt nots* of the Decalogue. Intellectual cleverness flourishes in the secrecy created by the resentment and fear of the slave perspective—and so does memory as providing the list of wrongs to be paid back. How does this fit into Nietzsche's observation that only nobles (or philosophers) can create values? Priests have only denied or negated already created values, and hence priests did not accomplish a full transvaluation.

The noble can become "evil" in protracted societal conflict coupled with constrained activity. Released from such protracted conflict, nobles become like lions, solitaries acting only in terms of their own strength and desires. The blond beast passage, famous from its Nazi appropriation, seems really only to describe nobles suddenly released from social constraint and their behavior under these circumstances.[4]

The problem of fitting the old valuation to the new is reflected in Hesiod's "ages," different ages being required to trace the downfall and degradation of the old heroes in a democratized Greece. Culture is the means of domesticating the noble utilized by the mob, not something forced on the mob by the noble. Culture and regression are therefore synonymous where culture is not unified. Nietzsche seems clearly to imply that an unbridgeable distance between noble and slave is healthy, allowing nobles to provide constant renewal of society by daring and original action that breaks the encroaching rigidities of forming traditions. But the triumph of the "maggot man" is equivalent to the overturn of this situation, is equivalent to nihilism and to exhaustion. Without occasional superior human beings, the thought of human society is suffocating. Man is getting "better" only in terms of the sick valuation of ressentiment, which prefers total leveling. Section 13 contrasts these two irreconcilable valuations. Strength is the natural expression of the strong; it cannot be withheld as the morality of ressentiment asks. "Free will" would erroneously suggest that the strong are free to be weak.

Nietzsche's discussion has become hopelessly abstract. If his genealogy is defensible, what impact does it have on the present? The image of strength he conjures up seems to belong to other times and places, the Hellenic age, for example. It is untimely in current society, a society in which it cannot coherently be exhibited. The "free spirit" can only ruminate and laugh, attempt to locate a personal style, or be silent, at least in our set of social constraints. While this position is consistent, it fails to envision relevant forms of action.

Nietzsche parodies a "rational" response in sections 14 and 15 to what he has been saying—a response that falls short of recognizing the full inner contradictions caused by the morality of ressentiment. Early ressentiment is not consistent and is caught in the perils of an incomplete priestly transvaluation. "Love" is "hate." "Weakness" is "strength." These things have to be found in small, quiet places in Christian thought. Various quotations, especially from Tertullian, give sufficient evidence that ressentiment is carried over to a presumed settling of old accounts during the second coming.[5]

The great clash of valuations in human history, as noted in section 16, has been that of the table of "good and bad" versus the table of "good and evil." The struggle has not been conclusive, although for the present the latter table seems to have the upper hand. A resurgence of noble classical valuations associated with the Renaissance has been depressed by the French Revolution. The appearance of Napoleon, however, seems to have shifted the balance somewhat back, Napoleon being a signpost to noble action. In this allusion to an eternal fight between two systems that cannot be compromised, we have an echo of Zarathustra. There are two opposed systems, each involving its own "good" and a contrast to that "good." Nietzsche finds a perspective from which they are both completely visible.

The affirmative system could return, erasing nihilism, as noted in section 17. We may already be aware that there is a possibility of rival value systems, that of worldly values being opposed to the demands of religion. Liberalism can suggest that rival value systems should be taken as equally acceptable, as schemes to be compromised. Nietzsche's minimal accomplishment here is to confront two systems from a perspective that can raise an essential question of philosophy: How is it possible to compare these systems in such a way that the comparison is not trivial? If it is a simple matter of Nietzsche's value table being set against the priestly value table, then Nietzsche shouldn't win trivially. In order to avoid triviality, Nietzsche must convince that Dionysian process exists and that it prevents the priestly table from having a further purchase on our experiences. This is why the doctrines of Eternal Return and will to power, Nietzsche's philosophical expression of Dionysian profundity, are crucial to Nietzsche's valuational claims, and that is why he worked so relentlessly at motivating their inevitability.

Is Nietzsche's priestly value table actually the value table of Christianity? Christianity is an enormously rich tradition, and envy or ressentiment can also be criticized from a Christian perspective. Along with the modern growth of Christianity, social formations have arisen in which social progress is fueled by bourgeois economic acquisitiveness and envy. It is possible to argue that ressentiment is part of a bourgeois mentality that has developed in modern capitalist countries with nominal Christian allegiances, but that ressentiment can be decoupled from real Christianity. It is also possible to argue that a society in which lower classes could envy the bourgeoisie arose from a structural change as social distances were closed in a totalizing economy and as the vestiges of noble and slave social layers came into direct contact. By contrast, real Christianity has nothing to do with the flat, humanitarian, benevolent, social reform ideas offered by modern compromised Christian institutions to temper naked greed. Real Christianity is an insight into terror and love, and it contains at least the vestiges of Dionysian feeling for profundity. Thus a Christian could accept Nietzsche's condemnation of ressentiment but see it as directed solely toward modern capitalist society and the social and private greed essentially connected to its economic structure. Nietzsche, in short, may have scored a bull's-eye with his arrow, but into a mistaken target.

An explicit exploitation of this line of argument is to be found in Scheler's *Ressentiment*.[6] Scheler analyzes ressentiment as appearing in bourgeois society because bourgeois society has grown so egalitarian that people can envy one another's places. By contrast, he notes, slaves in noble society would not have resented injury by their masters, as they couldn't imagine trading places, a point that utilizes Nietzsche's psychological claim in aphorism 18 of *The Gay Science*. Ressentiment is typically coupled with, and is an expression of, weakness. It would not be surprising to find women (especially older single women) and priests more frequently expressing ressentiment in comparison to socially dominant males. Christian values can be perverted or transvalued into bourgeois ressentiment values, but the core of true Christianity did not grow on the soil of ressentiment.[7] Again, Scheler here appropriates Nietzsche's notion that origins must be separated from the current valuation of concepts; a "break" has occurred in the typical expression of Christian concepts with the arrival of bourgeois society.

The Hellenes thought that love was the aspiration of the lower for the higher; true Christianity may reverse that. In Christianity, the loving noble helps the less noble without diminution of person. In helping, the more noble becomes "more like God." God is no longer the perfect unmoving source of movement; God is the moving, judging, caring, helping source of history, an active creator. True Christian love has nothing to do with ressentiment. Christian love springs from inner security and from spiritual plenitude. Benevolence does not help the person helped to become divine, it helps the person giving help to become divine. No anxiety is involved in Christian charity, as was often involved when nobles consciously stooped below their appropriate status. Ascetic ideals are also transvalued in Christianity as a means to an independent and unencumbered life.

Scheler agreed with the intellectual responsibility of this defense of a form of Christianity. Nietzsche could not find all Christianity with a single arrow. Scheler agreed that modern society represented a victory of the weak over the strong, but a victory over the spiritually strong in the Christian sense, not a victory over the noble. According to Scheler, Nietzsche misread Christian ethics as the confessions of envious priests, not understanding that envious priests had corrupted an existing rhetoric to their own purposes. Nietzsche's attack on Christianity is compromised by Scheler's observations. Nietzsche has the advantage of coming late, of being able to pillory the complacent herd of Christianity and the complacent herd of socialism. His social vision is too vague in detail to permit a conclusive resolution of the questions that need to be asked. One of these questions comes into view in the second essay of *Genealogy*. Can pain, suffering, and cruelty be eliminated in a transformed society? Clearly, Nietzsche will divide from these other possibilities on that issue, but the division remains abstract and conjectural as long as Nietzsche hasn't directly confronted concrete versions of Christianity and socialism.

In sections 1 through 5 of the second essay, Nietzsche notes that in order for promising to take place, human memory must be developed with a knowledge of causality, so that the act of promising can be connected to its fulfillment. Nature has bred this development; we can't change it by a mere act of will. To breed an animal that can be responsible, that can promise, requires breeding an animal sufficiently uniform to be predictable. Man's social nature has been bred to assist the end of social coordination. This process has been going on for a long time; its significance has only become apparent now. Nietzsche's subtext is that a full, drab uniformity signals humanity in a crisis.

A Nietzschean paradox presents itself here rather early, in section 3. The autonomous man of conscience is actually just the latest, most sophisticated version of the moral conformist, the product of centuries of cruelty and pain. (Quotation marks are used with great care in this section.) Nietzsche anticipates later discussion to the effect that the conscience is simply an interiorized form of social control, a superior form of control because it is internalized. There is nothing left "on the inside" in a person of consistent conscience to oppose it or to experiment with new options. The person of conscience becomes a predictable robot.[8] The pain that bred the conscience as an internalized control has been swept out of sight. The genealogists of morals have so far missed all of this. One reason that historians of morals have missed this is that they haven't noticed and haven't traced the vital clues given by proper genealogical study. Etymology and promising are now connected up. Promising was originally an economic contract, as we can learn from word roots. Failure to live up to the terms of economic contract was paid for in terms of pain inflicted on the debtor by the creditor. This was the mechanism that was then extended to a generalized form of social control.

Sections 6 through 10 observe that humans are now like tame domestic animals, bred through ages of beatings into submission and continuous hypocrisy. A look at the past shows how cruelty flourished and how it was intertwined with festivals, with gay times, with all of life. We can no longer comprehend this Dionysian excess, because we are driven by the illusion that we can eliminate pain and cruelty from life. Far from living in "better" times, we live in "worse" times, if Dionysus provides the test. Suffering is not bad; it is required for affirmation of life. Moderns make less pain seem like more by psychically isolating and dwelling on it, thinking through its significance. This is, of course, a sublimated attitude forced onto us by the triviality of our modern surroundings. Nietzsche wants to establish the connection between morality and pain. Virtue, in the absence of the divine spectator once necessary for its recognition, becomes a matter of human self-observation, especially focused on moments of pain.

Primitive economic debt, as noted in section 5, was transferred to other areas of the social sphere. We *owe* our community (generally) certain behavior in exchange for its protection from outside evils, or so the community would insist. At first, individual transgressions of social codes were met by expulsion. The penal code then evolved to find the exchange of equivalents within the society that can terminate and control what would otherwise be an endless cycle of violence based on revenge.[9] The moral notion of justice arises last and begins in a distinction between parties of greater and lesser power, moral evaluations compelling an appropriate settlement of debt without violence. This process culminates when "mercy" and "pity" replace the demands of a strict equivalence of justice.

Can we make all Nietzsche's comments on justice consistent? Nietzsche has already said that real justice involves a point of view and is not the calm and measured inanity presented on the basis of the table of good and evil. In the text we're examining, Nietzsche discusses social justice, the "oldest . . . moral canon of justice." Punishment is clearly for something that has been done, an act designed to balance the books of society. Nietzsche nowhere explicitly contrasts private and social conceptions of justice, but attention to context will separate these concepts sufficiently to preserve Nietzsche's view of the necessity and legitimacy of private (objective) justice against the demands of group uniformity.

What is the relationship of justice to revenge? Justice is not originally derived from ressentiment; it is a public matter. Even Nietzsche's paradigm judgments, made by an individual, are assessments of worth whose value is open to challenge and corroboration. Revenge flourishes in private. Justice originates as a social conception in the sphere of social life as a law that seeks to handle the potential disruption of reactive, violent feelings. Stronger powers seek especially to curb resentment among the weaker members of society, and the appearance of objectivity of the law is an aid to this. Successful legal codes screen out private feelings and settle disputes in a manner that is socially decisive. The last paragraph of section 11 discusses "just" and "unjust" as these terms are normally used *after* the law has come into existence. (That's why there are quotation marks here, since Nietzsche is discussing concepts based on moral tables that are not coincident with the moral valuations of nobles.) The law, because it formulates rigid principles for these purposes, is ultimately a restriction on life and part of the deadening weight of the past.

Section 12 contains an extremely important passage on origins, which deflates the notion that the genealogical tracing of origins can provide, by itself, a judgment of the present. The origin and the (present) purpose of something like punishment can be worlds apart.[10] Whatever the original cause, whatever the original purpose, structures can be obscured and transformed by later developments. This can be seen in biology, when an organ may originate toward one end, but then become adapted to another. No end is necessarily given with an origin, and teleological assumptions need to be rooted out of analysis. Even the assertion that punishment was devised for the purposes of punishment, perhaps a seeming tautology, can be false. The will to power, in short, constantly alters the meaning of whatever it operates on and everything associated with it. Dionysian process will ultimately destroy all rigidities of thought and social structure. Nietzsche thought that evolutionary scientists only stressed reactive adaptation to external conditions. This simplification ignores self-overcoming, self-adaptation to ends generated and projected from the individual, and all affirmative attempts to increase will to power from various power centers within Dionysian process.

Nietzsche returns to punishment in sections 13 through 19, noting that the *act* of punishment is more constant than its meaning, something that is obscured if we project our sense of punishment back onto its history. Due to the complex history of punishment, it is impossible to say what punishment is essentially at present, although we can untangle some of its historical strands. Once again, understanding ourselves is most difficult and perhaps impossible if we simply operate within traditional value tables or as though our understandings possessed a natural significance.

A typical reason for punishment, its supposed utility in making one feel guilty, is based on bad psychology. The criminal is made bolder (typically) and is well aware that the punished actions are not generally reprehensible. The criminal has just been unlucky, has been caught, and is feeling the effects of a more or less arbitrary assignment of punishment. The coherent criminal knows all this. Thus bad conscience and guilt are not necessarily produced by punishment and are quite independent of it. Guilt may occur independently in appropriately conditioned social subjects or may be a mechanism arising to make punishment bearable.

Nietzsche's own hypothesis is that bad consciences are the result of socialization—living in societies in which peace is normal. Aggressive instincts are thwarted by social control, cause unhappiness, discomfort, and even misery. When outward discharge is prohibited, the "inside" develops. This misery must be the prelude to something higher if humans are not to die out in a paroxysm of frustration. Nietzsche's historical conjecture concerning the arrival of liberating new social formations is the sudden conquest of one people by another. The cruelty of a new dominant class can be a spur to development. Self-conquest exhibits the same structural mechanism and works essentially through cruelty to oneself in the interests of self-transcendence. Returning to debts and debtors, Nietzsche notes that the origins of divinity are to be found in fear among members of a society that the founders of the society are owed a debt for their sacrifices. Sacrifice was an effort to pay back to ancestors the debt of sacrifice. The most powerful tribes would have the greatest debt and the greatest fear and would have transfigured their ancestors into the highest gods. Nietzsche sets these remarks into prehistory, perhaps to avoid the obvious objection that the texts of all known societies already refer to gods. Nietzsche's theory does not explain why the gods of Christianity and Islam should have become omnipotent when the societies "projecting" them seem originally to have been weak, nor can it explain why Buddhism never projected a god in the same way at all. Only Nietzsche's general point, that humans project gods, may be compatible with rigorous genealogy.

We now see in sections 20 through 25 how guilt and duty come to be connected with religious presuppositions. Bad conscience constructs a debt that cannot be paid, associated with evils that cannot be eradicated (original sin). One must withdraw from a worthless world (Buddhism) or recognize in some way that man cannot pay the debt. Christianity's God, who pays the debt, simply highlights man's inability to do so. Guilt before God is the ultimate self-torture, the ultimate self-cruelty, because it can't be expiated without divine complicity. The lack of perfection of the

Hellenic gods allowed them a more comfortable and shifting relationship to humanity. Where gods are projected by lower classes, they become projected beyond relevant upper classes and hence out of the real world.

Nietzsche has provided a description rather than an explanation of differences. His apparatus of social description is not complex enough to develop mechanisms for discussing the different forms of religion that have arisen in different societies.

The third essay of *Genealogy,* as we noted earlier, is a commentary on one line from *Zarathustra,* and it is a signpost to the future that Nietzsche's contemporaries seemed unable to read. This essay dramatizes the compression of the aphorism, indicating that power that an aphorism can unleash when interpreted by a dynamic and affirmative reader. The third essay completes the pessimistic leitmotiv of the earlier portions of *Genealogy* by leaving a message interpretable only in the future.

Ascetic ideals come from a (human) preference or perhaps a human necessity: that to will nothing overcomes not to will at all. Will to power expands, if possible, even if its target is deformed or fictive. This hasn't been understood. Chastity and sensuality are not antitheses, as is commonly thought, but are examples of the will being directed to different tasks. Desire is heightened by waiting, by ruminating, and by temporary chastity. A failed sensual will worship chastity because of this relationship but cannot escape the coils of the sensual by so doing. Wagner is a useful example.

Art comes from self-negation. An artist doesn't represent him- or herself in the work. The artist is thus *not* to be confused with the artistic product, the latter being more important. Neither the artist nor the product has an intrinsic meaning. Works require interpretation because the work does not start with a meaning that can be definitely spelled out, and so interpretation will vary with the contexts of any present moment in which the art work still exists. Artists are typically representing a morality, a philosophy, or a religion, coding it into their works for future interpretation. What of those artists who are philosophers? What can be said when philosophers pay homage to an ascetic ideal? In Schopenhauer's case, Schopenhauer's philosophy had the effect of providing an excuse for Wagner's moving toward a theory of the superiority of music over text. Schopenhauer is regarded quite carefully in sections 6 and 7. In following Kant's aesthetics, Schopenhauer saw what had beauty from the standpoint of the spectator as something not engaging our interests. Stendhal, an artist, knew better. One can only laugh at philosophers who assert that we can view representations of the female form only as "pure forms," as they have deluded themselves about the escape from sensuality. Schopenhauer, who stood closer to the arts than Kant, was not able to free himself from Kant's attitude. Schopenhauer, in speaking of freedom from sexual interestedness, reveals his torment. When a philosopher pays homage to an aesthetic ideal, the suspicion must be that the philosopher wishes to gain release from a torture by a pretense that it doesn't exist. Schopenhauer derived his happiness from his anger. If deprived of Hegel, of woman, and so on, he would have withered, contrary to what he consciously supposed. The ascetic ideal is a philosopher's rancor against something, for example, sensuality, and it is an expression of a desire for independence from that something. Self-deception is inevitably involved here, because the ascetic ideal is always moved by an absent center of desire or feeling.

Philosophers think finally only about themselves, completing what is a tendency to abstraction in artists; at least this can be said of those who have explicitly thought of themselves as pure philosophers. They think of the ascetic ideal as floating freely above life. The three great slogans of the ascetic ideal—poverty, humility, and chastity—are always encountered in the lives of great, fruitful, inventive spirits. These ideals are not virtues, as claimed by the apologetics of philosophers, but the painful natural conditions of their most creative existence.

The asceticism of poverty, humility, and chastity does not ultimately mark the deepest link between philosophy and the ascetic ideal. Values change over time, for example, suffering, which was once a virtue, but is now a vice. The philosopher was originally forced to adopt a virtuous disguise prepared beforehand by the ascetic ideal of the priest, sorcerer, soothsayer, or some other religious type. The reason is that the inactive brooding of these types allowed them to be out of temper with their times, and they had to engender a form of fear in others or be despised in terms of the social conventions of those surrounding them. To believe in their own ideas, innovators have had to be horribly cruel to themselves—creating their own hells so that new heavens could be created within. Early philosophers had to live within the identity of religious priests. Has this really changed? Has the philosopher still a need to assume a disguise? Who, finally, *is* Nietzsche's Zarathustra?

With the ascetic priest in view, we come to the ultimate representative of seriousness. The ascetic priest appears everywhere in human history, so that there must be some deep necessity for this continuous resentment against life, this deliberate willing of a decrease in physiological capacity for life. The philosophical version of this is a self-denying Kantian reason—a reason that can just comprehend that things are incomprehensible. But the development of strange perspectives yields new eyes and a new vision, and these alien perspectives are not simply to be condemned. They provide the leaven of history. A famous passage at the end of section 12 now asserts that the more eyes we have, the more complete our concept of something will be—but there is no such thing as an eye without "interest," an eye not turned in a particular direction from a particular location. This is Nietzsche's compressed image for his objective perspectivism. The highest eye is objective, sees everything that can be known to exist, until a higher eye is developed. To suppose one has imagined the highest eye is just delusive nonsense, although one may defend one's profundity of vision in the context of one's times. What can be seen from the highest perspective need not be rationally articulate. As Dionysian flux comes into view, vision may reach its highest point, while at the same time human language is further than ever from providing the resources to describe that vision.

Nietzsche's pain could hardly be more self-evident than in such passages, passages reflecting bitterly on his own asceticism. The philosopher, as opposed to the philosophical ideologue, seeks a vision that will unsettle history and permit an affirmative step into a new interaction with Dionysian process. In this Heraclitean image, Nietzsche wishes at once to be regarded as unique, as the real philosopher of his time, and yet *as* a philosopher, participating in the eternal return of the philosopher that is necessary if wisdom's desire for warriors against their times is to be fulfilled. Philosophy is neither good nor evil, neither good nor bad. Philosophy is born of one by the other, ceaselessly frustrating any easy valuation on any of the value tables.

The absurdity of ascetic ideals (including aesthetic ideals) is now manifest, but the absurdity can be seen to arise from a necessary conflict between life and some obstruction to it. The ascetic ideal is an artifice for the preservation of life. This is why ascetic ideals always keep springing out again—as life will always reassert itself. Wounds and even death focus a healthy attention on the desirability of living.

The vagueness of Nietzsche's conception of society causes trouble here. The articulation of false virtue makes Nietzsche's portrait compelling for second-echelon political and scientific figures. With respect to lower economic classes and their Christianity, the portrait washes out. The ascetic priest (the focus of Nietzsche's anger) is the representative of the herd campaigning against the strong. Nietzsche suggests that the priest often turns ressentiment back against the herd itself, unable to win a victory against the stronger, but driven by a need for a substitute conquest. Ressentiment turned by priests against the herd itself has often rendered the herd harmless and has thus created an almost accidental segregation of weak and strong within a society whose egalitarian ideology masks a passive and resentful passage through time. The priest may wind up in social bondage to the master.

Nietzsche does not worry about the dynamics of society as a whole. His concern is to protect the strong philosophers, artists, and prophets from the collective compulsions of the herd. The positive reaction of later artists to Nietzsche's philosophy seems more sensitive to his tonality than the Nazi appropriation. Nietzsche notes that priests cannot cure the sickness of society, as they are already bound over to a reigning value table. By inference, only philosophers, artists, and prophets remain with a purchase point for the transformation of society. But do they transform society by transcending themselves individually into Übermenschen? Nietzsche's social and political resources are too impoverished to solve this problem, and his most trenchant attacks degenerate into a descriptive analysis of a threatening social nihilism.

In section 17, Nietzsche notes that the priest is helpless because ressentiment does not provide a perspective from which nihilism can be conquered. The priest must suggest the classic ascetic route: act so as to reduce frustration by reducing will and desire to terms of the current valuation. An absence of suffering is an end to be achieved by reducing feeling, by reducing the possibility of a clash between desire and realization. Loss of self in mechanical work is a suitable deadening mechanism. This focuses the forgetting of self on the inauthentic rhythm of mechanical repetition, but memory is recalcitrant.

Section 19 is a development of Nietzsche's earlier views on lying and illusion. Lies can be dishonest or honest. Dishonest lying, an affected innocence coupled with censorship, is all too human. Affected by the strong as a way of concealing their strength, it becomes disgusting. Biographies of artists and prophets are now written so as to avoid all mention of the characteristic of strength, in effect conceding to the power of the herd. But the most powerful form of self-directed ressentiment is the orgy of self-pity associated with the concept of sin. The sick cannot avoid sin, and they cannot overcome it with the resources of ressentiment. In our time, with the notion of "sin" weakened considerably by the decline of Christianity, it's hard to feel the impact of these observations. The poor may be accused by their leaders of being indolent, but with few exceptions they are more likely to see themselves as victims of economic injustice and bad luck and not as sinners deserving their punishment. Nietzsche's real focus is on the strong. They are the ones threatened by the values of herd uniformity.

Finally, Nietzsche surveys the calamitous consequences of the ascetic ideal. It has produced physical sickness (section 21), literary sickness (the New Testament), and science. Scientists are literally the unconscious apologists of the ascetic ideal. Are the idealists the last opponents of the ascetic ideal, a way in which they would like to present themselves? Well—they are believers, but only believers that they play this role, a fact that ought to cause suspicion. They still believe in truth, and they are caught up in defense of the same value table that scientists exploit. Science and the ascetic ideal are closely linked. The scientist applies the relevant value table, pretending that perspective is not involved. This is most clearly seen in the rubbish that masquerades as scientific historiography. These historians ignore the interests that they ultimately serve. The ascetic ideal is the only significant human meaning, and it requires constantly renewed forms, since its ideals cannot hold in any fixed form against Dionysian flux embodied in the will to power. Nietzsche could discern no movement away from the nihilism of the ascetic ideal in his contemporaries. The silence of isolation may have begun to seem an onrushing necessity.

7

Society

To this point, we have looked at detailed passages in *Birth, Untimely Meditations, Zarathustra, The Gay Science, Beyond Good and Evil*, and *On the Genealogy of Morals*. These have supported an exposition of major lines of thought leading from *Birth* to Nietzsche's later writing. In the last chapters, we will consider the Dasein of the Hellenic noble as it is presented in the philosophical visions of will to power and the Eternal Return. But to proceed immediately to that task would be to suppress some aspects of Nietzsche's thought that have been mentioned but not developed. We have mentioned the lack of a concrete vision of social and political change in Nietzsche's aphorisms, and this lack has been crucial to criticism of Nietzsche to this point, but we haven't developed any detailed consideration of why his vision was truncated. The crude reason is that he attempted to measure surrounding society by means of his vision of Hellenic Greece. If one tries to imagine isolated Hellenic nobles, existing without a stable political system and without an integrated economic system, forming shifting alliances to solve immediate problems, one can construct the kind of social and political picture that dominates Nietzsche's approach to his surroundings, especially as it is sharpened by his disgust for an emerging capitalism. If one tries to imagine Hellenic nobles supported by their wives during periods of rest and convalescence, one can also construct the picture of gender relationships that Nietzsche seems to have regarded as optimal. Nietzsche's Hellenic visions simply didn't fit his surroundings, but the perspectives they provide allow for pungent criticism of democratic leveling and its dangers. We know that the noble lived with a different value table. In these next two chapters, we learn that the noble lived differently. The existential themes of the last four chapters cannot be illustrated quite so nicely by sustained readings of primary texts, since apart from some collected aphorisms in *Human, All Too Human,* Nietzsche's relevant reflections are diffusely scattered through the later aphoristic works and the unpublished work. The intent of these last chapters is to suggest that Nietzsche's Hellenic vision can give unifying perspectives on these scattered remarks. At the same time, the readings depend on a greater level of interpretive power than the earlier readings.

A glance at any of the indices of Nietzsche's works will reveal that there are three or four social positions that are constantly under discussion in Nietzsche's work: the artist, the philosopher, the scientist, and the saint or prophet. There is very little talk of kings and generals, businessmen and athletes. One also finds a sharp distinction between the social positions of nobles and herd men, and a recognition that women must be reckoned with, this last an obscure but compelling demand. These social positions have an obvious source in Hellenic society and its Greek successors. Nietzsche attempts to value modern society in terms of a Hellenic model and attempts to revitalize a decadent and decaying society with a Hellenic vision.

There are two distinctions relative to Hellenic society that Nietzsche has constantly in mind. The first is the distinction between the noble and the slave, and the second is the distinction between man and woman. In Nietzsche's view, society is threatened with decadence if either distinction is blurred. Both distinctions are required in an affirmative society. The difference between noble and slave is required as a source of value and as a means of controlling the pain and suffering of the slaves through the charisma of nobles. Slave work is required for the economic viability of society. Nietzsche's concern, of course, is for nobles, and his slaves are represented as an undifferentiated mass. Women are required as a stimulant for male curiosity, and they function to provide a healing place for the resting warrior noble.

The absence of all other major social roles except those originating in the Hellenic vision is striking. Nietzsche hardly mentions modern roles in government and business in his discussion, obviously thinking that all these roles were irrelevant to anything but continuing on toward a dreary democratic stagnation. Nietzsche's general view of a human society is that it is a relatively stable piece of foam in the wave of Dionysian process. The differentiable roles in society are those of the scientist, the artist, the prophet, and the philosopher. Without considering the affirmative and decadent versions of each of these, we can say something general about their locations. The functioning artist is typically in touch with Dionysian flux, mediating Dionysian flux through a valuation maintained by society that is ultimately threatened by this flux. The scientist, by comparison, is removed from the threatening profundity of Dionysian flux, and is patiently and rather mechanically developing the consequences of some valuation. Artists and scientists at a given time may be exact contemporaries, both working with a valuation that is the inheritance of some prior prophet's or philosopher's discovery. Affirmative prophets and philosophers apparently contemporary to the artists and scientists at some time are actually ahead of them. This may be because they can see further into the past that is contained in the present. An affirmative scientific philosopher can scrutinize the artist and the servant scientist, articulating their values, their roles, and their relationships, but the moving and shaking philosopher will be looking toward adaptive changes, as will the prophet in a somewhat more intuitive and less logical manner.

If these social positions are strongly marked, and marked as the positions determining the active or reactive direction of social change, Nietzsche also marks more weakly the positions of woman, slave, and noble. The noble has, rather surprisingly, an unclear relationship to the strongly marked roles. All these roles are contained in a kind of social bubble, a bubble that emerges on the surface of Dionysian process, retaining its shape for a while, but always threatening to burst and merge again with chaos. What is remarkable is that all talk of economic and political processes beyond allusions to the economic necessity of slavery is considered "dirty" and is swept out of sight, even though there is talk of economics and politics in the Greek historians. Nietzsche's vision of Hellenic Greece is peculiarly sanitary in its failure to consider political and economic life. Nietzsche simply fails to see any detail in those members of society whose Nietzschean function is to support the role of the noble, with a few exceptions for women's roles. Nietzsche's Hellenic society is dominated and moved ultimately by those who can feel the power and the threat of Dionysus. The nuts and bolts of social construction from more modern viewpoints don't come into focus at all. Most of our problems with Nietzsche on society are related to this peculiar fact, a fact that makes it difficult for contemporary philosophers to even notice that Nietzsche has a social and political philosophy. Nietzsche's political opinions are a bizarre conglomeration of disparate ideas to philosophers in the Enlightenment tradition. Nietzsche combines radical individualism and aristocracy without the mediation of rights or mutually beneficial utility calculations that comprise justice and liberty in the liberal tradition. Nietzsche, true to his intuitions, simply suspends the elements of his vision of Hellenic society without attempting mediation and simply denies that scientific elaboration of facts could ever bring unanimity of opinion and social peace, since the latter would represent a social structure so rigid that it would be destroyed immediately by Dionysian flux if it were ever achieved.

To situate Nietzsche, we need to consider a more complicated space of possibilities in social and political philosophy than that which comes to us from the liberal, Enlightenment tradition. To do this, we can imagine a line of liberalism whose end points are labeled *Marxism* and *capitalism*. Between these ideal-type end points we will consider a series of compromise positions that we will call *liberalisms*. In doing this, we accept Marxism's self-description that it provides a transvaluation of capitalism. Liberalisms attempt resolutions of freedom and equality in theoretical capitalism that may conceal, but not escape, contradiction. Common to all the positions on this line is the notion that economic and political processes are the springs of movement in society. At the end points, only economic process will be recognized, while all liberalisms (and all real life instantiations of these theories) will recognize a political factor as mediating between the pure types represented at the end points. In liberalisms, individuals must expend political and intellectual energy in the resolution of conflict in mutually negotiated checks and balances of various kinds. Built into liberalisms will be sets of checks and balances given by the intention to preserve promises and working relationships in spite of their pure economic irrationality as measured in the present moment. Liberalisms are constrained by the weight of history. The dignity of the individual and the virtues of self-chosen individual development are affirmed in liberalism. The end points of this first line have carried the weight of economic debate for some time, but they are also involved in a shadow political dispute based on their differing conceptions of economic process. Capitalism affirms hierarchy of opportunity and realized profits as the major motivation for growth and development. A pitiless selection process produces only the fittest survivors. This system, naked, would perish in a paroxysm of internal revulsion and fury even if the Marxist conception of a terminal revolution based on class conflict were theoretically inaccurate. Marxism affirms community of interests and needs and a vision of mutual support as the major motivation for growth and development. A relentless and comprehensive process of planning for all produces a society in which the needs of everyone are satisfied in communal happiness. This system, unmediated, would perish in a Dionysian entropic uniformity, according to Nietzsche, since the social system is incapable of absorbing sudden environmental changes. If pity must vanish at the end-point of capitalism, envy must vanish at the endpoint of Marxism. Because of this, perhaps no society of humans could ever be an instance of either extreme point, and Nietzsche's critique of both envy and pity, which are not values on the affirmative Hellenic value table, is symptomatic of his wide-ranging critique of the end-point ideologies. The glory of liberalism lies in its temporizing inconsistency. Considered just in the economy of envy and pity, social steering can be improvised from the inconsistent resources of the economy by pushing policy in any desired direction. Social hardship can be softened by an appeal to pity, and stagnation can be reversed by an appeal to the driving force of envy and the deserts of increased personal freedom. Any attempt to achieve theoretical consistency from a liberal point of view seems to drive one to a pure but inflexible ideology. There are theoretically consistent defenses of the ideal societies at each end point, where no one can actually live. The acid debates occur between ideologues at either end who point to a society not quite at the other end and then reveal the inconsistency of their target. Thus a Marxist may choose to see liberalism as the ideology of capitalism, arguing that talk of rights, duties, charity, and so on is an obscure veil thrown over the horrors of competition to the death. From the other end, the ideology of equality may seem to conceal the horrors of an insectlike uniformity or to be necessarily coupled with secret hierarchy. All this debate remains within the frame of economic and political consideration, and Nietzsche just doesn't fit in. Nietzsche is hardly a liberal, and he never says anything positive about the possibility that open debate could ever locate truth.

To locate Nietzsche, we need to recognize "doubles" at both ends of another line set at right angles to the first, creating four extreme points that define a convex space that can be filled with liberal inconsistencies. So far, we have only located one of the defining lines of this space, and we have no means of tracing a border around the space suggested by four end points. Let us consider the second line of definition. At one end, the double of Marxism occurs as Christianity or anarchism. The double of (socialist) anarchism is theoretically important. Anarchism sees Marxism as a prescription for political despotism, the latter coming inevitably from the hierarchical planning required for fulfilling the schedule of social needs without producing wastage in the form of superfluous production. Anarchism is prepared to abandon the state for a voyage of equality, without coercion and without a chartable future. This is what, theological differences aside, permits it to coincide with Christianity in the space under discussion. The objection that anarchism is not feasible in the real world, except possibly in very small communities not requiring extensive industrial planning, is overwhelming in terms of the value tables that drive Marxist and capitalist apologetics.[1] Anarchist practice could hardly meet this head on without producing hierarchy in connection with planning, so the practice of anarchists is precisely to avoid planning. Anarchists in practice can perhaps only form anarchist societies on a small scale, where money, trade, government can be eliminated. Often these societies have had to exist within larger societies, and the resulting friction has generally ruptured anarchic society, resulting in anarchists who participate as critics in a larger, liberal social organization. The Christianity of accommodation has existed within modern societies as a hierarchical institution, but it is important here to observe that the original social vision of Christianity was often that of a small community of individuals equal before God, whose attention was directed toward a presumed and important future and away from problems of earthly finance and planning. More stable Christian societies with a relaxed anticipation of the end of the world might attempt an organization around mutual love and sharing that resembles the theoretical socialist end point, insofar as sharing takes on an economic dimension. The anarchist/Christian end point on the second line is egalitarian, and hence is opposed to capitalism on that score, but it doesn't accept economic and political processes as the springs of social movement, and so it may be differentiated from the economic foundationalism of Marxism, as well as from the political compromising of liberalism, as a separate and singular position.

So far, we have considered a space of social and political philosophies determined primarily by a line stressing economic (and political) factors as the roots of social structure and movement, with Marxism and capitalism defining the end points. To this, we have added a transverse axis defined as denying the fundamental importance of economic and political factors, and we have identified anarchism as one of its end points, an end point sharing egalitarian ideals with Marxism but not with capitalism, in virtue of its distaste for hierarchy. We will locate Nietzsche's position at the other end of the line that has anarchism at one end point. A mixture of liberalisms can now be regarded as displayed in the rough convex space suggested by these distinct endpoints. We will not need to trace the borders of this space in order to discuss Nietzsche.

Nietzsche provides a "double" for capitalism. His position is opposed to the egalitarianism of both Marxism and anarchism, but it is also opposed to the economic hierarchy of capitalism. Economic processes were largely out of sight in Hellenic noble consciousness, and Nietzsche obliges in its recurrence with a version of anarchic individual competition geared toward developing a hierarchy of fitness in which the selection process is cultural, not economic. The progressive transcendence produced by cultural struggle is what brings a society the flexibility to adapt to changing circumstances. As in capitalism, there are a few individuals discernible at the top, the nobles, and an amorphous mass toiling to support the experimentalism that the nobles pursue to improve the fitness of the entire society. Wars release the power inherent in the innovations of the cultural elite by destroying older economic and social rigidities, hence bringing in bold new explosions of development. In this sense, destruction rather than conservation is central to social flexibility. Nietzsche's model is Hellenic. His nausea at leveling democracy and his approbation of philosophical leaders comes from his reading of Greek texts. Major Greek philosophers, such as Plato, shared these attitudes at an appropriately abstract level. A society in which compromise politics and economic processes ruled would have to be drab, dreary, repetitive, and boring.

Nietzsche's perspectivism plays a crucial role at this point. From Nietzsche's end point, Marxism and capitalism collapse into one another as accepting certain economic laws and assessing the future in the light of extrapolations drawn from these laws. Both must therefore end in nihilism, and they are equally reprehensible. Neither is aware of Dionysian process, nor of the necessity of transcending current conceptions of economic process. Liberalism fails because of its emphasis on public discussion, which Nietzsche had laid aside as mere babble as early as the first untimely meditation. Had Nietzsche noticed anarchism, although there is no evidence that he did in the sense in which we have described it, he would have thought its egalitarian overtones sufficient to condemn it. Thus Nietzsche thought that he had a higher perspective from which other social and political philosophies might all be located and judged, and all were found lacking. The lack in every case is a failure to take the effects of Dionysian process into account. Dionysian process will destroy all fixed structures, and the inevitable failure of fixed economic structures to stand over time provides a special case. But as the state is also a fixed structure, Nietzsche's position itself contains the seeds of an anarchism. A crucial question for Nietzsche's apologetics is whether his cultural hierarchy avoids the Dionysian by providing insufficient detail to seem rigid.

The notions of individuality and of collectivism need transvaluation when one moves from the axis of economics to the axis of anarchism. If

Marxist or socialist notions of collectivity provide a critique of any individuality that struggles against maximum social cooperation, capitalist notions of economic survival condemn any individuality that struggles against economic necessity to failure and elimination. It is not essential to capitalist apologetics that economic laws be known in advance. An evolutionary apologetics may applaud diversity of effort, allowing the (at least partially unknown) laws of economics to select superior strategies. There is a seeming waste built into this process, but it can be seen as the required waste of progress in an evolutionary model. A plethora of various forms is tried against an environment that selects the most efficient form, the others dropping out in the competition. The critique of Marxism or socialism is then that planners must be arrogant enough to suppose that they can infallibly plan for the future, or at least plan well enough to avoid economic disasters. Although individuals plan for themselves in capitalist apologetics, some of them are doomed to social sacrifice, that is, to failures that will illuminate the space in which success can be recognized. This line of thought might be developed to show that both Marxist and capitalist models are ultimately collective models in which individuality is punished when it conflicts with economic law, even though the notion of individuality is required for a self-understanding of social structure. There can be no coherent notion of a capitalist who does not function as an entrepreneur in competition against like others.[2] Both models therefore contain a robust reference to an essential social collectivity, and it is the notion of an individual that is secondary and problematic, being a kind of singularity in a space of coordination and potential conflict.

On the axis of anarchism, the individual becomes central, and it is the notion of a social collective that is secondary and problematic. That this requires some transvaluation is obvious, since the secondary notion of an individual taken over from the axis of economics can't function here as conceptually foundational except at the cost of contradiction. At the anarchist end of this line, there are several possibilities for individual development, and the egalitarian nature of the ideology is really only the denial of political hierarchy or economic hierarchy for the purposes of control. Whether the individual considers others in decisions remains an individual decision, and this vision is less socially coercive than its Marxist foil. What's missing is an account of what will select individual variations. Anarchists may speak of everyone doing what he or she would like to do, as though these choices were free, and there is little discussion of failure as measured against a real world. Critics of anarchism have often suggested that this is why anarchist conclaves can achieve longevity only when they exist inside a larger viable society that can shield them from the direct shocks of a hostile environment. Nietzsche's anarchic individual is measured against Dionysian process, a process that provides a measure of flexibility and hence of affirmation. His anarchic individuals are selected by a process that will make them uniform in flexibility and affirmation, each measured against Dionysian flux. At the top of the hierarchy, there will be one Übermensch, even if there are many instantiations of this most flexible type. They do not measure themselves against each other, and they do not differentiate themselves by rational discourse with each other or by direct competition. The Übermensch thus provides a regimentation of the Hellenic noble, since competition between Übermenschen provides practice for the requisite flexibility of adjustment, not to each other so much as to the unexpected turns of Dionysian process. Any society, always presenting some traditional rigidities against Dionysian process, must continually change and adapt. Everything below the level of the most flexible individuals will corrode and fall away over time. The Übermenschen achieve coordinated action only because each adjusts to process in the place within Dionysian process that they occupy, without planning coalition politics for the future. It is process that causes coordination in conjunction with flexibility. Nietzsche doesn't discuss the details of social and political structure because all such structures are transitory and contingent. His social and political vision is of a collective of Übermenschen buffeted by reality into a smooth and coordinated accommodation to change, a highest level above which there is nothing to describe. Below that level, nothing will stand for long.

The roots of this account lie already in the first untimely meditation. When Nietzsche is still constrained by history to talk about societies and nations, he distinguishes between a genuine, uniform culture and a culture that is a pastiche of bits and pieces of other cultures. The nonuniform cultures will pull in different directions, like liberalism, in the face of onrushing Dionysian process, and hence must suffer diminution. A unified culture will present a single vector that is coincident with the directional flow of Dionysian flux if it survives. But when this characterization is spelled out, Nietzsche's deepest fissures come slowly into view. If the Übermensch represents a vector, then some calculation into the future from the present moment must occur to explain the alignment. The Übermensch can't just be lucky in positioning if self-discipline is to play any role. But this keeps some history alive as a basis for calculation. If history and calculation are reduced to the zero point, the Übermensch would be selected by luck. Another way to put this is to notice that any comparative measure of affirmation requires a time lag. The affirmative superiority of the Übermensch must be compared over time to less adaptive strategies for confronting Dionysian process. If the vector disappears, and the Übermensch is simply the adaptive survivor, totally without history and simply going with the flow, only a moment of which presents itself, Übermenschen can never be identified in advance but will be recognized only after the flow has occurred and revealed its path. Nietzsche's view here seems to collapse structurally into the competitive struggle associated with capitalism, a struggle that demands the elimination of pity, except that Nietzsche's process of selection is not primarily economic. Economics and culture, however, both act over time, and that is sufficient to suggest that rigidity can perhaps not be bred out of living creatures. Affirmation of *whatever* comes can't necessarily be planned in advance of time, as time may eliminate the affirmer. The tension here is terrific. By comparison to others, the Übermensch represents an end point, an end point selected by Dionysian process for the lightest history and the greatest flexibility. But as the present moment becomes the only frame accessible to the Übermensch, an enormous confrontation of opposing impulses increases in intensity. Nietzsche's end point may contain the same unlivable contradictions as the other end points, and his claim that humans can't be Übermenschen threatens to become a conceptual triviality. A society of Übermenschen is flexible by default; no structure is provided that would be rigid in the path of chaos, and yet a society without structure is a notion difficult to bring into a concrete image. This topic will be taken up again in the last chapter. Just inside Nietzsche's end point remains the original vision of Hellenic Greece, a society driven by hierarchy in which privileged cultural social positions will provide the leaven of change. Both the extreme point and this vision inside it deserve a wider place in driving social and political philosophy, for they increase the variety of ideal types that can be brought to bear on theoretical discussion.

We have now described and contrasted four positions of political and social ideal types: Marxism, capitalism, anarchism, and Nietzschean hierarchy. In addition, these ideal types suggest a somewhat amorphous space of compromise representing the various livable confusions of liberalism. All the extreme, theoretically consistent positions are latent within the confusions of liberalism, the latter here taken as any uneasy, inconsistent amalgam of two or more of the ideal types. As cultured, civilized scholars, we may feel that there is something inherently grubby in any exclusive reduction of social interaction to economic or political terms. We can also recognize the appeal of liberty (individual freedom of action) and justice (some type of formal equality), even if economic and political processes seem somehow foundational. In developing any of these impulses, the drive to theoretical consistency can lead us out of the morass that is liberalism, into one of these relatively ideal, consistent, but flawed political visions. Nietzsche seems to have been drawn along such a path. The extreme points fail to include a reasonable image of the necessity and cost of political interaction in any large society, condemning themselves to utopian schemes in which the interaction of concrete human individuals with eccentric preferences is avoided. Debate among the ideal types is complicated and often proceeds by the shady practice of placing an opponent just within liberalism's contradictory domain and arguing the consistency of the home base position against the contradictions of the opposing liberalism. This is to adopt the strategy of science, making the ideal the measure of the real, which Nietzsche diagnosed but lapsed into himself. Nietzsche defended his utopia against others on the grounds that it had once existed in Hellenic Greece before the time of Socrates. But his conception of the Übermensch represents an idealization of that historical vision, an idealization in the direction of self-awareness of Dionysian process. The Greeks had had a light historical tradition, but the Übermensch extends the tendency to an asymptotic point: the Übermensch will live without history. Nietzsche's purified vision of Greece, constrained by rational polemics against existing views, loses the notion of society altogether and may threaten conceptual chaos. Even if chaos is avoided (and Nietzsche courted a chaos tuned to reflect Dionysian profundity), Nietzsche's ideal Hellenic society may be as unrealizable as the utopian visions he so cogently criticized from his own perspective.

This structure helps to explain Nietzsche's spleen, and also the spleen directed against Nietzsche. A Marxist may well argue against competitive capitalism, but he or she will argue on the common assumption that economic processes are fundamental.[3] The capitalist vision can be seen from the Marxist perspective as mystified, but comprehensible and wrong. This allows sustained, patient, detailed confrontation with the errors of capitalist apologetics, economic forecasts, and so forth. By comparison, both the anarchist and the Nietzschean seem irrational in a manner that is difficult to articulate. They do not recognize the root assumption of the centrality of economic processes. A Marxist must see Nietzsche as an irrational, hazy defender of capitalism, because Marxists can only look down the line of economic and political considerations. In fact, Nietzsche has a position sharply critical of capitalism, as well as of Marxism.

If Nietzsche's vision is distinct, how could he have supposed that he could establish the superiority of his perspective over that of the other perspectives, apart from the negative critique that actual societies were instances of liberalisms headed toward nihilism? The horrors of actual societies, especially of contemporary European societies, receive a devastating critique in Nietzsche's descriptions. But Nietzsche has other weapons. What of the utopic visions of the other ideal types? Their outstanding characteristic is that they lie only in the future, in a future that cannot be accurately described. Particularly for the Christian conception of heaven and the socialist classless society, no historical instantiations are known. One attempts to describe the transformed humans that will inhabit such societies, but one's visions of the new humans (unlike any that we know now) is uncertain. A clearer vision lies necessarily in the present. The arguable superiority of Nietzsche's vision lies in the fact that his perfect society has already existed and has left a complicated record that allows us to clarify its outlines, with an acceptable hermeneutical margin of uncertainty. This enables us to have a detailed vision of where we should be heading: toward a social formation proven to be superior by a clear historical vision that cyclical time will allow us to instantiate again.

Nietzsche's great enemy in this respect is Plato.[4] Plato's perfect state embodies a hierarchy in which people find a natural place given their abilities, and it is a state dominated by philosophers. But Plato's vision, while Greek and antidemocratic, was decadent in Nietzsche's terms. Plato's vision was reflected back from a conjectured world of being as devoid of wars, devoid of Dionysian flux. The ideal state has generals and an army, but there is no sense that the state could be devastated by acts of war. Plato's society was to be preserved against change by the truths of the forms and by an educational system devoted to the cyclical reproductions of the same. Nietzsche needs a Platonism on wheels, and he must break the dikes, inundating the Cretan City with a Dionysian flood. Greece needs interpretation, but Plato had it wrong. To sidestep the awkward fact that Plato was Greek, Nietzsche affirms again that we are most confused about ourselves. Nietzsche's insistence is that only he has the distance to see through Plato back to the Dionysian origins of Hellenic culture; only he is able to understand why Plato opens centuries of reactive decadence with his postulation of religious being in an effort to freeze a reactive portrait of a rational Greek life at one crucial point in its development. It is this reflexive distance that gives Nietzsche a higher perspective.

Nietzsche's argumentative strength is that he opposes the flaws of actual societies, and the conceptual problems of other utopic solutions, with his vision of Hellenic society. His utopic vision is constructed with believable historical detail. But is his reading of Greece correct? Here is one final place to cash Nietzsche's perspectivism. No reading is provably correct: that's the fundamental principle of Nietzschean hermeneutics, so we shouldn't be able to catch Nietzsche out pretending to have a provably correct Dionysian reading of anything. Nietzsche's view works as a piece of aesthetics; our problem is to know whether it is merely aesthetic fantasy, or whether it can be realized in life. Nietzsche's nobles are, ultimately, fully concrete Platonic ideals, but we don't know whether there could be any. We don't know whether Nietzsche is forced into a form of Platonism by an inability to locate the Übermensch in this world. The holism missing in Nietzsche's social and political philosophy is compressed inside the wholeness of his image of the Hellenic noble. In aesthetics, appearance and reality can coincide as there are beautiful aesthetic objects to be taken as examples. But can we project the ideal Hellenic noble into our real world? Nietzsche's answer relies on the body. As we move toward a personal realization of this ideal of Hellenic Dionysian unity, Nietzsche thinks we feel ourselves becoming more whole, more powerful. But is there a path of monotonically increasing felt harmony that charts the course to the Übermensch? If so, isn't Dionysus, ultimately, benevolent?

Nietzsche's problem is ironically posed by the necessity of consistency. He does not strictly reverse Plato, privileging the world of becoming over the world of being, as the inversion of a contradiction is also a contradiction. Instead he collapses the world of being into the world of becoming, or at least he does this as consistently as thought will allow, providing a negation of the whole structure. When this has been accomplished, the fecund tension of a contradictory metaphysics is lost. Nietzsche is constantly approaching this asymptotic point, where the power of speech is lost and the ambiguities of writing are inescapable. The bounds of logic drove his vision of Hellenic Greece to the breaking point, but provided a social and political vision that we can unearth from the record of his torment.

We have already noted that instantiations of Marxism, anarchism, and capitalism tend to become tempered and turned back into liberalisms by social realities. What happened to Nietzsche? It would seem that the mad Dionysian biological metaphors can't be driven to the asymptotic point of complete competition. The grim consequences of Dionysus for existing society fade for some curious reason when Nietzsche discusses the role of the artist and the philosopher in his vision. Even if the development of these higher types is slowed by an undesirable contact with reactive types, the

Dionysian metaphor suggests that struggle should increase hardiness, or fitness—especially if a doctrine useful for others is being developed. Similarly, there is no mention of struggle between artists and philosophers in Nietzsche's social vision—a struggle that ought to be stimulating and progressive given Nietzsche's biological intuitions. But Zarathustra is alone, and his thoughts are not developed in competition with the thoughts of other Übermenschen. There are not other, equal thinkers with different ideas. There is no action over time that can demonstrate affirmative superiority. When we attempt to go all the way to the asymptote, there is no basis for talking about competition between ideas or feelings among the Übermenschen. We have to turn back into liberalism, or realize a situation not so dissimilar from Plato's utopia, in which there is only one world of being. There is only one Zarathustra, who is having (literally) religious visions. No wonder epistemology is quiet in Nietzsche's texts. Nietzsche could not establish on his own grounds that he was the only one in touch with Dionysus. Greek *agon* disappears between *Birth* and the world of the Übermensch. This is a way of feeling despair that the Übermensch will not be reached, will never occur, and can only be used as a navigational point to steer away from a leveling liberalism. To know that the *Übermensch* won't or can't appear requires the forbidden apparatus of metaphysics, a temporal picture large enough to guess at the future on the basis of presumed regularities. The felt optimism of *Beyond Good and Evil* wasn't, however, a conviction that increased over time, and *Genealogy* drops into bitter pessimism. No wonder that Nietzsche was hopelessly suspended between these visions in his final years of silence.

Nietzsche's vision of the Eternal Return prevented him from becoming a modernist, from assuming that endless novelty and progress was possible in principle. Cyclical temporality rules out all constant progress as it had in Hellenic times. Nor is Nietzsche well assimilated by postmodernism, since the eclectic pastiche that passes for culture in typical postmodernist moods would be inconsistent with his concept of the kind of unified culture that could win temporary delay in the struggle with Dionysus. Nietzsche regards economic movement as the result of cultural aesthetics, and not vice versa, but the possibility that aesthetics can drive economics would hardly sustain an interest in postmodernism unless postmodernism could establish that it was an overcoming of nihilism, and not its end point.

If Nietzsche sustains a Hellenic vision, as suggested here, it is a legitimate question whether such a vision in a nineteenth-century context makes him a social and political crank. He may have enlarged the space of social and political philosophy, while remaining fixated on an asymptotic ideal point. To a large extent, this judgment is reflected in his shifting and ad hoc antipolitical postures with respect to the events of his day. Nietzsche feared the state because it seemed to him to threaten an imposed and bogus culture. Later social and political thinkers who have been concerned to preserve some notion of culture along with a modern state structure have at times grappled with Nietzsche's pessimism.[5] There can be no objection from Nietzsche's viewpoint to appropriation; he could only object to appropriation that is not affirmative. In this connection, we can return a last time to the prominent fascist attempt to assimilate his vision.

That Nietzsche's vision of society is intrinsically fascist has been repeated or intimated often enough. Fascists have attempted to construct their own cultural wombs, and in many cases they seem to have treated themselves as a noble elite within a theoretically transformed social structure. This is the closest point of parallel. Nietzsche's Übermensch is not a führer, utilizing state police to enforce obedience to his orders, and Dionysus could hardly lay off the thousand-year Reich. Nazi culture could never have appealed to Nietzsche. If other intellectuals reached an accommodation surrounded by a Nazi order by cynically accepting its manifest cultural deficiencies, it is useful to remember that Nietzsche, if he was suspicious of those who did not recognize the valuational roots of their thoughts and actions, was not concerned to trick fools but to expose them.

Nazi readings must shift emphasis from self-development to a philosophy of power. This shift is facilitated by concentration on Nietzsche's unpublished writings, while suggesting that the published works were a series of masks of some sort. A great deal of fancy footwork is required to carry this through in view of Nietzsche's published critique of German culture and his attacks on forms of anti-Semitism, and it is not clear how Nietzsche's individualism and class division in a noble society can be made compatible with a vision of a people (*Volk*) led by a führer. The textual solution is to emphasize selections from Nietzsche as the essential Nietzsche, a move that is made easier by Nietzsche's aphoristic style. Nietzsche is no more responsible for the Holocaust than Caesar is responsible for the boredom of high school Latin class. Efforts to forge links between thinkers and their caricatures or misappropriations are always in the service of some form of conservatism, some idea that if radical thought were to be eliminated, peace and good will would flourish naturally among human beings, a conviction totally at odds with Dionysian notions of profundity.

Ultimately, the piecemeal insights of Nietzsche's aphorisms are more shocking, more rewarding, more disturbing for our attempts to justify social and political philosophies than thinking of ourselves as though we were Übermenschen. The society of Übermenschen simply can't come into focus; the Hellenic world from which the concept is abstracted could not escape either envy or pity, to judge from the textual evidence. If Nietzsche lost sight of this in his intoxication, the human side even of the Hellenes is always there to turn us short of Nietzsche's ideal. Perhaps, ultimately, Nietzsche's deepest Dionysian insight is that we *do* have to proceed without certainties, without theories in which we can place much trust, an insight that gradually forces us away from his own vision of Hellenic Greece. The asymptotic social ideals point to means of temporarily decentering a complex muddle that practice alone cannot find a means to escape. From moment to moment, a series of idiotic and indefensible thrashings about may be our only means of keeping our social noses above water, above Dionysian flux, with no certainties of continuance attached. If all of the extreme points are fatal to humanity, Nietzsche's discovery of another extreme point has still given us a larger space in which to maneuver in searching for a flexible and satisfying form of social existence.

8

Women

In this chapter we will discuss the position of women in society as an example of the complexities that should be advanced when Nietzsche's views on social positioning are considered. Somewhat analogous treatments could be advanced for other locations, such as that of slaves, whom Nietzsche took as essential to all economic structures, but the status of women is easier to bring into comparative scrutiny with the status of women in our own society. We take the discussion of the status of women to suggest all the other problems that present themselves in considering Nietzsche's views on social differentiation.

It is often assumed that Nietzsche is a misogynist. The obvious passages supporting this view have been exploited by misogynistic writers since Nietzsche's time as truths that Nietzsche dared to speak, but that others have conspired to cover over. Yet other commentators have seen Nietzsche's misogyny as a symptom of latent homosexuality.[1] Nietzsche, on the basis of the same passages, becomes the bête noire of many feminists.[2] In our time, the emergence of explicit philosophical discussions of gender relationships and homosexuality in connection with recent social movements has made Nietzsche a name to reckon with in all of these circles and has undoubtedly added a perspective on Nietzsche that could hardly have been anticipated by Nietzsche when he was writing. Any desire to see gender relationships as currently instanced in society altered pushes one toward interpreting Nietzsche as an ally or as an opponent, producing a bias in one's hermeneutical stance that is difficult to control. Without denying the apparent textual basis for Nietzsche's supposed endorsements, one can legitimately muddy the waters a bit. When we look at

Nietzsche's many passages on women, we discover that his so-called misogyny is a complicated matter. To begin with, if we compare Nietzsche to his contemporaries who also discussed women, we can see differences. Schopenhauer hated women as he hated noise, any of either being negatively valued, and he did not discriminate. For example:

> That woman is by nature meant to obey may be seen by the fact that every woman who is placed in the unnatural position of complete independence, immediately attaches herself to some man, by whom she allows herself to be guided and ruled. It is because she needs a lord and master.[3]

Nietzsche is never this crude. Where a misogynist draws no distinctions, hating all women, Nietzsche's emotions are modulated.

Let's look at one of the famous texts from "On Little Old and Young Women" in *Zarathustra*: "Everything about woman is a riddle, and everything about woman has one solution: that is pregnancy." Taken out of context, this sounds like Nietzsche is advising that a man should consider women as machines for making babies, and to modern ears this sentence is ugly and daring in its defiance of civility. But the context complicates matters. Whose pregnancy, for example, is being discussed?[4] We know elsewhere that Nietzsche believes that the attraction of women, or of truth, can impregnate man with intellectual curiosity, making a man pregnant with new ideas. Thus, even if male/female differences are fixed and natural, there is a complicated economy of impregnation and birth existing between them, and babies do not exhaust what humans bear.

This passage, after a development in which, to be sure, man's happiness is projected as willing and woman's as obeying, with the intention that in this way *conflict* of wills, the source of unhappiness, can be eliminated between gender positions, culminates when the little old woman (an explicit description of an experienced woman who knows how to articulate her thoughts) acknowledges the force of Zarathustra's intuitions, and gives Zarathustra a truth: he is to take a whip when he goes to women. Now, of course, Nietzsche is the author of this woman's observation, but what is he trying to say when he allows the old woman to speak? This "tiny truth" is to be kept quiet, and it is introduced as a "truth" born of this woman in this complicated image, or it will speak too loudly. Does this mean that the tiny truth is profound and shocking, and needs to be covered over because it justifies battering women? That doesn't feel right to any sensitive reader, not least of all because it is so blatantly stated. It would seem rather that this tiny truth (quiet truth, infant truth) is one that only a few wise people could correctly understand. Distance from women is required for their usefulness to Zarathustra's task. He loves and hates them simultaneously, his love being greatest when the distance of hate is maximized, and this interweave of love and hate is what is to be expected on Dionysian grounds. Repeatedly, women and life, or women and the Dionysian process, are identified in *Zarathustra*. Too close an approach threatens loss of individuality, loss of identity, loss of the ability to give birth to the thought of the Übermensch. On the other hand, life resents Zarathustra's relationship to wisdom. The whip may be the symbol of a crude domination. Indeed, in the famous photograph of Lou Salomé, Paul Rée, and Nietzsche, it is Lou who holds the whip, driving the men forward. Does one take a whip to create this motivating distance, because the woman will always forget the whip? Is the whip to be applied (metaphorically) to oneself as a discipline, to preserve distance? These possibilities are sufficient to indicate that the "misogynistic" texts have no automatic interpretation.[5] Their "normal" interpretation is produced by the misogyny that is brought to their reading.

Is it possible to effect some summary of Nietzsche's many statements on women that does not reduce him to a simple misogynist? Certain points seem to stand out. Nietzsche believes that the male/female split is a deep biological difference, always marked strongly in animals and marked strongly in humans as well. This marking is always accompanied (in animals) by a differentiation of function. In birds, for example, male and female are differentiated in plumage and in behavior. In humans, this seems somewhat reversed. If the male receives the beautiful plumage among birds, this is awarded to women as a cultural artifact. At this point, the line between biology and culture is blurred.

There can be different cultural expressions of the male/female contrasts, emphasizing traits that could be collected around different masculine and feminine gender identities. This is shown historically by the obvious contrast in these identities between ancient Greece and nineteenth-century Europe, for example. Once again, Nietzsche prefers the Hellenic model of society and defends it as optimal for the business of motivating artistic, philosophical, and religious creativity. Nietzsche is aware that various gender relationships are possible, but he believes that his Hellenic model produced both the greatest men and the greatest women (for example, Ariadne) that the world has ever known. This model is based on modest women who are aware of surface (who know that profundity is an illusion) and who are therefore more in tune with the Dionysian realities that cast up social structures. As in the case of slavery, Nietzsche, developing the perspective of the male noble, supposes that those filling the other roles can be happy and affirmative, simultaneously aware of Dionysian flux, under these arrangements. The trap here would be to argue (on what basis?) that Nietzsche is wrong. In not accepting Nietzsche's perspective, what needs to be developed is the perspective of others, especially that of the Hellenic women in Nietzsche's dream. Would they, and would their slaves, have agreed with Nietzsche's claims?

In aphorism 425 of *Human, All Too Human*, Nietzsche says that women could be made over into men in every sense other than the biological. This could occur, at least in every advanced European country, given suitable educational resources. But the result would be a useless period of chaos. This is sufficient to indicate that gender relationships can take different forms. In the historical, European version of gender differentiation, men and women cannot understand one another, because each reacts to a projected ideal as though it were the actual other.[6] The Apollinian and Dionysian possibilities are communicated to children through dichotomized roles, permitting the inconsistencies vital to creativity to be transmitted to (at least) male children in the areas of the mind, and to (at least) female children in areas necessary for the biological continuance of humankind.

Only the male perspective is explored by Nietzsche, but this is not a simple matter of blindness. As in the case of scholarship, Nietzsche felt he could judge only on the basis of his own experience. Nietzsche does not openly explore the possibility of androgyny in the sense that both perspectives might be accessible to all human beings, the one becoming accessed by consciousness, and the other repressed. He treats the process of socialization as conventional, but as irreversible once it has taken place. For men, mothers provide the foundations of religion, conformity, and morality, while fathers liberate and indicate how traditions can be altered and overcome. In Nietzsche's account, mothers supply their male offspring with intellect (!) and gender images, while fathers add will and a certain rhythm of thought. For Nietzsche, women are complicated, being as mothers at once typically further from nature than men in preserving Apollinian traditions (this a legacy from Schopenhauer), but closer to nature than men in displaying a Dionysian concern with the species and with process. Because of this, women are especially complex, and valuations of women must depend on the assemblage of roles that they adopt in individual cases.[7] It is the range of these possibilities that defeats any slam-bang charges of misogyny.

Nietzsche, as always building on a favorable valuation of Hellenic society, is opposed to the relative loss of differentiation in gender roles in modern society and was appalled by the prospect of a socialist society in which gender identity could become a matter of choice. Nietzsche saw the logic of feminism as pushing toward gender equality and more women scientists, and he did not like what he saw. Nietzsche would be, by extrapolation, opposed to all feminisms that push for equal representation in various current social arrangements. He would be much more in line with feminisms that argue for a divergent, genuinely feminine set of insights that would be essential for the correction or improvement of a society otherwise headed toward male scientistic control.

Women had never been treated with so much respect, with so little feeling for gender differences, as they were in Nietzsche's time, in an era of increasing democracy, according to Nietzsche's observations. Women are surrendering their differential roles as women, and so both men and women are degenerating as democracy and socialism advance. Women's influence decreases, Nietzsche thought, as women's rights increase. De-feminized women would be just as boring and uniform as demasculinized men. What we see in such observations is Nietzsche's preference for a Hellenic society of differentiated gender roles.

In order to continue the discussion of Nietzsche on women, we will survey some of the many aphorisms in which Nietzsche discusses women, in order to develop a sense of the range of his concerns. Nietzsche's Hellenic model is explicitly noted in *Human, All Too Human*, aphorism 259. In Hellenic society, public culture was male dominated, and women existed in the private domain. Men and women were educated to different tasks. The youth and desirable superficiality of Greek culture is related, in Nietzsche's mind, to this sharp division, in which men were devoted to the development of virtue in (male) youths. A higher place was given to women in art than in life, something that can prove misleading to those who do not understand the mechanisms of artistic production. The task of women elsewhere was to counteract overstimulation by the production of beautiful, powerful bodies.

In a later aphorism, aphorism 356, Nietzsche observes that when one lives in complete dependence and doesn't work, bitterness will develop toward those on whom one is dependent. This kind of bitterness and dependency is more common in women than in men for historical reasons. Nietzsche here explicitly avoids the supposition that social gender differences are natural.

Aphorism 227 of *Daybreak* presents a similar idea. Clever women who have been kept in a secluded environment are examples of spirits that will take revenge when the opportunity presents itself. This is a historical deformation, rather than a gender essence. Women share some propensities for revenge with priests because of their historical lack of power.

Aphorism 75 of *Daybreak* is relevant to an understanding of this motif. Something about Christianity is not European and not noble. This is reminiscent of the problems caused by the Dionysian flood that Greece needed to fend off with stronger Apollinian forms, as noted in *Birth*. Christianity has a savage, destructive aspect not always noted in its modern theological forms. For Nietzsche, chastisement is bad, and so is (by itself) seclusion from the world. Set against the whip passage, it's pretty clear that Nietzsche is *not* in favor of chastisement, but considers it reprehensible.

Comparing the present with antiquity, we've exchanged friendship for sexual love, as Nietzsche notes in aphorism 503 of *Daybreak*. Sexual passion requires that the love object be the sole object of passion, with a consequent constricted focus of thought that prevents creativity. This aphorism is concerned to see the current relationships as historically different from those of the Hellenic world, and as different in a way that threatens the possibility of ongoing creative ferment.

Aphorism 131 of *Beyond Good and Evil* notes that the sexes deceive themselves about each other, because at bottom they honor and love only themselves (or their own ideal, to put it more pleasantly). Thus man likes woman peaceful, but woman is not essentially peaceful, however well she may have trained herself to appear so. Men and women are not able to understand one another if this is so, and indeed their perspectives on one another are both false, as they have to be because of their partial nature. Nietzsche is struggling for a higher perspective in which they can both be represented, without requiring that such a perspective be completely objective.

Men actively corrupt women by creating female images to which women are then expected to conform because of the social power of men, as Nietzsche states in aphorism 68 of *The Gay Science*. Men will, and women are pressured to conform to their will. The alternative would be a clash of wills, frustration, and chaos, or so it is thought. Men need to be better educated. This observation suggests that Nietzsche was not satisfied with the current arrangements and wanted to establish new images and better arrangements based on his Hellenic model, where presumably the roles might be assigned without continual pressure to force compliance.

Females are considered the productive beings among the animals, and males, the "beautiful" sex, or so Nietzsche suggests in aphorism 72 of *The Gay Science*. This biological distinction is reversed among humans, as we noted above. Pregnancy in the male (spiritual pregnancy) is as close as males can come to the feminine character.

Aphorism 352 of *The Gay Science* notes that we can't dispense with the masquerade called *clothes*. Without clothes, appetite would be discouraged. We dress ourselves up with morality, both men and women. This is part of Nietzsche's perspectivism, the fact that we see ourselves, not as we are, but as mediated through images. Coupled with the fact that we view projected images in the other sex, the result is almost complete gender skepticism, gender chaos, and gender opposition.

Each sex has its own distinctive prejudices about love—hence equality would be nonsense. This is the kernel of aphorism 363 of *The Gay Science*, which defends the necessity of asymmetry while encouraging a functional asymmetry that would increase will to power. Neither sex presupposes the same feeling and the same concept of "love" in the other. Women mean total devotion, soul and body, without reserve. Men, in return, will not surrender their rights as long as they remain men. These asymmetries are important. If both sides renounced themselves, we would have empty space. For a man, wanting (which can be stalled by a woman) terminates with having, and a man will not readily admit that a woman has no more to give him. However much Nietzsche's language here offends current sensibilities (and it does), what he says should be put into the philosophical context of looking for matching desires that need not be frustrated, so that the struggle between the sexes is not a form of rigidity that must be swept quickly away by Dionysian process.

Aphorism 406 of *Human, All Too Human* observes that a satisfactory marriage must contain a component of friendship, because most of a marriage is a long conversation. This point explains why Nietzsche thinks a good marriage is possible despite the *aporia* of romantic love. Romantic love was not involved in the noble Hellenic marriages that fascinated Nietzsche, and Nietzsche found romantic love, with its conflicts and resolutions, deceptions and intrigues, destructive of genuine human relationships.

Women's sudden judgments are often interpreted as oracular intuitions, Nietzsche notes in aphorism 417 of *Human, All Too Human*. But the world is so complicated that a good will can always find sudden judgments to be true at some level. As usual, Nietzsche avoids the position that there is a basis for determining the truth of articulated intuitions, so this is merely the dismissal of an egregious piece of folk wisdom.

Aphorism 425 of *Human, All Too Human* allows the possibility that one could make women into men through education, switching cultural gender roles, but over a period of several hundred years in the three or four most civilized countries in Europe. (There may be a sarcastic appraisal of "civilized" involved.) Not, of course, in the sense of a biological reversal, but in the sense of a cultural and social reversal. Women could take on all manly virtues and strengths, but also correspondingly manly weaknesses and vices. Could humans survive the transition? This would be a time in which wrath would reduce science to dilettantism, philosophy to idle chatter. Nietzsche, in privileging hierarchy, sees disaster unless a new power is found for women, a power not related to their old place in custom and morality, and a power that couldn't be released by a mere reversal of social roles that was independent of some deeper transvaluation. Hierarchy is clearly more important for social adaptability than gender relationships, which, even if inverted, would leave everything the same and couldn't produce a better society.

Women and artists are both suspicious of science, and in this sense they can be grouped together as oppositional to the false superficiality of the presumed explanatory depth of science. Aphorism 204 of *Beyond Good and Evil* makes this perhaps surprising observation. Women and artists jointly resist the call to profundity, wishing to stay on the surface. While this might sound as if Nietzsche accuses them both of superficiality, his explicit love of the Hellenes for their resistance to scientific temptations and their profundity in staying on the surface supports the idea that Nietzsche sees something profound in a woman's instinctive dislike of science. His own wrath extends therefore particularly to women who would become scientists.

Aphorism 60 of *The Gay Science* presents a crucial image. A man, embroiled in his noisy affairs, sees an untouchable, quiet beauty glide by, embodying a desire to move quietly *over* existence, over its surface: A woman has this unapproachable calm in which the man fantasizes his best self. This effect is produced by the distance involved in the image. On board, there is a noise, noise that would destroy this dream image. The distance of the feminine is what produces the fantasy required for creativity, and this distance is maintained if the veil is not touched. Breaking the distance would be a disaster, especially for the fantasy required in the creative process, the dreamlike state that permits Dionysus to be glimpsed.

The last specific passage of our survey will be that of the often cited Preface to *Beyond Good and Evil*. Suppose that truth is a woman.[8] This famous supposition of Nietzsche's must be approached with caution. Nietzsche doesn't hate truth, and in terms of the double concept, he means to speak the truth. Truth increases will to power, but that must not be

confused with the hardened "truth" of science, a conservative regurgita-
tion of an already given value table. "Truth" is not a woman; quite the
opposite. Scientists and philosophers have already vanquished her, but she
is hardly worth having. Can the other truth be a woman? The suspicion
can arise only for a philosopher who has made an attempt to understand
women. Dogmatists have been inept, clumsy. If truth were a woman (what
kind of a woman?), they could not win her with their methods. Dogmatists are too crude, too quick. A quick look and the veils are imagined
away, and an edifice of thought is all too quickly constructed. A subtler,
less assured approach is necessary, coupled with an awareness that conquest always is temporary, provisional, uncertain. To suppose that truth
could be a woman is not the supposition of a misogynist and not a simple-
minded affirmation. The thought of truth as a woman means that the
chase of what is elusive has strung the bow and has produced the tension
required to prefer perspectivism to dogma. The resultant fecundity, which
could never have been produced by a frontal assault, permits the optimism
of the successful lover to burst into "aftersong." Nietzsche's preferred
truth is transitory and linked to the surface. Both women and truth are
linked only to appearance, for Nietzsche, but this is a positive valuation of
both from his perspective. It should be remembered that the Preface of
Beyond Good and Evil is written from the perspective of the free spirit,
who still expects to win over both.

    This survey of aphorisms concerning women should be sufficient to in-
dicate that Nietzsche sees major differences between the position of wom-
en in the Hellenic society that is his model, and the position of women in
modern democratic societies. If Nietzsche pours scorn on women who are
democratic levelers, this is not itself misogynistic, as he pours scorn on
democratic levelers of all kinds. Many of the passages seem to suggest
quite subtly that women are capable of transition to new forms more in
synchrony with Dionysian process and that his negative phenomenology
is of women as they have been, not as they could be. This brings his
remarks into conformity with his views about the arrival of the Übermensch, and indeed nothing explicitly said about the Übermensch necessi-
tates that the Übermensch must be male.[9] The possibilities for women can
be heard only by Nietzsche's inner ear, or perhaps exemplified in his brief
relationship with Lou Andreas-Salomé and in his positive valuation of the
modest women of his Hellenic vision. All of this seems a distinct under-
tone when one examines a sufficient range of Nietzsche's comments of
women. The passages we have examined are actually a small selection
from Nietzsche's numerous references to women. Many of the most dam-

aging passages cited by critics of Nietzsche have not been discussed, but the purpose of this survey is not to defend all of Nietzsche's remarks, not even as nineteenth-century majoritarian social phenomenology, but only to defend Nietzsche against charges of misogyny developed out of a single-minded perspective that would seek to place his works on a new *Index Librorum Prohibitorum.*

The intention of this chapter to muddy the waters of Nietzsche exposition by noting the variety and complexity of Nietzsche's remarks on women has now been accomplished, and in one sense this chapter has ended. This is explicitly *not* to end with an endorsement of Nietzsche's social vision. Here the central theme has been to show how Nietzsche's views developed out of his vision of Hellenic society. With respect to his contemporaries, Nietzsche was a dreamer. The alternatives are hardly reducible to Hellenic greatness, on the one hand, and democratic nihilistic leveling, on the other. If Nietzsche offers an unworkable pair of alternatives, he does offer a genuine possibility for consideration. He is correct that there is no transcendental basis on which to rule him out as a simple misogynist. The task is not so much refutation of Nietzsche as the development of other perspectives in which greater formal social and political equality of gender roles can avoid the dreary uniformity of opinion and action that Nietzsche ascribes to his democratic alternative. To know more, we need more developed perspectives, to take a page from Nietzsche's book, especially perspectives that recognize that a Hellenic vision will not fit smoothly onto the social, economic, and political realities of the twentieth century.

The argument here has been that Nietzsche's philosophical insights begin in his vision of Hellenic society and that they terminate in the transvalued metaphysics of the will to power and the Eternal Return, doctrines that completely erase the weight of the Hellenic past in a philosophy suitable for any time. One question is whether those doctrines can be understood without their social roots. On Nietzschean grounds, the answer has to be negative, since the philosophy has to be in the service of some value table, and the value table could not be completely abstracted from social attitudes. In the remainder of this chapter, before initiating a study of will to power and the Eternal Return in the last chapters, we can confront the relevant question by looking at Heidegger on Nietzsche, and then at Derrida's critique of Heidegger on Nietzsche. The relevant difference, and the reason for anchoring the discussion in these readings, is that Heidegger completely ignores gender, whereas Derrida makes an explicit attempt to theorize its importance. Heidegger attempts to master Nietzsche's texts, imposing an order and assigning Nietzsche a fixed place as the last metaphysician. If the reading is coercive, the Nietzschean question is whether it is life enhancing. If Derrida completely respects Nietzsche's texts, leaving them in a delicate suspension, this suspension doesn't mirror Nietzsche's hermeneutics of engaged reaction, and once again one can raise the Nietzschean question of whether Derrida's reading is life enhancing. These questions provide a suitable background for explicit consideration of the doctrines of will to power and the Eternal Return.

Whatever the nature and final valuation of Heidegger's philosophy, Heidegger was involved in a long confrontation with Nietzsche, a confrontation of undoubted importance to the development of Heidegger's philosophy, if not of importance for the "turn" that some commentators see as essential to understanding Heidegger's development. Heidegger sees Nietzsche as inverting Plato, making the world of becoming central, and placing being in the world of becoming. The study of Being (*Sein*) in Heidegger's sense, doesn't yet appear in Nietzsche, that is, the study of what can give the existents studied by metaphysics meaning. Heidegger's investigation doesn't place Nietzsche into the metaphysical tradition by a detailed examination of Nietzsche's relationship to Kant, Hegel, and so on; rather Heidegger uses Nietzsche as a crucial general representative of subjectivist terminations of the metaphysical tradition in order to develop his own philosophy of Being.

According to Heidegger, the thought of the Eternal Return comes first, and grows into the thought of will to power. After this, the will to power is the dominant theme of Nietzsche's ontology. Heidegger's approach makes Nietzsche a thinker (in Heidegger's sense), that is, someone who develops one (or a very few) basic thoughts. Nietzsche makes life the focus of his thought, developing the essence of life as "will to power" utilizing some notions of *correctness* as *suitability for growth* (instead of a traditional notion of truth as an eternally correct assertion) in the form of a biological metaphor. The value claim here (in *correctness*) derives from Heraclitus, and it explains why value, rather than knowledge, is at the root of Nietzsche's philosophy. Nietzsche's biologism actually conceals a prior decision as to what exists—one that is in line with metaphysics and (ironically) in line with modern science. Hence Nietzsche falls victim to a value table, the same error he correctly notes as crippling other metaphysicians. Nietzsche's biologism is anthropomorphic; he humanizes the universe. Humans schematize and fix their thoughts just enough to satisfy practical needs. At the same time, human art shows that humans have overcome a purely animal status, so that Nietzsche's biologism is no mere acceptance of what exists, but dwells on the possibilities of self-control and self-overcoming. Heidegger's reading of self-control stresses that if one doesn't control oneself, one will experience external control.[10] The task of Heidegger's Übermensch is to take over control of the machinery of technology, rather than allowing it to control us (the situation in which the last men of *Zarathustra* find themselves). Clearly, Heidegger's reading stresses a notion of self-overcoming. It is this Nietzsche, Heidegger's Nietzsche, that fuels the later deconstructive appropriations of Nietzsche's texts, especially as the playful, experimental aspects of self-overcoming that can be found in Nietzsche's texts are brought to the fore.

One must confront the suspicion that it is Heidegger's own systematic thought that forces Nietzsche back into the metaphysical tradition. Nietzsche's thought is restricted to existents when Being comes onto the scene. It is no accident that Heidegger turns for confirmation of his views to a reading of the late fragments, and treats the will to power as having a factual, almost scientific status, rather than as being an illusory attempt to display or intimate Dionysian process. What Nietzsche says early about Dionysian process, and what remains of Dionysus in late fragments not discussed by Heidegger, corrodes the edges of existents, and points curiously toward an ontological monism that can be thought to have similarities to Heidegger's Being. The repression of the Dionysian image is required to force Nietzsche into a more metaphysical position, but it can't be justified against the full range of texts. Heidegger's oedipal resolution involves some clear misreading of Nietzsche. Heidegger's own subtleties before texts, his proclivity for early Greek philosophy, his strategy for overcoming the subject/object dichotomy, his desire to have a historically flowing philosophical ground, all owe a great deal to Nietzsche. We have argued here for a systematic interpretation based on Nietzsche's sustained attention to the conflict between the value table of the Hellenic tragic vision and the value table of the scientific modernity that surrounded Nietzsche. This conflict is essential if one is to realize the will to power and the Eternal Return as Nietzsche's developed philosophical statements of the affirmative consequences of the Hellenic tragic vision for his own time. By concentrating on the *Nachlass*, Heidegger loses touch with the roots of Nietzsche's views in *Birth* and truncates his account. This can be seen by the absence of most of the topics we have considered so far as essential to Nietzsche's confrontation with his times in Heidegger's account, and by the astonishing fact that Nietzsche's many observations about women make no impact on Heidegger's discussion whatsoever.

Derrida's hermeneutical stance could hardly be more opposed to that of

Heidegger.[11] Derrida would keep all the Nietzschean texts in equal suspension, refusing to streamline consideration on the basis of Nietzsche's
or Heidegger's or any reader's perception of what is less important and
what is more important. What is important is often almost accidentally
revealed, a point that Nietzsche wouldn't deny. Derrida would raise the
embarrassment for the Heideggerian reading that it presents at best a
caricature of Nietzsche's thought, a caricature that skips over large tracts
of subject matter on which one can discern Nietzschean traces, a fact that
is an embarrassment because of Heidegger's self-conscious hermeneutical
sensitivity. The terrain of argument is partly that of the consequences of
the absence of woman in Heidegger's account, and Derrida's remarks here
are perhaps more concerned to note the destructive effects of hermeneutical method on a body of text than they are to develop Nietzsche's views
about women, no matter what a first impression may indicate. Derrida
has quite explicitly cited *Spurs* as a work primarily about textuality—not
about Nietzsche's philosophy.[12] In fact, *Spurs* is about Nietzsche's styles,
about Nietzsche on women, about Heidegger, and about Derrida himself
(as well as the views of some of his students)—all at once.

In *Spurs*, Nietzsche's awareness of "lying," his views about truth as
metaphor and illusion, are bracketed out, phenomenologically speaking,
and nothing of what Nietzsche says substantively about women is really at
stake, although Derrida's account explicitly accepts the general idea that
Nietzsche's views here are as multifarious as there are individual texts to
be cited. To attempt to put this in a nutshell, *Spurs* demonstrates that
woman cannot be captured as an essence by the terms of philosophical
discourse, by the metaphors on which it rests, and that Nietzsche's peculiarly decentered presentation of texts on *woman* can be read as his
intimation of that fact. Indeed, the simplest reading of the astonishing
claim that *woman* will not have been the subject of *Spurs*, is that Nietzsche's styles indicate that *woman* cannot be the subject of any discourse—
and ultimately this means that *man* could not be a subject either. So to
speak, rather than producing discourse, men and women are produced by
it. *Woman* doesn't designate something that is then interpreted in the
discourse about women. Designation is a rigidity that comes after the
founding metaphors of the discourse have been chosen. Nietzsche is
therefore a precursor (and one of the few) of Derrida's attempts to decen-
ter philosophical discourse from its apparently privileged and unambiguous semantical status.

Heidegger, who had sensed this in Nietzsche and who had provided
hints of Derrida's position in such notions as the crossing out of Being, or

the trace of Being, failed to deconstruct Nietzsche's discourse and fell back into his own system. Recognizing that Nietzsche was correct in diagnosing the originary metaphor of Western metaphysics in the privileging of being over becoming, Heidegger failed to discern the precedent chaos of possible meanings and substituted his own privileged notion of Being (which, for Derrida, gradually deconstructed itself as Heidegger elaborated it). A certain portion of *Spurs* is devoted explicitly to a parody of Heidegger's attempts to discern fixed meaning where only an irreducible hermeneutical complexity prevails in Nietzsche's actual texts. To elaborate slightly on this, it must be added that Heidegger failed to trace out the real accomplishments of his deconstructed Nietzsche. The reading proposed here, which accepts much of the import of Derrida's critique, imposes its own constraints on interpretation by leading the reading of Nietzsche relentlessly back to Dionysian process, a strategy that allows an account of Nietzsche's development and a statement of important Nietzschean views without ever stabilizing its accounts in a foundational level of meaning.

On Derrida's view, words do not have central, fixed meanings and secondary, or tropical, meanings, as our dictionaries suggest. This means that translation is a problematic notion for Derrida, often achieved by the sheer juxtaposition of texts in different languages. *Spurs* illustrates this quite well. Consider just the obvious difficulties with the first two sentences after the heading *Distances*.[13] In French, *style* and *stylus* are the same word, a fact that requires the translator to try adding "or a stylus" to the second sentence, long after the obvious pun of the first sentence leads naturally to the second sentence. This is an extremely minute, but obvious, example of what happens to Derrida's style when its playfulness and involuntary segues are subjected to the rigidities imposed by the translating language. Spurs attack and defend; there are attacking and defending, or distancing, spurs. The defending side of this ambiguity, extensively explored in *Distances,* is completely lost in English. The effect of women depends on the distancing involved in their perception by men. Women are veiled—they have no essence from which it is a matter of retreat or approach. Like truth, women cannot be pinned down to an essence of femininity, and *writing* is associated with both, an eternal postponement of unambiguous knowledge.[14] Truth, suspended in quotation marks, is a mere surface, like woman, whose superficiality is related.

A long passage culminates in a description of three women: the castrated woman, the castrating woman, and the affirming woman.[15] The castrated woman is hostile to women's sensuality, imitating men in a rush to science. This, of course, robs woman of her style (her defense, her veil). The castrating woman plays with truth to get what she wants by convincing men of the illusion that their perception of woman is true. She uses "truth" without believing in truth. Both the castrated and the castrating woman can at least be located with respect to the discourse of truth. Each has an essence, but it is not the essence of woman. A digression in Heidegger establishes that woman does not appear in Heidegger. This also applies to truth. Originally, philosophers had been truth. Then truth became an idea, and receded, like woman, from the grasp of men. Christianity explicitly excised threatening woman from its discourse, as did philosophy. Philosophy excises her as representing falsehood (versus truth), or as nontruth (irrationality). But a third, affirmative woman, cannot be written here. She must affirm herself in man. An affirming woman cannot appear in the discourse, but only in its margins or folds, its ultimate heterogeneity. This woman can have no essence, given the foundations of the discourse, and hence always threatens the stable metaphors of metaphysics. Nietzsche's discourse senses this, being satisfied neither with the castrated system nor the castrating system. Nietzsche is always looking at woman from some perspective, but recognizes that no perspective permits the essence of woman to come into view. In loving the affirmative woman, however, he at least partially escaped misogyny in an uncertain text.[16]

Derrida, having now completed a discussion of Nietzsche's styles (his veils), returns to Heidegger. Heidegger had to avoid the decentering question of woman in claiming to have read Nietzsche, to have identified Nietzsche against his will in the space of truth. The Nietzschean fragment "I have forgotten my umbrella" is a part of Nietzsche's textual corpus, and an undecidable part.[17] Heidegger has to forget Nietzsche's forgetting to give a definitive reading—but the aim is wrong. There is no definitive reading. This is what we learn from Nietzsche's excruciating heterogeneity, remembering (rather than forgetting) that Nietzsche noted that he was not taking woman as a subject—a different matter from not discussing woman, which is what Heidegger accomplishes. The subject of woman is not simply tacked on to Nietzsche's discourse as a gratuitous expression of misogyny. To begin with, the differences Nietzsche notes among women's roles in his Hellenic vision, which we surveyed first, are essential to his critique of contemporary society. But the confrontation of Derrida and Heidegger shows that complex issues are at stake. If Nietzsche had assigned an essence to woman, the structural core of any misogyny, he would have fallen into contradiction with his views on Dionysian process and affirmation. Consistency with those views required Nietzsche to make the complex observations concerning women that he does, and any failure to notice this makes it ever so much easier to force Nietzsche into a controlling metaphysical assignment.

Heidegger and Derrida place Nietzsche into a supporting role that isn't, by itself, incompatible with Nietzsche's conception of how we must utilize the past if it is to have meaning. Heidegger's repression of the heterogeneous texts dealing with women is essential to his hermeneutics of mastery. Heidegger positions Nietzsche as the last metaphysician, but his reduction of will to power and the Eternal Return to a single doctrine, as well as his teaching of Being, means that Heidegger, if he escapes the Western metaphysical tradition, himself produces a kind of *ersatz* metaphysics that does not permit him to link Nietzsche to metaphysics while escaping such linkage himself. Derrida, in producing an attack on the metaphysics of mastery, produces an open conception of reading that makes the life-enhancing aspect of Nietzsche wither into complete hermeneutical freedom of interpretation. Where Heidegger had taken a determined position on technology, Derrida prefers to unsettle fixed interpretations in the service of the heterogeneity of the complete text and produces no reading of will to power or the Eternal Return. In both readings, the status of women becomes a counter in a wider game of philosophical controversy. The status of women as a sign of Nietzsche's social vision has to do work against the background of Dionysian process if Nietzsche is not to be silenced, and if the substantive outlines of his philosophy are to come into view. In the last two chapters, we shall attempt to look at will to power and the Eternal Return outside the realm of hermeneutic controversy, but our reading cannot be innocent. Will to power and the Eternal Return complete the philosophical version of Nietzsche's Hellenic vision, providing Nietzsche's way of living in the social and political present without carrying along a detailed knowledge of the Hellenic past.

9

Power

The doctrines of will to power and the Eternal Return are closely associated with Nietzsche, but they are often based on fragmentary texts that Nietzsche didn't publish. Their legitimacy might therefore seem questionable. From the perspective developed here, their legitimacy can be grounded in the fact that they complete the arc of development that begins with the description of Hellenic nobles in *Birth* and develops into the prophetic projection of the noble as Übermensch in later texts. The completion depends on a philosophical reworking of the earlier insights. Dionysus is, from the beginning, an Apollinian fiction, and a fiction that could only be concretely experienced by a Hellene. Will to power is a philosophical description of the world of Dionysian flux, but one that is independent of a specific historical location. The Übermensch is a prophetic projection, a fiction, who would experience Dionysian flux directly, but the experience of the Übermensch cannot be concretely described in language. The Eternal Return expresses the affirmation of the Übermensch in a philosophical attitude.[1] In short, in Nietzsche's last fragmentary efforts, the mode of prophecy gives way to the mode of philosophy. Dionysus and the Übermensch no longer receive explicit reference, since a conception of life is being put forward that is independent of the weight of history, even if it had been found in historical deliberation. Nietzsche is the first Hellenic philosopher, and these doctrines present the value table of his Hellenic philosophy.

These philosophical doctrines may seem to reposition Nietzsche as a metaphysician, even if he avoids the metaphysical tradition that preceded him, but a defense against this easy repositioning can be developed from

Nietzsche's philosophy of life. Insofar as these doctrines are conceived as having only intellectual content, they have not been understood: that is the defense. These are not doctrines to be stated and proved, nor doctrines from which theorems are to be derived. Nietzsche has assumed the mantle of the pre-Socratic (premetaphysical) philosopher; *he* is speaking, and followers are urged to live in a certain way, not to think along certain specific lines. These doctrines stand like aphorisms; they are to be developed by living their implications. Dionysian chaos is something one feels, that one has an awareness of, without having a scientific description, since it escapes the net of language. Nietzsche's avoidance of metaphysics reduces to his avoidance of a philosophy of cognitively defensible ideas. Nietzsche's doctrines of will to power and the Eternal Return represent the transvalued philosophical awareness of Dionysian process. These doctrines are suggested by a philosophical critique of Nietzsche's vision of Hellenic Greece, and they cannot be correctly understood save as a development out of that vision.

No description of Dionysian process can be other than fictive and false, so that in presenting his images, Nietzsche is not really placing one doctrine in the place of another. The hypostatization involved in language use is unavoidable, and hence the inadequacy of Nietzsche's statements, and his awareness of that inadequacy, must be kept constantly in mind. He is pointing to something that he believes human language cannot describe. If Nietzsche's attempt weren't self-consciously fictive and inadequate in these terms, it would play the role of an ontology. If it weren't also self-consciously fictive and inadequate, the Eternal Return would provide an axiology and an epistemology for Nietzsche's philosophy. Nietzsche is not a skeptic about the existence of Dionysian process nor about its consequences for philosophical doctrine; he is skeptical that his vision can be expressed at all, and certainly skeptical that assertive language, as opposed to artistic suggestion, can communicate his vision. Nietzsche's *contrast* of his vision with conventional ideas can only be intimated by the aphorism and the genealogy. When his vision alone is in central focus, language loses an anchor, and his terminal silence may be read as an expression of that fact. This side of Nietzsche, akin to traditional forms of mysticism in its repudiation of the adequacy of language and rational thought, can nevertheless be defended against the easy charges of relativism or skepticism that the scientific value table will automatically generate when confronting Nietzsche's aphorisms.

If we make Nietzsche into a radical, pluralistic monist, we can assign him a place in metaphysical history, but this can be done only at the expense of ignoring both the hierarchy of power centers in Nietzsche's doctrine of will to power, and the immanent holism that interconnects all these power centers as part of Dionysian process. Will to power, as a philosophical representation of Dionysian process, presents a radically decentered, vibrant, biological metaphor for history. One cannot predict where affirmation will arise. That is crucial to the notion of decentering. A new species of plant, pushing its way somehow and somewhere out of a slagheap that would not seem capable of sustaining life, is an appropriate symbol of the force of Dionysian process in Nietzsche, a force that can be held in check temporarily, but cannot be permanently controlled. Like a species that produces so many young that they must fight with each other to ensure species survival, the force of Dionysian process can produce internal clashes that seem reactive. Nature is blind, and its direction of movement is accidental. To this extent, Nietzsche offers a transvaluation of both Hegelian history and the evolutionary biology of his time.

Nietzsche's biologism was opposed to what he knew of Darwinism, precisely because Nietzsche's acute intuition saw that Darwinian selection was for a "fittest" type that would be an average representative of its species against prevailing selection pressure. For evolutionary change to occur, Nietzsche realized that new forms, not very fit at their inception, must be cast up and must somehow survive. (The embryonic Übermensch, and this resonance is important, must be cast up; the survival of the Übermensch is what is problematic.) If Darwinism saw species as passively adapting to their environment as selection takes place, Nietzsche stresses that the boundary of species and environment, and the boundary of biological individual and environment, is dynamic and is being pressed on from *both* sides. Forces from *inside* the boundary attempt to act on the environment, to increase the will to power of the species and the individual out of an internal dynamism. Although his remarks are vague and philosophical, Nietzsche seems to have sensed that mutation (or something like it) was necessary to trigger change and that some explanation of the emergence of new species needed to be added to Darwinian adaptation. In all of this, he produced his most penetrating specific critique of the science of his time.

It is an irony of history that where Nietzsche produces his most penetrating attack on actual science, Dionysian process points to a mechanical and individualist residue in Nietzsche's conception. Nietzsche's intuition was that an individual selected in the current environment might be doomed to quick extinction as a result of environmental change so that fixity of structure had to be modified or eliminated in the light of environmental change over time. His dynamism thus opposes the value of fixed structures, and his philosophy becomes a relentless criticism of conservation of values. Nature's strategy in a changing environment is to hedge against the future by providing a mix of types in the present environment, gambling that one of them will prove selected against any environmental change. Various mechanisms of mixing genetic material constantly preserve the diverse assemblies of different individual types that are tried out against the environment. And there are substrategies that Nature can employ. With lower animals, Nature's strategy is to present a variety of types, within a species, each of which is relatively short-lived and rigid, as a hedge against change. With higher animals, one strategy is to lower the rigidity of the individuals, while lengthening their life span, hoping that complexity and flexibility of response will allow adaptation to environmental change, thus hedging against what could be its devastating impact. On Nietzschean grounds, we can't rest content with the personification of Nature as a rational planner, but we must still accept that Dionysian process in the guise of Nature casts up a variety of strategies for continuation of some parts of the process at the expense of other parts, and that these strategies involve more than attention to the present moment when survival is being contemplated.

The root problem is this. Nietzsche wants to find a form of life that adapts perfectly to each new moment by accepting it as it is, and not allowing itself to be steered by the hysteresis of the past in the present, as humans may take a wrong direction under the steering of history. As this form of life seeks to increase its power, this flexibility allows it to seize any advantage that the moment presents. In comparison to cultural rigidity, the Übermensch will not be constrained at all by the past, and not constrained at all by an expectation of the future. Looking at the broad changes across species, we note that many organisms have nearly only precoded responses to the present, which means, philosophically, that they are responding now as though they could infallibly anticipate the future. In humans, reason allows a vision of the past to suggest a future for which one can plan and against which one can correct for error as one's plans prove inadequate. But human reason is not theoretically the best planner against all futures. Nietzsche emphasizes the rigidity of human reason, seeing it frequently captured by unnoticed value tables, and he downplays its hierarchical or reflexive possibilities. A rigid rational planner planning for the wrong future may be swamped and destroyed by the wills to power in an antagonistic array. Nietzsche is always alert to make that observation. So to speak, reason is only a good weapon against a rather stable environment that shows but small changes or trends to the human who learns to read it and adapt to it.

If humans exhibit different kinds of reason, and cultural differences represent that variety, Nature would again be stressing diversity as a hedge against uncertainty. But if Nature thinks in terms of the species, and is perhaps not concerned if particular species forms die out against a changing environment, Nietzsche's expression of will to power stresses adaptation at another level, that of the individual. Nature selects for species; Nietzsche wants to select for superior individuals. But if the environment is Dionysian chaos, it also defeats Nietzsche's strategy. The question is whether one can construct an individual that is in some sense guaranteed to adapt successfully to clashes with other wills to power by relying on maximum flexibility. The Übermensch expends will and energy precisely on feeling Dionysian process and in never coming out of tune with it, escaping destruction, so to speak, by remaining in the eye of the Dionysian hurricane. Nietzsche deals with dynamism and uncertainty by the theoretical construction of an organism without rigidity, the Übermensch, and he's driven to this by a desire for consistency. He wishes to describe the one type of creature that need not fear any tricks whatsoever from the voiceless god of creation and destruction. Rigidity can bring us down, overwhelming us in a Dionysian rage that crushes opposition. But there is perhaps an obverse, that complete flexibility may also prove a disaster for the Übermensch, not allowing the Übermensch to exist, ever, for more than an instant. This is the paradox that screws Nietzsche's line of thought to the sticking point.

Suppose that short-term trends were all deceptive, so that rational planning for the future is impossible. Under these circumstances, rational planners would all be completely mad from a Dionysian perspective, but in spite of that, some particular mad planner might get lucky, constructing under the illusion of reason just what it turns out is required by the actual future as it unfolds. For a particular time period, collective illusion may cast up a lucky winner, whose "rational" plans just happened to fit the turn that reality happened to take. As time periods pass, a series of lucky winners might sustain humanity, earning a great laugh from a Nietzschean perspective in which each is seen to be completely deluded about the connection between thought and success. Nietzsche wants to replace reason with will to power, the perspective of the vital interests of expansion of the individual. The individual, a congeries of potentially conflicting wills to power, may control inner conflict to produce an organism perfectly adapted to the moment. Will to power (for the individual) would express itself always as the will to (increase) power in the present moment, that is, as a will that is free to seize any opportunity for increasing power that the moment offers. This is precisely the strategy assigned to the Übermensch, but Dionysian process is so corrosive that it brings this conception down as surely as Nietzsche had used it to establish the folly of reason.

The problem is this. It's possible to imagine that the sequence of maximal growths in power at each instant over time is not as maximal as some other path that involves some nonmaximal growth points over an extended period of time. Once we assume that momentary fluctuations are never reliable guides to the future, this possibility can't be avoided. As a conceptual experiment, we can imagine two species of giraffes existing in the same environment. The taller species increases the length of its neck at every opportunity, and as we can assume that the tallest trees are taller than its neck at each point in time, at least at the start, it always has plenty of food and succeeds in increasing its population at the expense of the shorter giraffes, who have been rather lazy about exercising and eating, and simply succeed in staying alive, scavenging on the few leaves that are left at an appropriate height. Now let us assume that the taller giraffes catch up to the tops of the trees, eat them bare, and then discover that they're too tall to bend down to the level where a few of the shorter giraffes have managed to stay alive. If we assume that the taller giraffes don't kick the shorter giraffes to death in a rage as they die out, and they might not since they're not human beings, we can envision a triumph of sloth over exercise and muscle, and this is the absence of an environmental change that favors the one over the other. As long as there are divergent paths through time, some of them involving forms of rigidity designed to smooth over short-term fluctuations in the environment, the question of a best strategy becomes open, and some independent measure of increase in will to power is required if we are to talk sensibly about local accommodation as producing the desired strategy. Nietzsche has simply not provided such a measure, and so his intuition remains vague, even if it is sufficient to cast doubt on the superficial optimism of the Enlightenment reliance on human reason. Dionysian process, if it casts up Übermenschen, should no doubt cast up a variety of Übermenschen, some more aggressively adaptive in the short run than others, but Nietzsche is out to describe a single type guaranteed to survive, and he intends to produce that type if it is possible. Ultimately, however, Dionysian process must laugh at the coordinated adaptation of the Übermensch, just as it does at the pretensions of reason. The Übermensch, struggling against this realization, is a resolutely tragic conception.

Will to power is Nietzsche's clarified vision of Dionysian process.[2] Nietzsche sometimes uses "will to power" as an expression without an article, and sometimes he refers to "the will to power," suggesting that there is but one will to power, which takes many different forms and hence functions as a metaphysical principle. This variation is one reason why "will to power" has not been capitalized here, since it is not so easily identifiable as an expression with a constant reference, like the Eternal Return. The whole of what exists, the world, the Dionysian flux, is *the* will to power. In this sense, "the will to power" is simply a collective name for everything, but this everything can be broken down into wills to power in Nietzsche's organic metaphor, individual, shifting centers of power within this process. Nietzsche could not have admitted a set of definite wills to power as existents over time without falling back into a mechanical atomism, and this is one reason why he couldn't use models from physics to establish his claims for will to power and the Eternal Return, because the models available to him embodied atomistic premises. Nietzsche's models were intuitively drawn from his conceptions of chemistry and biology. Nietzsche also had to avoid the substantialization of wills as attached to individuals. The concept of will in Nietzsche expresses his biological dynamism, and it does not repeat the philosophical idea that will is primarily a faculty of human beings. Everything that is organized even for a moment wills to increase its power in confrontation with its surroundings. Wills are abstractions that locate conflict between parts of the Dionysian process. What something is can only be recognized by the part it plays in such conflict; how it expands or contracts in power as time flows by. The world is not grounded in the will to power; the world is an ungrounded, unlawful clash of events in which some wills to power come, at least temporarily, to dominate other wills to power, and within each will to power, lesser wills to power might also be struggling for expression. This view is consistent with Nietzsche's complex usage of expressions for will to power. It is incumbent on those who want to see Nietzsche as a metaphysician to explain coherently why he would ever drop the article; his concern for textual detail suggests that it couldn't be a matter of simple carelessness.

Textual support for the perspective argued for here is available in the published work.[3] We begin by considering aphorism 36 of *Beyond Good and Evil*. This paragraph uses both "will to power" and "the will to power" as expressions, and it is cast in a subjunctive mood, requiring delicate handling. In the first paragraph, Nietzsche repeats his claim that science regards the world as a confusing appearance whose real features are to be given by mechanical causation. The mechanistic world is broken down into existents and forms of causation, a suggestion that Nietzsche notes within mechanical science the break between explanatory reasons and explanatory causes, and within the latter the break between causation by heat, light, magnetism, electricity, and so forth.[4] Nietzsche suggests a reduction in which the entire world, including its inorganic and mechanical aspects, can perhaps be explained as a clash of desires, passions, or wills. Everything can then (possibly) be explained at a single level of appearance, and with a single principle of action: organic confrontation. Nietzsche suggests that the apparent diversity of the world is an expression of conflict in a primitive unified (Dionysian) process. Nietzsche's mysticism is nowhere more evident than it is in this passage, which repeats the structure of mystical accounts of the formation of a differentiated world from an undifferentiated primal form.

Nietzsche notes that it can't be proved that the thought experiment of the first paragraph must fail, and that the experiment must be made. With respect to science itself, Nietzsche adopts the perspective that its own conception of method requires that all possible experiments be undertaken, so that it is driven to think out Dionysian possibilities by its own valuational principles, if they are to be explicitly applied. The concept of will now makes a sudden, unifying appearance. To work out the experiment means postulating "will" as the only cause, the quotation marks indicating an abstractive fiction. But "will" cannot act on matter, and here Nietzsche accepts the definitional trivialities of science, so that "matter" must be seen as "will" if the experiment is to succeed, rather than the reverse prejudice of science. Nietzsche, continuing in the third paragraph, suggests "will to power" as the reference of this view and notes that this is *his* view, or rather this is his *sentence*, since he is asserting. If will to power could be worked out as a coherent and comprehensive doctrine, so what? Would it be merely the inversion of a mechanical doctrine that could reduce "will" to "matter?" If, as wills, we express will to power, if we were matter, on the same hypothesis, wouldn't matter express will? A subtle asymmetry appears here. Nietzsche suggests that the scientific view, the view of the spectator of mechanistic processes, can't be closed in on itself, since the scientist must pretend to stand outside the process he is describing in order to produce an account of it as knowledge. There is no such outside perspective point in reality, and the scientist suffers from a self-deception. In Nietzsche's case, any perspective is an expression of will, expended in a struggle with other wills. The perspective is real, i.e., *in* the world that it describes, and it doesn't fall (as a perspective) into the trap of claiming to be knowledge—hence the use of the subjunctive mode, which avoids a universal claim to truth. Nietzsche is only inviting others to try on this perspective, to attempt (also) to see things through it.

Earlier, in aphorism 22, Nietzsche had suggested that nature's conformity to law was essentially a bad reading of nature from a scientific perspective. It is not something that is given; it is not the text of nature but a projection into nature of democratic desire that nothing be above anything else, that everything be equal before the law—in society and in nature. Nietzsche then describes hypothetically someone who might be able to interpret everything as hierarchy and will to power—the same possibility that is explored in the thought experiment of aphorism 36 that we have just considered. He makes two simultaneous moves. The view of the world as Dionysian flux or will to power does not mean that the world can't have a necessary course, although that course won't be capturable in typical scientific laws. In short, chance and necessity can be suspended; pure chance gives a course that is as necessary as the rule of law, and it can be appropriately described. The Eternal Return is an expression of both chance and necessity, a transvaluation of their apparent opposition. Nietzsche's other move here is to claim no more than that his view is an interpretation. Why does Nietzsche welcome the suggestion that his view is only an interpretation? Because he is prepared to live with the clash of interpretations, supposing that some of them can be proven superior to others. What he cannot live with is the idea that foundations are necessary and that they express an absolute framework or perspective. Once attention has been brought to the evaluation of perspectives, Nietzsche is on his home ground. If every power center has a perspective, the world can be will to power, that is, an assemblage of power centers. Monism is compatible with pluralism to that extent, with the existence of temporary and possibly antagonistic power centers, shifting as the process is described. The world is not the assemblage of perspectives. All perspectives give what knowledge of process there is, but it is relentlessly fictive knowledge, even if some fictions are superior to others.

Nietzsche's biological metaphor is presented clearly in the latter part of aphorism 12 of the second essay of *Genealogy*. After noting that the origin of something and its current significance may have nothing in common, Nietzsche connects this with hierarchy and with a general view of biological development. Nietzsche is determined to stamp out teleological history. The various parts of a thing, a custom, an organ, a creature, can take on an almost chance significance over time, depending on what happens within the larger whole of which this is a part. A very brief characterization of Dionysian process as clashes of wills to power is followed by the observation that the destruction or elimination of a part may be part of an increasing strength and perfection of the whole. (Humans are no exception—their complete elimination in favor of a new species could constitute an advance.) Nietzsche suggests that advance might even be measured by the mass of things that are sacrificed to it. Implicit in this is the emergence of hierarchy; less important parts are sacrificed to the harmony of a ranking whole. If a whole were a democracy of parts, so to speak, it would not matter which parts disappeared, and progress would be meaningless. The direction of progress is given by the perspective of increasing wills to power, a valuation consistent with Nietzsche's perspective.

Nietzsche notices here that a part may appear of no particular significance, a part that can come to play a great role if the larger organism containing it develops in a certain way. The evolutionary time lag suggested here is used by Nietzsche to criticize Darwinian adaptation in anticipation of the scientific critique that Darwinian theory did not contain the resources to explain the origin of species. But Nietzsche doesn't turn this weapon on himself. If the significance of the present can't be known until some time in the future, the present can't provide any clues to adaptation that preserves maximum adaptability in the face of all possible futures. If the Übermensch is to increase will to power, the Übermensch must guess or be lucky. Should the present not have an orientation, should it always return, the Übermensch can try to live on, but there are no coordinate points for charting flexibility, and the Übermensch is threatened by conflicting characterizations of the present, or by conflicting feelings. *Amor fati,* love of fate, Nietzsche's positive affirmation of whatever happens, threatens by itself to collapse into passive adaptation.

According to Nietzsche's view of will to power, the real world consists of dynamic quanta, all of which stand in a dynamic relationship to all other such quanta. When we add Nietzsche's assumption that the total amount of energy in the universe is limited, partly because the notion of constantly increasing energy would make no sense, it's clear that these quanta are in a *struggle* with one another. An increase in power at one center means that power must be diminished somewhere else. But as there are no stable power centers, and larger power centers may be subdivided, the dynamic conception is a philosophical realization of Dionysian and Heraclitean flux. The universe breaks down into wills to power, which experience only what they encounter, but which all are linked by a network of such experiencings. There is no general scheme or philosophical plan of the universe beyond this loose notion that it is everywhere similar to the part characterized by my own experience.

Will to power is the philosophical refinement of Dionysian flux, already noted in *Birth*. The agonal relationship between nobles fades into will to power in the sense that the outcome of the struggle between nobles is determined by struggles within them. There is no difference between inside and outside in that both are fields of clashing wills to power. The successful noble (where Dionysian flux is held constant and doesn't determine success as an external variable) is the one who masters self, and this notion will have to take on a special meaning in Nietzsche, for whom the "self" in the received cultural sense is an illusion, the product of a linguistic fiction. Successful noble action is flexible and unified at the same time, which means that it is undertaken as a coordinated bodily movement in response to the exigencies of the present. Mastery of self cannot be determined (if supple) maintenance of the same ideas and rules of action over time; such mastery would fall victim to Dionysian capriciousness. Mastery of self has to be submission to whatever is required at a time without regret, without a countervailing hedge. Success in increasing power does not come from developing rational plans against the outside, but in tuning the inside so as to find the flexible and integrated response to those power centers that one encounters. Will to power is most powerful when it is most cunning, sly, and free. But what can produce the tuning?[5] If it were chance, a consistent Dionysian philosophy without the notion of the Übermensch would be possible, but the desire for the Übermensch, the desire to become the Übermensch, the desire to live in conformity with the possibility of the Eternal Return, produces an interpretation whose drive for consistency leads Nietzsche inevitably into inconsistency. If being and becoming are suspended in the Eternal Return, consistency and inconsistency are also suspended in these last philosophical insights.

Wills to power are sorted out by the dice throw of chance according to whether they are reactive or active. Consciousness is always a rigid and reactive force; this is why we have come to lose touch with our bodies, and both memory and habit have contributed to this alienation from self. Wills to power differ in quantity, and these differences result from the will to power acting over time. The will to power affirms or denies, ultimately, hence defining the path of force with respect to nihilism. Major problems for this interpretation involve such questions as how reactive forces can triumph over active forces (or enlist them in support of reaction), and how differences in quantity between forces can be differences in quality. This last question is the root structural problem of all monism, adapted to this account.

Nietzsche's view has led Deleuze to suggest that we need to reformulate our language of explanation in a Nietzschean context, asking "Which one is *x*?" instead of "What is *x*?" The conceptual resources to answer the latter question do not exist, since we cannot know Dionysian process, but the former question requires only that we somehow be able to indicate centers of power within the process. We need to consider the world under the theme of will to power, looking for the forces that account for what we observe and studying their active and reactive types. Nietzsche might have been uncomfortable had he found himself at this point, since his doctrine suggests, as we have seen, that the clash of forces lies beyond our ken, and, beyond feeling the direction in which power is exerted, we can only explain by inventing causes.[6]

That we are individuals is an Apollinian illusion, since will to power situates us in Dionysian flux, but the push to unity of style returns us to a notion of individual survival over time. Nietzsche simply cannot theorize collective actions or collective planning, since it would involve the transfer of information between locations in the flux, and there is no neutral language for such a transfer. When democratic humans act collectively, they must act reactively, opposing Dionysian flux, and they may coerce the affirmative individual; but such collective reaction will not stand over time, and its standing at all is no indicator of truth. This solves the problem of why the strong should be protected against the weak, but at the price of a dubious strategy of unity. It is precisely in collective action that a mix of strategies may make sense against an uncertain future. In Nietzsche's ontology, there are only individuals *in* flux; there are no collectivities that can stand against flux by offering a continuously renewed mix of reactions and by trimming away what is nonadaptive, thus retaining a constantly changing definitional structure.[7] The breaking point for Nietzsche's doctrine is really the strange unified individual that his Dionysian strategy requires. The unified individual may be stronger or weaker than any individual that depends on a mixed strategy in the short run, but successful unity can't be predicted or constructed given the terrible corrosion of Dionysian process over time, and short-term success can always be followed by disaster on the next cycle. Nietzsche made Dionysus so unpredictably powerful that control becomes an impossibility. If we need to be aware of the precarious nature of human existence, if we need to avoid a silly science optimism, there are still other value tables to develop than that associated with Nietzsche's Übermenschen. Will to power, ironically, functions like an "invisible hand," a subtle confirmation of Nietzsche's elective affinity with capitalism, but a sign also that the individualism that is ideologically extolled over collectivity is ultimately empty.[8]

Nietzsche's difficulties with collectivity were already contained *in nuce* in his original vision of Hellenic Greece and his early remarks on culture in *Untimely Meditations*. If culture is the unified life of the people, it doesn't transcend them. But cultures are designed to create a womb that acts as a shield against Dionysian destruction. Much of culture escapes direct selection. Cultures are unlikely to be selected on whether their members drive on the left or the right, or on whether (Nietzsche's example) preferred sexual plumage is male or female. In biological theory, it is individuals who live or die, but species that adapt or fail to adapt to their environments. Nietzsche's biologism is intuitively brilliant, but in error. Even in the inorganic realm, perception is not infallible; it is selective. The individual responds to certain features of the environment that it can read, but it may be unable to sense changes in the environment that spell its doom. A totally aware body may be inadequate to sense all the features of Dionysian flux that are open to it. This is one reason why individualism and collectivism can't settle their dispute on the terrain of philosophy.

There is no "will" in itself in Nietzsche, directed toward future goals. The "will" and the "person who wills" are fictions that are created to give a narrative account of what happens. If we will, what happens is independent of our efforts and just happens. If we get what we want, we're lucky. There are, in fact, no permanently true natural laws in Nietzsche's views. Natural laws (as in science) are too crude to get at the fine structure of events. What we normally think of as organic and inorganic processes are all expressions of the will to power, expressing itself as the attempt by everything that exists to transcend itself. A human is a congeries of wills to power that can conflict and typically do conflict. Each self-overcoming provides a new interpretive point; that's why all wills at this microlevel are associated with perspectives. All differences in the universe result from the differentiation provided by wills to power, especially in their strength. Aristocracy, for example, is desired by strong wills, and democracy is desired by weak wills. Weak wills have to take strong stands in order to operate, whereas strong wills (great spirits) can act in a coherent but powerful and low-key way.[9] Will is control of one's own powers, not control (domination) of others. It can result in self-transcendence. The "will to power" is a metaphor, since in its expressions there is no coherent "I" that wills. The will to power accepts (in any particular case) the accidental, repetitive nature of things and attempts accommodation of its strength to what happens. Increase of power must come from increasing unity of the individual, allowing the individual's movement to coincide with the direction of Dionysian flux, rather than partially resisting it through internal disunity. The will, as it is ordinarily understood, is an illusion, along with the agent who wills. If this is forgotten, will to power seems simply turned to the outside; it seems an attempt to control *other* power centers as though there were no problems at home. Nietzsche's will to power is not so much control *over* Dionysian flux and other power centers as it is control in reaction to Dionysian flux. It is this accommodating control that is willed by the most consistent power centers as a means to expansion and longevity. One cannot stand against Dionysian flux, so one joins it with a vengeance.

The real world of flux must escape language. Language falsely reifies flux and exists only as an army of clashing metaphors, to be used with caution. Therefore, more and more adequate philosophical language must become more and more charged with contradiction as a Dionysian philosopher tackles the contradictory problem of consistently describing what can be sensed of the universe. Nietzsche's awareness of philosophical superiority is based on the idea that he is *aware* of perspectivism. Where others encounter the world *through* perspectives, Nietzsche claims his perspective to be aware that all encounters, insofar as they can be expressed in language, are perspectival. Nietzsche's perspectivism, at a metalevel of awareness, must lead to Dionysus. To speak, we must adopt a linguistic mask, and hence a name, effecting a unity of person that doesn't correspond to the reality of will to power, nor to the reality of Dionysian text. Nietzsche doesn't speak to us in his texts; "Nietzsche" speaks in his texts, and when "Nietzsche" constantly reminds us of that, Nietzsche has a chance to allow us to sense the existence of Dionysus, who can't speak in the text. A cheerful, consistent, optimistic perspective can prattle on, unaware of itself. A perspective aware of itself, aware of perspectivism, must attempt to increase power by incorporating perspectives, and becoming more adequate to the Dionysian vision which alone can explain perspectivism. But as it becomes higher, more adequate, it becomes *more inarticulate,* as language doesn't contain the resources to express a full vision of Dionysian flux. Nietzsche's perspectivism is a transvaluation of Hegel's absolute system. When you put perspectives together from a high point of view, as Nietzsche notes, you don't create knowledge, nor do you get an increasingly more detailed *account* of Dionysian flux. What you get is an increasing awareness, an awareness increasing with the scope of the account, without gaining any detail of the Dionysian process. Zarathustra is largely silent on his mountain; he speaks to humans when he descends to them.

Consciousness, which relies on language, is a particular error which needs to be downgraded by the Dionysian philosopher in favor of integrated bodily responses. Nietzsche is the philosopher of the hands, the ears, the eyes, the nose, the feet, and finds pure reason the silliest of the possible guides to action. He admires the inorganic world where communication is perfect and action immediate; error begins with organic life. The concentration on the body pushes the organic toward the inorganic in the service of a life of minimum consciousness and felt reaction—but this integrated body is also a fiction. In the absence of a developed philosophy of the body, the body is merely an idea, a conceptual ideal point, since the body can harbor warring wills to power without the intervention of consciousness. Nietzsche means to put out a signpost to feeling with one's own body.

Nietzsche presents the advantages of unity as though they were obvious, but the problem of time frames that plagues his general conception of evolutionary process undercuts his philosophy of life. Going with the flow, so to speak, may result in the best short-term gains in power, but there is no guarantee that mixed strategies won't have greater survival value over time in a constantly shifting environment. And all this waives the question of whether or not there is one direction to Dionysian flux. The eddies and countercurrents of a stream, Dionysian or not, may not provide a clear direction of flow when one encounters the stream at a point, through a perspective, but we can waive this criticism and still find Nietzsche to be in trouble. If the Übermensch is unified and uniformly adapts (in all of the Übermensch's power centers) to every shift in the direction of Dionysian flux, the Übermensch is drained of any substantive content, and the continued application of the same name over time is a mere fiction in the worst sense. A continued identity, an *awareness* over time that one is an Übermensch, can't be sustained against this flux. Nietzsche's account of staying on the surface heightens paradox here to the breaking point. Adaptability and awareness point in different directions, and the problem of knowledge, Hamlet's uncertainty mentioned in *Birth,* can't be resolved. What Nietzsche accomplishes is the transvaluation of Platonic, Cartesian and of scientific outlooks that will explain change through the varying relationships between fixed entities. If Nietzsche's conception has problems, he has decisively unmasked the pretensions of the ruling value tables, and a war of interpretations can begin.

10

Return

The Hellenic noble, experiencing the tragic, was affirmative *despite* an awareness of Dionysian flux. If will to power expresses Dionysian chaos in an ahistorical form, expresses the view that there are no laws, only chaos and change, how can one be affirmative? If, as *part* of will to power, we urge ourselves to become what we are, to perform a life of health, why should we gear up if chaos makes that performance, at best, temporary? Will to power takes history to the zero point: there is always only chaos. The minimum history designated in the second untimely meditation, and required for affirmation, is then provided by the Eternal Return, and it is a history of ourselves, of what we can affirmatively grasp and feel. At the last stages of Nietzsche's development, there is still only Dionysian process (will to power) and Apollinian illusion (the Eternal Return), the latter making the former bearable to animals with cognitive powers. The Eternal Return continues the suspension of *Birth* as the Apollinian vision of will to power. The Eternal Return answers the question of how we could live as nobles lived. The Eternal Return is a vision cast up by will to power, but neither reducible to the latter, since will to power as the Eternal Return is reactive, nor incompatible with the latter, since will to power will repeatedly erase specific visions of the Return.

Cognitive opposites are neither permanently oppositional in Nietzsche's view nor resolvable in synthesis. They remain suspended until Dionysian flux destroys both of them. The reason for this, so to speak, is that language and its conceptual structure can never fit chaos. Sanity/insanity, good/evil, finite/infinite, fact/value, chance/necessity, past/future, affirmation/despair, and health/sickness are among the pairs that are subject to Nietzschean suspensions. The Eternal Return implies these suspensions; that is why it is a key Apollinian vision. What we will now we must will forever. What has happened must happen again. What will happen has already happened. If will to power can't be articulated as doctrine, the Eternal Return can be more so, but compatibility and incompatibility between them are also suspended. The affirmation of the tourist, saying "wow" to every new experience, is *not* Nietzschean affirmation. Nietzschean affirmation involves the simultaneous realization that what we confront will disappear (will to power) and will remain forever (the Eternal Return). Nietzschean affirmation depends on despair. This is what we have to understand: Why is it that the Eternal Return produces at the same time the deepest despair and the highest joy? The Eternal Return and will to power can't be the same thought or completely different thoughts; only a complex interaction could produce this suspension of reactions in the ahistorical noble.

Extant readings of the Eternal Return tend to make it a scientific claim, raising the question of its compatibility with will to power and with modern cosmology, or, to make it a moral claim, urging a flexible and affirmative approach to life despite an awareness that the picture of existence underlying it is probably illusory. Both approaches oversimplify the logical relationship between will to power and the Eternal Return. It should be clear that from Nietzsche's point of view, no logical relationship could capture the relevant suspension of insights.

One path of interpretation on this basis is to take the Eternal Return as a piece of scientific cosmology, as an attempt on Nietzsche's part to replace a science historically allied with Christianity with a Hellenic science allied with Dionysian process. The dangers with this should now be obvious, since it's clear that Nietzsche could not have consistently developed a discursive Dionysian science. But there are other problems. Although Nietzsche discusses in his notebooks whether the Eternal Return could be proven in some sense, he never publishes a proof.[1] His writings describe the Eternal Return merely as the only way in which the Übermensch could encounter Dionysian process. His notebooks may then be taken as expressing an interest in the amusement that a scientific "proof" of the Eternal Return, or even its possibility, would create. Any attempt to make the Eternal Return a piece of discursive cosmology runs into the problem that Nietzsche's resources are inadequate to establish the Eternal Return unless some atomistic doctrines are added to will to power suggesting that there are only a finite number of power centers, each of which can take on only a finite number of power states or levels of power.

It is clear that Nietzsche's organic conception of will to power blocks this line of proof, whether Nietzsche was completely aware of that or not. But to start down this path is to assume that Nietzsche would have wanted to develop a replacement scientific cosmology, and that the failure of such a cosmology to materialize reduces Nietzsche to a metaphysician in a bad sense, or to someone who urges an existential attitude toward life on us without any supporting argument much stronger than that we will like it, or that it will be good for us. The cosmological path is determined to lose Nietzsche's own conception of the *coercive* subjunctive importance of this doctrine, ultimately seeing it as a mistake, or as a mere prophetic call to a different style of life.

Danto, for example, has argued that Nietzsche's "proof" of the Eternal Return (finite universe plus infinite past time yields Eternal Return) is invalid.[2] If Nietzsche actually advanced this proof, this is one of the things that can be said for certain, as Simmel had originally shown.[3] Consider two wheels touching at a point and fixed to parallel axes so that they rotate together, continuously touching, but in opposite directions. If each of them has an arbitrary mark, and the marks are coincident at the start of the rotation, then if the wheels rotate in an irrational ratio, the marks will never again be coincident. Therefore infinite past time plus a finite universe do not need to yield a physically cyclical cosmology. Danto tries to fix up the argument by suggesting that finite states or configurations are needed, not merely a finite universe, if the argument is to be carried through. (In the example of the rotating wheels, since each position of the mark is regarded as a different state, each wheel has an infinite number of states.) Sterling argues that Danto has misread Nietzsche, and he proposes a consideration of energy designed to repair Danto's argument consistently with the Nietzschean texts.[4]

Soll has argued that future recurrences could have no meaning for this life, raising the question of what identity would mean across cycles.[5] If I won't be able to remember what happens now, why should I take the future into account, as in Nietzsche's affirmative ethics? If I am able to, how can I balance the two events against one another? (This seems to lose the subjunctive moral force of Nietzsche's use of the return.) Sterling says "replicas" will return—memory can't accumulate because then the cycles wouldn't be identical, since the persons in each cycle would remember their past selves. A person then is and is not identical with future replicas.

Zuboff makes similar points. Zuboff does not hold (and Sterling agrees) that in a nondeterministic universe, the Eternal Return would have no implications for values or morality. Once again, this occludes the subjunctive aspect of Nietzsche's language.[6] Nietzsche says to act *as though* the Eternal Return were true, not to act *because* it is true. Nietzsche clearly kept centrally in mind the judgment that the Eternal Return was a fiction.

Magnus notes that Sterling loses the subjunctive connection between cosmological and prescriptive aspects of the return—and also assumes that our present existence is our first time around.[7] Eternal Return is simply the recommendation to adopt the being-in-the-world of the Übermensch. This can stand as a capsule summary of Magnus's book.[8] But why should we adopt the existential attitude of the Übermensch as Magnus suggests? The doctrine as he expresses it has no compulsive force, even if Magnus is correct that Nietzsche shared his prescriptive attitude. Physical proofs, if valid, would coerce one to act as the Übermensch on prudential grounds. If they're not valid, we can't have Nietzsche's prescriptions without some grounds for their purchase on our attention.

Schacht observes (along Danto's lines) that the physical proofs are wrong, but doubts that Nietzsche would have been impressed by this.[9] Nietzsche's major employment of the device is to use it as a test of one's strength and disposition to life. Schacht suspects (reasonably enough) that the origin of the idea is in Heraclitus.[10] Heraclitus's cyclical universe just moves from entropic calm to great energy and back again, without any necessity that the same sequences should repeat.

All the analytic treatments recognize the centrality of the doctrine—but give it such a reduced reading that its centrality for Nietzsche casts some doubt on the cogency of his thought. Nietzsche clearly thought that one couldn't be indifferent to the idea of the Eternal Return, that one must be either joyfully transformed by it or cast down into despair.[11] On any strong cosmological doctrine, the future should be a matter of indifference, since I can't control it, and since it's not therefore relevant to me now, and I should either be resigned or indifferent to it at the present moment. Urging an existential attitude in the teeth of such a process has little prescriptive force, and Nietzsche is not a prophet who is likely to propose rules of guidance on such a slender basis, or to recommend a self-overcoming that is a knowing self-deception.[12]

The root difficulty with the lines of interpretation we have considered so far is that they proceed from the assumption that Nietzsche was attempting to prove the truth of the Eternal Return, and that failure of a proof pushed Nietzsche toward existential doctrines. But this path of interpretation should never be entered; the very first step is the mistake. We return here to Nietzsche's perspectivism. He isn't trying to prove the Eternal Return; he simply uses its possibility as the most acid attack possible on teleological history and history that traces the significance of past events into the future. Proving the Eternal Return would mean finding a perspective from which *all* the cycles could be described; Nietzsche did not think that such a transcendental perspective was a possibility. Imagine that things have all occurred an infinite number of times before. This value scheme, compatible with the present moment, and indeed with everything that we can be said to *know*, requires a different way of living than that suggested by other value tables. Indeed, the Eternal Return eliminates the concept of a value table as a fixed set of values. We have to approach the Eternal Return as a highest perspective from which the fixity of all previous values tables can be analytically determined and exposed to the ravages of Dionysian process. The subjunctive force of the Eternal Return, its perspectival nature, is clearly marked in the texts. That Zarathustra announces the return is itself an indication that it is not to be proven as doctrine, but is to burst into consciousness as a compelling valuational point of view.

It is possible to interpret Nietzsche as proposing a way to live, not a reading of the unfolding of the universe. We should consider the world as endlessly unfolding without purpose and not as actually repeating in cycles. That Nietzsche wished to deny purpose or plan in any unfolding is a certainty. In view of this nonteleological unfolding, the Übermensch could not divine the future and has to value knowing that this is impossible.

A version of this subjunctive reading has been proposed by Nehamas.[13] In spite of what Nehamas takes to be Nietzsche's careless phrasing, close reading suggests to Nehemas that Nietzsche is only committed to the following weak claim that if he were to exist again, then everything about the world (good and bad, including the 'small man') would have to exist again. In any event, all the psychological doctrines that Nietzsche draws from the recurrence can be drawn from this weaker claim. The weaker claim is equivalent to the assertion that events in the universe are so tightly connected that everything that has occurred and will occur in the universe is implicit in the present moment. The conditional assertion, "If my life were to recur, it would recur in exactly identical fashion," is not an assertion of cosmology, but a piece of metaphysics, so that this subjunctive reading places Nietzsche back into the camp of metaphysics. Its significance is that there is no "essence" of a person contrasting with contingent features. All a person's properties belong equally to him or to her. A different life in any respect would be the life of a different person. Now we see that if we accept any part of ourselves, we must accept everything and the entire world; if we reject any part of ourselves, we must reject everything. This would explain why joy and despair are the only appropriate responses to discovery of the Eternal Return. (The metaphysical connection of everything to everything else Nehamas takes to be equivalent to the will to power.) This life and this world are the only life and world we could have, so that Nietzsche's repudiation of other worlds is nicely saved on this reading.

Now, unless there is nothing in our past to regret, this does not lead to affirmation. But if there is a moment at which I would want to be again, all the past is affirmed at that moment by the metaphysics, because it is all connected to that moment. The past can only be redeemed in this way, by finding a harmonious moment whose affirmation affirms an entire life. (Most commentators believe that what recurs can only be a subset of what has happened, a subset selected because it can be affirmed and perpetuated.) The process of interpreting one's life as it occurs is potentially a never-ending task, looking for a moment that would allow complete affirmation. If the hermeneutical task is to see the unity in our lives as an aesthetic phenomenon, Nehamas thinks that the problem is that the affirmative person could turn out to be morally repulsive. The objection is an analogue to the old problem of whether an immoral person can have a logically consistent set of beliefs. This problem is a serious one for rational ethics, which attempts to use reason alone to differentiate between moral perspectives that are assumed to occur on the same level. Whether the analogous problem arises for Nietzsche involves a careful consideration of the perspectives from which moral judgments are made, and of their relative heights. That humans might find the *Übermensch* repulsive, for example, is not really a problem from Nietzsche's perspective.

Strong also rejects the return as a cosmological doctrine, arguing that it is a vision occurring to individuals in which eternity is present, as in the scene at the gateway in *Zarathustra*.[14] This would make Nietzsche's vision novel, and not a repetition of Greek or oriental ideas. We need a relationship to time which is conceived of neither as a circle nor as a uniform straight line running forward and backward from where we are. We need to evolve a form of life in which humans are self-conscious (as opposed to animals). The doctrine of the Eternal Return will detect nihilism in those who cannot fully adopt such a stance. We must change or disappear—that's the significance of nihilism. A certain orientation to the world produces the Eternal Return, and nothing can be said about the Eternal Return as an objective feature of the world. That's why there aren't proofs of the doctrine. The Eternal Return functions as a separation mechanism for locating the parts of our lives that can be affirmed and perpetuated. Strong's differences with Nehamas are evident in the face of this selection.

The best clues as to how to be in the Eternal Return are given textually by the failings of the "higher men" in *Zarathustra*. Their affirmations are not sufficiently comprehensive in scope and they are not sufficiently selective. They must deny, change, feel, transfigure, and overcome self. Strong returns to the Heraclitean play image. The world is a game in which necessities provide the constraints of play, although they are not experiences as necessities. The high men do not gamble and accept the outcome; they resent bad outcomes. One wants to play, and must play the game, according to its constraints—so that play makes obligation and desire coincident. Laughter is the sign that the past has been willed again and accepted. Strong then introduces a "simple example" of the attitude stemming from the return, the attitude adopted in . . . skiing! When skiing well, we experience freedom, power, lack of constraint, in a joyful affirmation of our acquired skills. Knowledge has been made instinctive, but just that which is to be perpetuated. (All good knowing is knowing how, to appropriate another jargon.) In skiing, Strong says one conquers time, and those portions of one's life not directly relevant are excluded from interference at the time of skiing. (Apparently Strong always enjoys a good laugh when he falls down.)[15] Strong feels that we should constantly work toward such instinctive behavior, and that this is Nietzsche's doctrine. Further, this task would never be completed, so self-transcendence is a constant requirement. But how could we code in enough habits to anticipate all the circumstances we might confront? And aren't habits just the kind of rigidities that the Übermensch wishes to eradicate? Skiing may be regarded as a set of skills that we use to feel our way down the slopes, reacting smoothly to new contingencies, but the example doesn't seem to generalize very far, and it's not clear what set of habitual skills would allow us to feel our way through political contingencies in a politics of transfiguration.

The subjunctive readings of Nehamas and Strong depend on one's ability to survey one's entire life, either to affirm it as a whole or to affirm aspects of it. But our lives are what they are. We have to accept them as they are, in one sense, even if we would not want to repeat them exactly again, if that opportunity were to present itself. An Übermensch cannot be a human being who would affirm an entire life. The resources for surveying past and future, and finding satisfaction in all of the details are features of a metaphysical value table that is not Nietzsche's, partly because it involves the importance of long-term memory. The Übermensch can't wish to save an entire life against Dionysian process. The Übermensch could not be concerned with a memory as extensive as that required for such a choice. To become what we are, we need to become beings who can constantly adapt to Dionysian process, who react to what is confronted at the moment without steering against the current flow due to rigidified rules of conduct. Subjunctive readings threaten to return us to the metaphysical quagmire that Nietzsche was so anxious to avoid.

The suggestion made here is that the strains imposed on Nietzsche's doctrine of the Eternal Return push its interpretation in two incompatible directions that Nietzsche ultimately could not resolve. Various conflicting existing readings of the Eternal Return can be grouped as partial realizations of these two interpretations insofar as they deal with specific textual material. Referring to these general interpretations as the pessimistic cosmological theory and the optimistic moral theory, respectively, we will immediately see why despair and joyous affirmation are the only legitimate reactions to the meaning of the doctrine, and are not existential attitudes that can be suggested as appropriate responses to it. The Übermensch, grasping the doctrine, is driven toward both of these poles.

The pessimistic cosmological theory is an interpretation of the Eternal Return stressing the origins of Nietzsche's views in his vision of Hellenic Greece, in this case, in his preference for cyclical cosmology. There is waxing and waning in the universe, but no permanent progress, no unalterable change. "Chance" causes individuation, but necessity rules in the long run. Identity is not a viable concept; it is always an illusion. The universe may return to the same state, pass through the same cycles, but we can't know this—it is, however, a possibility that we must confront. Everything belongs to a Dionysian process, and individuals must return to this process. The sequence past→present→future cannot be defined. This cosmology is exactly the cosmology of the great Hellenic tragedies, although tragedy reveals only the existence of the process, not its full cyclical nature.

On this view, there is no reason to believe that the Übermensch will ever appear. Willing the Übermensch is simply willing the destruction of the human, the completion of nihilism. The Übermensch has never existed and will never exist, but the human will eternally return. Contemplation of this causes Zarathustra great pain. On this view, the Übermensch can be described as the end of the human, the point at which contradictions in any human era are brought to the breaking point. The Eternal Return can't be expressed, although it is a real moment, the moment of return of a human cycle to Dionysian process. The Eternal Return is a signpost to the Dionysian process that ultimately brings everything down, affirmative or reactive. Übermenschen are recurrent terminal points that are never fully instantiated. Nietzsche and the Übermensch disappear just when they seem to conflate, just when the Übermensch struggles to be born. If Dionysian process could cast up the Übermensch, it should have happened, and not only would there have been an Übermensch, there should be one now. The Eternal Return forces the Übermensch not to appear, because the vector of history must and yet cannot exist at the location of the Übermensch. The Übermensch will not adopt a perspective, will not know that the vision of the Übermensch is perspectival, yet the Übermensch is not a metaphysical abstraction because it is the human perspectival attempt to express the moment of reconciliation of the human with the Dionysian. The doctrine expresses a permanent tendency of the will to power as best it can be expressed in human language.

Klossowski's interpretation comes close to a realization of the pessimistic cosmological doctrine.[16] Klossowski discusses the moment at which the return presents itself, whether to Nietzsche, to the Übermensch, or to anyone. At this moment, the self existing before this realization must dissolve away, just when the possibility of the return presents itself, and one remembers previous lives and the possibility that one will live again. As long as one is *someone,* the return is not evident. When the return is evident, one is many—one is not someone-in-particular. The return cannot be stated in the voice of a single person. In willing to return at a particular point, one wills that the past leading up to one can occur again, thus redeeming it. Klossowski intimates that the return (as a doctrine) appears just as we fuse with Dionysian process, repeating the insight of *Birth,* but in a modern, Nietzschean form. (This ties into Klossowski's general hermeneutical view that there are no first and last times, no identities like "this is me," no originals and copies [the essence of Platonism being transvalued], no authentic texts or proper meanings.)[17] The instant that presents the return seems at first unique, providing the opportunity for this affirmative willing, just before the dissolution of the self.

Klossowski presents a Dionysian ontology in which signification arises as part of chaos with a partial self-identity—like bits of foam on a wave. (The wave, the sea are Nietzschean images which constantly reappear in Nietzsche's texts.) The rise and fall of intensity can interpret itself, giving rise to "signs," i.e., repetitions (nearly exact) of the same movement. We are all movements on the surface of the same process. The code of everyday signs is an artifact that "forgets" this situation. The strong flux of energy corresponding to the tonality that reveals the return overpowers this transient set of signs. The image of the vicious circle forms at this point, as this most powerful flux is attempted an interpretation. (That there is no final interpretation issues from its invitation to repeat the cycle.) Under the sign of the circle, *the* self is gone. Meaning and the Eternal Return seem to coalesce. We can't think this: so it appears only in this moment of high tonality. The will (that imposter) is also gone, along with thought. The will of the individual is not "responsible" for acts of the individual. The will to power is the humanized version of the vicious circle, but the Übermensch is the subject, just passing into awareness of the circle. The Übermensch is not stable here, but passes back into alterity, into a recognition of the circle as a chance revelation all of whose parts must be willed again in a new fictive subject.

The optimistic moral interpretation stresses the origins of Nietzsche's views in his assertion in *Birth* that he is the first to understand tragedy, and it appears in many other buoyant and optimistic Nietzschean passages. So we do have joy or depression—and pessimism/optimism is held in a suspension that avoids triviality. Individuation is perhaps a chance occurrence, but its continuation depends on a willed unity, willed control, willed values. The universe is permanent becoming. From one moment to the next is the real cycle, one that selects for affirmative willing. The same individual can survive in its affirmative aspects. Here we do not have complete nihilism, but a concept allowing for the Übermensch to appear.[18] The Übermensch can appear as a form of self-conscious affirmative style. The Übermensch affirms everything, not making a selection. There has never been an Übermensch, but perhaps Zarathustra (i.e., Nietzsche, or someone just about to appear) could be the first Übermensch. The transvaluation of values can be accomplished so as to force a new era. On this view, the *Übermensch* can't be described (because he/she/it is "beyond" the human and human language), but the Eternal Return can be expressed as the endless return of becoming; being *as* becoming. Episodes can't be compared across time; there are no categories for that which escape illusion. To support the optimistic view, we can't just dismiss the passages talking about cycle; we need a construal of the present. In effect, we must argue that past and future are "contained" in the present. The former is easy. Part of the present is the past—as the past appears in the present in such passages as that provided in "On the Vision and the Riddle" in *Zarathustra*. How can we get novelty in the future? Well, the future is also in the present as the fragments that will compose it. (There is nothing new that will appear under the sun.) To say that this spider has occurred before alludes to this fact. Nothing begins to exist at an instant; everything must appear before itself (or before it appears) in the process. Not everything in the moment is contemporaneous. The vision of the prophet or the Über-mensch, for example, is well in advance of the vision of those surrounding. This sense of time has firm roots in Hellenic Greece.

Drawing on texts from the *Nachlass*, Deleuze has observed that Nietz-sche's cosmology only forces the view that the universe had no terminal or equilibrium state, a conclusion based on the infinity of past time, which suggests that this state would have already been reached.[19] An equi-librium state would have been reached and held, but we are still experienc-ing Dionysian flux. (Where modern cosmology only accepts a finite past time for *our* universe, an adjustment is required. Perhaps other universes must be postulated, but cosmology is not inconsistent with Nietzsche's views, and big-bang evolutionary models are manifestly consistent with Nietzsche's philosophical insights unless one adopts a strict cyclical cos-mological reading of the Eternal Return.) In short, Deleuze takes Nietz-sche's cosmological insight to be that becoming is permanent, an idea that can be traced to Heraclitus. Returning is the being of that which becomes. The present moment can pass only because it contains past and future. What must be added to Heraclitus is an evolutionary reading of affirma-tion and negation.

Deleuze doesn't quite say the following. To conceive Eternal Return as exact cyclical repetitions involves the idea that we can conceive exactly the same event occurring at two different times. But such a conception is a hopeless abstraction and can't be the basis of Nietzsche's doctrine. We only experience this moment and whatever of the past and future lies in it. There is no problem with the past being present in the moment, leaving traces in it; nor with the future being contained in the moment as the redemption of its fragments. Thus everything "appears" before it appears, so to speak, so that the eternal repetition of the same, i.e., of the mo-ment—which cannot be compared with other moments (even if parts of *it* can be called "other moments," as in dealing with the past) because there is no viewpoint (perspective) outside the moment—is compatible on this reading with the textual resources.

As an ethical doctrine, Deleuze's Eternal Return is a new synthesis: whatever you will, will it in such a way that you can also will its eternal return. Much laziness, stupidity, cowardliness, resentment, and so on, drop out under this construal. Still, reactive forces that are willing to go to the limit of what they can do negatively are not necessarily eliminated by this. A second selection is involved. Reactive forces repeatedly tested against becoming must be destroyed. Nihilism is vanquished by its own reactive nature when tested against constant becoming. Only something that can change its nature, that is, become itself, can survive.

On the optimistic construal, the Eternal Return has little to do with psychology; it has everything to do with the way the Übermensch would experience existence. The pessimism of the cosmological reading is determined in a conjunction of Christian values, fear of the absence of progress, and a view of cyclical time. This cyclical time is not a facile transvaluation of linear time. The same moment doesn't recur at different times; we have rather different moments in which the past is exposed and erased at the same time. This is not the solution of the dwarf. If we could expunge the Christian view of progress, we could leave history, but we would also abandon affirmation. The Übermensch would be adaptively reactive, hardly a realization that could provoke joy, even in terms of the Nietzschean value table. Avoiding the vestiges of past valuations, we still can't avoid despair with respect to the pessimistic interpretation, and if we can avoid the fear that contingency may delay the arrival of the Übermensch, we can't avoid anticipatory joy on the basis of the second interpretation. Thus the two reactions described by Nietzsche seem suspended unless we can find some way of privileging one of these interpretations.

At this point, Nietzsche's perspectivism breaks down. If every human judgment essentially involves a point of view, the effort to transcend humanity by working into the viewpoint of the Übermensch seems to strike a dead end in the exhaustion of our language. Merely surveying, merely transvaluing human value tables, does not force a high enough perspective on us to transcend all human points of view. The uncertainty of the existence of the Übermensch seizes up the machinery of Nietzsche's thought. Neither of these interpretations, the pessimistic nor the optimistic, can "see" the other, can interpret it, or can offer a higher perspective; and neither interpretation can be coherently stated in discursive language. The Übermensch is barely seen to be a possibility, but not a possibility that is also a necessity. If thought is driven to its limits here, it is because thought has risen to the highest consistent perspectival transvaluation and has burst its moorings in an asymptotic apocalypse.

How can we choose between these two theories? As we are in the moment, necessarily, perhaps we never can. That would explain why the reaction is either joy or despair, and why these reactions alternate as dominant. The Eternal Return is the necessary superposition, so to speak, of these two possibilities. *This* is why we can say that the self disappears at the instant of realization, into Dionysian process, in the one case, into the

Übermensch, in the other. When the Eternal Return is realized, in any case, the self disappears; it no longer exists. This is why only the optimistic Zarathustra remains at the end of *Zarathustra*, fading into the Übermensch, his double having disappeared into Dionysian process, but still haunting the book.[20]

Did Nietzsche choose between these two theories? Perhaps he couldn't. Perhaps he stopped speaking because he realized that the moment of experience could never select between these two theories and that the effort to articulate them was equivalent to an *aporia*. The drive for truth was not central to Nietzsche in the form in which such contradictions had to be resolved by evidence. In this sense, Nietzsche had repudiated science. The drive for resolution was also not central to Nietzsche in that he could suspend views whose synthesis would be demanded by the dialectic. It was in this sense that Nietzsche had repudiated Hegel in refusing to be forced toward consistency from the complexity of his feelings. That a regard for consistency might have forced him into a depth quite reminiscent of the suspensions of *Birth* is a sign that his last ten years of silence were of a piece with his first views of the Dionysian.

Cast up by will to power, the thought of the Eternal Return destabilizes itself, coding a necessarily temporary view of eternal process. As a cognitive insight, it maximizes the weight of the past, presenting the possibility that everything might have happened just this way innumerable times already, and then it provides the implosional resources to cast off this heaviest insight. Everything is different and the same; this suspension allows us to suppose counterfactually that everything has always already happened innumerable times this way—the way we're experiencing it— and then to laugh it away. All my lives have been lived and will be lived; there's just no telling what will come next. Even if the same Dionysian state were to recur, it might be interpreted differently. There is therefore no burden of the past and no constraint of the future. We're free because necessarily anything might happen.

Cast up by will to power, the thought of the Eternal Return completes the transvaluation of all values. There are no religious or scientific eternal truths; the Eternal Return must be willed, and rewilled again whenever it recurs, since the last time will have been forgotten. The thought of the Eternal Return must be able to occur at any time; it is not an insight obtained *after* a belief state is reached, and subsequently retained. Its occurrence doesn't *permanently* alter our lives. If we are to live so as to will now to live again this way here *in* Dionysian flux, the Eternal Return cancels the transcendental perspective attempted by Christianity. The Eternal Return cancels a finite past and a finite future, meaning that the present can't be located by an asymmetry in time, thus transvaluing all the relevant religious and scientific tables of value available to Nietzsche. The Eternal Return isn't the abstract negation of other metaphysical doctrines; its corrosive nature can command the label of transvaluation that Nietzsche chose to apply.

If the Hellenic noble and the Übermensch are fictional personae, will to power and the Eternal Return are fictions addressed to *us,* signposts to a transvalued mode of existence. That they end in a destabilized confusion is required by consistency, since otherwise an inadequate language would have written itself into coherence, as Hegel's language attempts to do. Nietzsche diagnosed a greater threat to health, and this is ironically shown by the thin content of his writing. In not explicitly attacking the philosophical succession, he lost the weight of a foundation in a tradition of previously settled doctrine. In deliberately transvaluing in an originating mode, he had to speak like a prophet, producing a vision that must seem obscure in its ordinary language expression. Nietzsche requires more daring interpretation because he attempted to stick with consistency along a course that he knew would ultimately suspend inconsistency with consistency. His sanity became a gift to others; and he achieved the singular status that he sought.

The critical Nietzsche can be devastating. We could surely live better if we were different, especially, as Nietzsche emphasized, if we lived without ressentiment. And Nietzsche makes us aware, perhaps more than any other philosopher, of the precarious value tables and will to power that drive our apparently dispassionate philosophical reflections. Nietzsche does not theorize why the current value table has stood so long, possibly because the clear focus of genealogy loses detail; it loses forms of Christianity and Judaism, for example, that are oppositional to capitalism. Nietzsche's dynamic suspension of will to power and the Eternal Return seemingly provides the existential energy for self-transcendence, but at the expense of flattening out the opposition, and of being unable to suppose that nihilism could also transcend itself in order to hang on for another century. But humans do seem to need to transcend themselves to survive, if current extrapolations from political conflict have any value. Humans are most ridiculous when they are most serious, as at political or religious high moments. Laughter and change are desiderata: that much can be granted outright to Nietzsche.

In the end, however, Nietzsche remained captured by the language that he despised. Flexibility over and against the vagaries of Dionysian flux sounds good in *our* language, but, as we have seen, it is ultimately vacuous. Emphasizing the body sounds good in *our* language, and seems a sensible correction to philosophies of pure reason, but there is no such thing as *the* body. There are various bodies, and some of them don't have the resources to reach health from terminal illness. Therefore, there is also no philosophy of the body any more than there is a philosophy of mind. Nietzsche's philosophy cuts deeper than food faddism, but it can't eradicate pity, which it senses as a crucial problem. Pity, unlike ressentiment, connotes social bonds that Nietzsche fails to theorize. Would healthy Hellenes have to have healthy children? Nietzsche seems tempted by an affirmative answer, and falls into biological naïvete. Life cannot reduce to struggle and self-transcendence: the individualistic element in Nietzsche remains too strong—the symmetric moment to the power of Dionysian flux. Nietzsche was unable to theorize symmetric relationships between men and women, or productive forms of social cooperation and friendship. The Eternal Return can affect only an individual consciousness; it cannot affirm social formations or entire epochs. Those of us who would not emulate Nietzsche's isolation, or his terminal decade of silence, but who are moved by his passionate attacks on prevailing convention should turn to the development of new value tables that transvalue the present inanities of human convention, urged on by a vision of Dionysian flux and grateful for Nietzsche's spur.

Notes

Introduction

1. Nietzsche may have stage-managed his own biography by overdramatizing his illnesses, even in letters to friends, in the service of his doctrine that great accomplishments are born in suffering. See Ehrlich, "Suffering in Nietzsche," for an exploration of this possibility. As Ehrlich notes, we never know when Nietzsche is wearing a mask, or what the mask might be. In spite of Ehrlich's account, it seems reasonable to suppose that no one who has experienced university teaching and bad reviews can be an untempered optimist, and I see no reason to doubt the general claim that Nietzsche's life was subject to prolonged bouts of physical illness, especially eye troubles. The trajectory of Nietzsche's thought to be developed here abstracts from the influence of friends such as Wagner, Paul Rée, and Lou Salomé who undoubtedly caused deviations but do not seem to have altered the general orientation. Whether Nietzsche might have agreed with the developmental plan of his thought proposed here is doubtful, since he probably overestimated the magnitude of local changes in his thinking. It is helpful to remember that Nietzsche was well aware that we have the greatest difficulties in assessing ourselves.

2. In the nineteenth century, German philologists studied all Greek culture, including Greek philosophy. Nietzsche's early work deals importantly with the history of Greek philosophy, and in particular with the texts of Diogenes Laertius, the biographer of Greek philosophers. Nietzsche, who was also familiar with important modern philosophers, later applied for a chair in philosophy, but did not obtain it. Nietzsche's philological contributions are controversial. He is often omitted from histories of German classical scholarship. For positive assessments, see Flashar, Gründer, and Horstmann, *Philologie und Hermeneutik im 19. Jahrhundert,* and Reinhardt, *Vermächtnis der Antike.* O'Flaherty, Sellner, and Helm, *Studies in Nietzsche and the Classical Tradition,* contains articles assuming that Nietzsche's place in scholarship is secure.

On the other hand, no reference to Nietzsche appears in von Wilamowitz-Moellendorff, *History of Classical Scholarship*. This is the same philologist who, early in his career, wrote an extremely negative review of Nietzsche's first book.

3. This useful contrast, suggested by Nietzsche's own reflections on nomad thought, has been developed in lectures by Edward Said.

4. See Nelson, "Nietzsche, Zarathustra, and *Jesus Redivivus:* The Unholy Trinity," for an interesting survey. For a comparison of Nietzsche and Kierkegaard, see Grau, "Nietzsche und Kierkegaard." A consideration of Nietzsche's theology occurs in von der Luft, "Sources of Nietzsche's 'God is Dead!' and Its Meaning for Heidegger." The early study of Nietzsche by Lou Salomé, *Friedrich Nietzsche: The Man in His Works*, emphasizes a religious reading of Nietzsche's works.

5. Can Nietzsche and Marx be reconciled? By pulling the texts of Hegel, Marx, and Nietzsche this way and that, a surprising number of interesting permutations show up. Horkheimer and Adorno ignore Nietzsche's social and political views and use him to attack shallow scientist Enlightenment thought, including positivistic versions of Marxism. Their goal is to generate a more reflective Marxism that one can presumably locate in Marx or most of his followers. Those who see Nietzsche as a profoundly antidialectical thinker, for example Deleuze, may not think that Nietzsche is useful in such a project, retaining the break between Nietzsche's and Marx's conceptions of a better society. Others have argued that Nietzsche's casual acquaintance with true socialism caused him to judge socialism falsely and prevented him from realizing that it is only a socialist society in which true Übermenschen can develop and in which everyone is potentially an Übermensch. This remarkable view, expressed in Koigen, *Die Kulturanschauung des Sozialismus*, requires a determined hermeneutical posture. The same is true of those attempts to argue that Nietzsche is the witting or unwitting apologist of capitalism who prefigures the repressive ideology of Nazism, such as Lukács in *The Destruction of Reason*. Perhaps these possibilities will indicate how complex the issues are, and why we shall have to return to them below.

6. Nietzsche's impact is shown indirectly by the vitriolic disputes between his readers, which are probably not equaled in the secondary literature on any other philosopher. (The secondary literature on Marx and Hegel would have to be considered.) As an introduction to the madcap acerbity characterizing Nietzsche studies, the reader could glance at Nordau, *Degeneration*, p. 417, which argues that Nietzsche's prose is indistinguishable from prose produced by those now recommended for the most serious psychoanalytic treatments, the debate triggered by MacIntyre's "Nietzsche's Titanism," which last argues that Nietzsche went insane from thinking Nietzsche's thoughts, or Dannhauser's "Trivialization of Friedrich Nietzsche," which argues that the modern Derridean readings of Nietzsche have nothing at all to do with Nietzsche, a conclusion also drawn by Fischer with respect to Danto's analytic Nietzsche in his review of Danto's book in *Journal of Philosophy*. Perhaps some of this nastiness is in place (and the validity of these claims is not being assessed here), but when Nietzsche's name is mentioned, the switchboard does light up.

Chapter 1. Greece

1. Winckelmann (Johann Joachim Winckelmann, 1717–1768) wrote extensively on classical art, and especially on the Greek conception of beauty. His conception of ancient art as embodying serenity, elevation, rationality, and simplicity came to be a dominant view concerning what was classical. For Nietzsche's attitude, see paragraph 4 of the section "What I Owe to the Ancients" in *Twilight of the Idols*. Nietzsche's transvaluation of older attitudes is somewhat paralleled by the recent transvaluation of a serious Mozart into a luminous teenager in *Amadeus*. A basic account of the influence of Winckelmann's views on German intellectuals can be found in Butler, *The Tyranny of Greece over Germany*. Lessing's somewhat intuitive differences from Winckelmann (discussed by Butler) should particularly be noted in view of the high regard that Nietzsche had for Lessing.
2. The account given by Dodds, *The Greeks and the Irrational*, stresses the irrational side of Greek life and is more indebted to Nietzsche than the single citation of Nietzsche makes evident. A full discussion of this question would require a consideration of the views of Hamann, Herder, and then such romantics as Hölderlin and Novalis. See the discussion in Baeumer, "Das moderne Phänomen des Dionysischen und seine 'Entdeckung' durch Nietzsche."
3. The negative reviews of *Birth* by his fellow philologists effectively ended the early promise of Nietzsche's academic career. One motive was jealousy. Nietzsche had obtained the chair of philology at Basel on the promise of his talents and the support of his teacher Ritschl before he had completed the doctorate. Reviewers in some cases obviously resented Nietzsche's meteoric academic rise. Others found the polemical role that Schopenhauer and Wagner play in the discussion tasteless, viewing the book as a mixture of (pure) philology and journalism, and as a case of special pleading. Nietzsche may have deliberately provoked this, since he was opposed to the notion of pure philology and to the validity of received scholarship. See the discussion of Nietzsche's philological approach in Birus, "Nietzsche's Hermeneutical Considerations."
4. A psychoanalytic account could be supplemented with anthropological material concerning the importance of dreams in other cultures. All that is necessary to see the importance of Nietzsche's point is that dreams may present or code truths that are not accessible to normal, waking consciousness in our culture without the intervention of efforts at interpretation.
5. Because of music, tragedy is not subject to the full strictures against *linguistic* fiction. Conscious thought, as is well known, is at odds with simultaneous musical performance (although it may be involved in learning performance). What Nietzsche says about temporality and music may seem surprising at first, but it could be set into a coherent aesthetic theory. Although we hear music over time, Nietzsche's point is that we also hear it all at once, the significance of the present note of a melody, for example, being determined by the rest of the notes of the melody. (The Eternal Return is almost prefigured in the response indicated.) In comparison, the viewing of paintings or sculpture is more cognitively integrated over time. Nietzsche suggests that music is

produced by Dionysian process (not by the conscious artist) and that language is inadequate as a means of representing musical feeling.

6. Nietzsche's remarks take into account the absence of musical notation for Greek music. Music was always already Dionysian, involved with the possibilities of bodily movement. Vogel, *Apollinisch und Dionysisch*, argues for the obvious—that Nietzsche's views of Apollo, Dionysus, and Greek music are indeed fictions and that they controvert some of the "facts" of serious classical scholarship.

7. A hint of a treatment of comedy is also sketched at the end of section 7 of *Birth*, comedy providing a way for art to mediate nausea before absurdity. On this view, Apollinian mediation is common to comedy and tragedy, and they are more closely related than their traditional separation in the theater suggests.

8. Nietzsche's views here are primitive. Suffering can confer dignity on humans in both the Judaic and Christian traditions. In the Judaic tradition, suffering as atonement was ennobling, and the successor notion of the imitation of Christ in Christianity also confers dignity on suffering. See Bowker, *Problems of Suffering in Religions of the World,* for a discussion. Nietzsche's polemics against Judaism and Christianity constantly stumble against the problem of variety within these traditions. His views concerning evil are consequently only partly on target. For an extended argument that Nietzsche, although a great philosopher, completely failed to find real Christianity, see Scheler, *Ressentiment.*

9. There is a suspicion that only mechanical careers within science and scholarship can really fall victim to Nietzsche's attacks, although as a statistical matter, most scholars and scientists may not be so far from Nietzsche's portrait. Nietzsche here makes Socrates the focus of his attack, but the complicated relationship between Socrates and Plato means that a reading like Kierkegaard's in *The Concept of Irony* could exempt Socrates and make Plato a more appropriate target. Later in his career, Nietzsche tends to shift his attacks toward Plato and away from Socrates, perhaps because he senses the complications. See Dannhauser, *Nietzsche's View of Socrates,* for an extended discussion.

10. There are many parallels, including the fact that the possibility of talking animals already occurs in *Birth*. The point will be developed below.

Chapter 2. Style

1. Nietzsche explains this in the third essay of *Genealogy of Morals,* an essay that might well be taken as the last meditation of *Untimely Meditations.* But by this point in his career, Nietzsche's pessimism had deepened. He feared that his message, like that of the Hellenic nobles, might not reach his contemporaries and would have to travel over time to reach a respondent thinker uncorrupted by the philistine straitjacket of conventional thought and language. In this sense, the arrows of his aphorisms were being released over the horizon of his time. For an insightful study of the aphorism, see Krüger, *Studien über den Aphorismus als philosophische Form.*

2. David Friedrich Strauss (1808–1874), the subject of attack in the first untimely meditation, was famous at the time for a biography of Jesus, an important fact for grasping Nietzsche's strategy. After hearing Hegel lecture in Berlin, Strauss became a Hegelian theologian. Strauss's first position was at the theological school attached to Tübingen University, where he lectured in philosophy. The philosophy faculty objected, possibly because the lectures were popular with students, and refused Strauss a regular appointment to the philosophy faculty, where he wished to teach. Strauss resigned lecturing in 1833 until the matter could be settled. While free from lecturing duties, Strauss rapidly completed *The Life of Jesus,* which was published in two volumes in 1835 and 1836. Its popular success also made him even more unacceptable for a university post. (There's an ironic parallel here between the career impact of *The Life of Jesus* and *The Birth of Tragedy.*) In 1839, Strauss was appointed to the chair of dogmatics at Zürich. The local peasant population, furious in its understanding of the unorthodox implications of Strauss's biography of Jesus, descended from the surrounding hills armed with sticks, staging a demonstration against the appointment. This demonstration ultimately brought down the Swiss government. (Ideas have consequences. Q.E.D.) The book that Nietzsche attacks comes late in Strauss's career, after Strauss was supporting himself as a freelance writer. Nietzsche, who early in life had been an admirer of the iconoclasm of *The Life of Jesus,* was rendered nauseous by the shallow optimism of the late works. For Nietzsche, repudiation of Christianity should be followed by tragic insight, not by scientific optimism. Nietzsche was also revolted by Strauss's humanism, the idea that there is something unchangeably, inevitably "human" that makes life ultimately justifiable, no matter what. Nietzsche found Strauss's lazy electicism repugnant, as is indicated explicitly in the untimely meditation. Finally, Nietzsche was also attacking someone who had publicly attacked Wagner, and Nietzsche may have been responding to a request from Wagner to balance the books.
3. Considerations of space preclude a study of Nietzsche's attempts to fuse philosophy with poetry. See Grundlehner, *The Poetry of Friedrich Nietzsche.*
4. See also aphorisms 59, 113, 293, 300, 335, 344, 351, 353, 355, 373, and related aphorisms 93 and 270 in *Daybreak.*
5. The third essay of *Genealogy* is an explication of a brief "aphorism" from *Zarathustra* that is quoted at its beginning. See section 8 of Nietzsche's preface to *Genealogy.*
6. If the romantic hero/heroine suffers because of great sensitivity in boorish and crude surroundings, you can tie the young Europeans to romanticism *if* you accept the idea that the young Europeans crave to suffer. The question of whether romantics craved action and were worried about the sufferings of others is also problematic. Further, central romantic writers (Schlegel, Novalis) were not much discussed by Nietzsche. It seems dubious to cite the romantics (or any subset of them) as the specific focus of the attack.
7. There are a few trickier points related to the English translation. Kaufmann's translation runs at one point as follows: "to find in their suffering a probable reason for action." *Probable* doesn't seem right. The sense of the original seems more adequately rendered by replacing *probable* with *convincing.*

8. In *Birth*, scientific culture is traced back to Socrates, who had transvalued the tragic culture he found around him. The scientist or scholar in the resulting scientific culture has no grasp of Dionysian truth. Looking at the imagery of section 15 of *Birth*, we see that scientists as a group will each dig their own holes, gather their own precious stones. A sublime metaphysical illusion, that causality is explanatory, drives scientists again and again to the limits of science, where science would have to turn into art. Science is driven by a mechanism, the utility of individual truth seeking, which disperses scientists in different directions but ultimately prevents them from collectively overstepping the boundaries of science. By contrast, the seekers of a unified culture are united in the direction of their vision, and they stand on the same ground. The seeking of scientists cannot be extended or synthesized into an affirmative culture because their orientations are diverse and their perspectives irreconcilable at the same altitude. If Nietzsche does not permit scientific cooperation, he also fails to recognize that science might become a series of paradigmatic schemata that can adjust to changing data domains in new investigative techniques. Nietzsche's science criticism would have to be rethought in the twentieth century.

In the domain of scholarship, Nietzsche at least managed a critique of his predecessors that can be filled out along orthodox lines. Nietzsche is clearly aware of Kant and Hegel, and in fact prefers Kant's relative clarity. But from Nietzsche's perspective, Kant's position is constrained into a coherence of synthetic a priori rules by privileging abstract scientific knowledge. Kant's epistemology mirrors the tunnel vision of science. No wonder that he is unable to find a connection between phenomenal and noumenal realms, for example; his starting point is too divided, too restricted, too partial. It is not the total human being that generates the rules for Kant, but merely one human faculty. For Nietzsche, the entire bodily experience is involved in the generation of values, and different bodies will generate different schemes of value. Nietzsche's wrath is invoked by the obscurity and eclecticism of Hegel, especially by the emasculated vision of Greece that Hegel attempts to synthesize with Christianity. The notions of absolute spirit and (ultimate) identity of concept and conceptualized, which involve superhuman conceptions of knowledge, obscure the localized human origins or values almost completely. Hegel wants flux *and* certainty; Nietzsche believes that they are contradictory in the sense that philosophers have thought them. If Nietzsche and Hegel abstractly deny the same doctrines of Kant, they wind up in quite different locations. Most secondary sources contain some discussion of Nietzsche's relationship to earlier philosophers. For example, Deleuze, in *Nietzsche and Philosophy*, discusses the relationship of Nietzsche to Kant and Hegel. See also the comments in Breazeale, "The Hegel-Nietzsche Problem." A comprehensive discussion can be found in Kaulbach, *Nietzsches Idee einer Experimentalphilosophie*, and specialized topics are treated in Goedert, "Nietzsche und Schopenhauer," and Kaulbach, "Nietzsche und der monadologische Gedanke." For a recent comparison of Nietzsche to Hegel (one that, contrary to Deleuze, sees Hegel as the more incisive metaphysician), see Houlgate, *Hegel, Nietzsche, and the Criticism of Metaphysics*.

Chapter 3. Prophecy

1. Gary Shapiro, "The Rhetoric of Nietzsche's *Zarathustra*," suggests such an approach.

2. No exposition of Lacan can be attempted here. For access to the fundamental Lacanian view I allude to, see Lacan, *Speech and Language in Psychoanalysis.*

3. There is a shift in German terms here, *Gelehrten* being used instead of *Wissenschaftler,* the latter being the general term for a scientist or scholar usually occurring in Nietzsche's prose. In this context, the former term seems to connote an especially important, revered, and conservative scholar.

4. Later, in *Beyond Good and Evil,* section 58, scholars are presented as dwarfs beneath whom there can be no form of human life. The idea that only personal experience can legitimate judgment, which we met earlier in the second untimely meditation, also appears in *Beyond Good and Evil,* section 204. Nietzsche's (and Zarathustra's) preference for heights can be read, incidentally, as a preference for the perspective of the noble, situated at the top of the social hierarchy.

5. The last phrase in Kaufmann's translation before "Thus spoke Zarathustra"—"And what I want, they would have no right to want"—might seem a little strange. What would "they would have no *right*" mean? This phrase hypostasizes an abstract right, which isn't suggested in the original. "And what I want, they cannot want" seems to make better sense in context.

6. See the detailed discussion in Schlecta, *Nietzsches Grosser Mittag.*

7. Our discussion remains entirely on the surface of portions of Zarathustra's imagery. Higgins, *Nietzsche's Zarathustra,* and Lampert, *Nietzsche's Teaching,* are two recent commentaries on *Zarathustra* worth consulting. Higgins suggests that Part 4 of *Zarathustra* follows the pattern of Menippean satire. An extremely elegant and succinct reading is presented in Gadamer, "The Drama of Zarathustra." Even if no academic chairs devoted to the study of *Zarathustra* have been funded, as Nietzsche once suggested, many problems of interpretation, and some quite unexplored perspectives, remain. For example, the importance of the midnight sun and of mountain top moments of insight in alchemy suggests resonances with *Zarathustra* that haven't been coherently investigated. Whether *Zarathustra* is great literature is controversial; that many of its images remain obscure is hardly controversial. Nietzsche would have enjoyed (and probably intended) the opacity of his text to the learned.

Chapter 4. History

1. Foucault is in more or less complete agreement that the modern subjective personality did not exist before the nineteenth century. See Foucault, *The Order of Things* and *I, Pierre Rivière, having slaughtered my mother, my sister, and my brother . . . : A Case of Parricide in the Nineteenth Century.* In Foucault's view, the modern "confession" develops along with the appropriate subjectivity. Horkheimer and Adorno single out Odysseus as offering a presentiment of the modern personality type. This type spreads through the

population with the development of early capitalism. Jaynes, in *The Origins of Consciousness in the Breakdown of the Bicameral Mind*, has an even earlier date, but a slightly different project, as he is looking for the origins of one form of consciousness, not necessarily a modern personality type. All these studies are compatible with Nietzsche's observations that a modern subjectivity is quite incommensurable with Hellenic tragic culture. The talk of instincts becoming second nature in section 3 of Nietzsche's text can be regarded as an adumbration of the development of the notion of the unconscious.

2. Here is a point of application for Nietzsche's appeal to movements of self-expression. For Nietzsche's impact on modern educational reform, see Cooper, *Authenticity and Learning*. Nietzsche's call for self-development was often picked up by progressive circles whose ideology was otherwise apparently inconsistent with Nietzsche's views. See Thomas, *Nietzsche in German Politics and Society 1890–1918*, for an account of Nietzsche's use by German socialist and feminist theoreticians.

3. Nausea in the face of modern life is later taken up by the Frankfurt School and by Heidegger. The suggestion that people are interchangeable, without true centers, appears in Frankfurt School analysis in terms of an image of people as Yale locks, with private combinations, i.e., soulless machines performing similar functions. Conformity and pseudoindividuality are discussed extensively in the section of *Dialectic of Enlightenment* called "The Culture Industry." See Adorno and Horkheimer, *Dialectic of Enlightenment*, pp. 120–67 (the Yale lock image appears on p. 154). Authenticity is discussed extensively by Heidegger in contrast to the inauthentic nature of normal, everyday life. See, for example, section 38, "Falling and Thrownness," in *Being and Time*, pp. 219–24 (English translation). Adorno and Horkheimer were pointed in a quite different direction from Heidegger. See the critique of Heidegger in Adorno, *The Jargon of Authenticity*.

4. Nietzsche's attractiveness to some philosophers has been his refusal to specialize, his insistence that philosophy maintain the widest possible scope of personal interest combined with lightness of scholarship. Löwith, a German Nietzsche scholar, objected to considering Nietzsche along with Marx and Freud as modern *philosophers* of suspicion. For Löwith, Marx is an economist who sees philosophy as a form of ideology. Freud is a psychologist who sees philosophy from the outside, as a form of rationalization. Nietzsche also seems to see philosophy as a psychologist, however, philosophical systems being apologetics for previously selected value tables. In any event, Nietzsche does not appear, as Freud and Marx do, in any standard histories of scientific disciplines, unless hermeneutics be considered a science. For a discussion, see Ijsseling, *Rhetoric and Philosophy in Conflict*, especially chapter 13, pp. 92–102.

5. The scholar is a eunuch rather than a woman.

6. Popper, for example, who believes in historical laws, finds the following to be of interest: "You cannot make a revolution without causing a reaction," and "You cannot, in an advanced industrial society, organize consumers' pressure groups as effectively as you can organize certain producers' pressure groups."

Humans act in such a dizzying variety of ways (despite culture, ideology, lack of resources) that no interesting historical laws of unrestricted scope have been formulated to date. For references and a discussion, see Ackermann, *The Philosophy of Karl Popper,* p. 171.

7. The mechanism is obvious. As religion is compartmentalized, and religious needs appear only among other needs, the drive toward institutional power produces compromise statements embracing hostile dogmata. The result is religion presented in the guise of advertising trivialities. See Luckmann, *the Invisible Religion,* and Ackermann, *Religion as Critique,* for detailed discussion.

8. Quantum and relativity physics produced breaks with past science and have brought to scientific consciousness the idea that scientific progress is probably not ongoing and cumulative. A more complicated but persuasive view is maintained in Bellone, *A World on Paper,* where it is argued that revolution in physics reaches back to the nineteenth century. Nietzsche could not have been aware of this, although the situation is compatible with Nietzsche's view of historiography. Nietzsche's blanket view of science must be revised against these developments.

9. See the introduction to Kenner's translation of Hartmann, *The Sexes Compared* (and other essays). Darnoi, *The Unconscious and Eduard von Hartmann,* is another useful source of information.

10. See von Rahden, "Eduard von Hartmann und Nietzsche." Apparently Nietzsche had read Stirner and accepted his individualist anarchy as a move away from Hegel's absolutism. See Schulte, *"Ich impfe euch mit dem Wahnsinn"* (pp. 53–61). In spite of suggestive parallels, Stirner's egoistic idealism is not consilient with many of Nietzsche's most important opinions.

Chapter 5. Transvaluation

1. See aphorism 335, where Nietzsche suggests that "know thyself" must mean "know the world," as we are furthest from an understanding of ourselves. Honesty compels us to turn to physics or chemistry. *Physics* connotes the study of nature as the only source of knowledge that can solve the problem of what we should do, and the Eternal Return will indicate the shape of the new physics. Nietzsche felt that physical laws would change with Dionysian process over time.

2. This is explained in advance in section 6 of "Reason in Philosophy," which just precedes this passage in *Twilight of the Idols.*

3. Hermeneutical theorists divide between those who think that definitive readings are possible, for example by discerning authorial intention or utilizing interpretive rules, and those who argue that readings are always vector resolutions between a reader and a text at a point in time, none of the readings having a timeless validity. An objectivist version of the latter possibility is developed (from Nietzschean roots) by Heidegger and then Gadamer, who argue that meanings are projected from a text by a suitably educated reader, but that the process of conflating these meanings into a final consistent reading cannot be completed.

4. See the list provided by Nietzsche in aphorism 201 of *Beyond Good and Evil*.

5. We have had this image of scientists and scholars as mechanisms before, for example in "On Scholars" in *Zarathustra*. A newer image would involve a computer metaphor, no doubt, but this hardly changes the nature of the problem that Nietzsche alludes to. Early philosophy of science, based on the suggestion that a methodology of science could be isolated and exploited to explain scientific progress, was ruled by a positive valuation of emotion-free science, providing a caricature of Nietzsche's caricature. In recent years, the idea of complete scientific objectivity has come under attack in forms that provide an ironic vindication of Nietzsche's intuitions.

6. Out of compulsion, it needs to be noted again that Nietzsche's charges seem only to apply to routine science and not to revolutionary episodes in scientific thought. No set of rules can fix the direction of scientific advance, a point now conceded almost universally by philosophers of science, even if some social steering of scientific goals is conceded.

7. Many similar views with some uncanny parallels, such as references to Greek supremacy, were expressed by Oscar Wilde. See the essay "The Soul of Man under Socialism." This can be found in Wilde, *The Artist as Critic* (pp. 255–89). Convergence of opinion between Wilde and Nietzsche has frequently been noted in the secondary literature on Nietzsche.

8. Secularization is discussed in Luckmann, *The Invisible Religion,* and Ackermann, *Religion as Critique,* along lines indicating that Nietzsche's intuitions are still compatible with current empirical research.

9. Nietzsche has in mind the religion seminars of the German university and the presence of scholar-theologians in this academic context.

10. The hammer of philosophers, mentioned here but developed more extensively elsewhere, is used not to smash things but to tap them to see if they are hollow. Nietzsche's view that nihilism stems from attempting to stabilize a detached value table is illustrated by his brief critique of Kant in sections 10 through 12 of *The Antichrist*. Kant's philosophical morality is a partial paralysis of reason in the service of an insidious theology, and its acceptance with jubilation was at the hands of those with a vested interest in the retention of the Christian value table. Kant's defense of the "true" world was to argue not for its provability but for the fact that it couldn't be refuted. For Nietzsche, of course, foundational values are neither provable nor refutable, so this maneuver is trivial. Virtues are taken by Kant to be legitimately proven only insofar as they are prompted by a feeling of respect for the *concept* of virtue, shifting the attachment of will from Dionysian process onto the preservation and extension of abstract fictions. As mechanisms of duty, our desires and pleasures are cut off from a healthy motivational link to action.

Kant's attempt to suspend science and Christianity and Hegel's attempt to synthesize Greek and Christian values are phony patchworks (for Nietzsche) based on entirely conventional readings of sources. We cannot deduce from a value table whether an affirmative or reactive use of the table is being made by a person who accepts it. Affirmative use can be made of both the Greek vision and the Christian or scientific vision. Socrates and Plato had effected a transvaluation that was at first affirmative. An affirmative use is one that develops a position of constantly increasing sensitivity to the world around us. The actual universe is a universe of Dionysian process, a fact that is not denied by Plato or Socrates. Platonism, however, supposes that this universe of Dionysian flux is too unstable to be knowable and opposes to it an intelligible world of forms that can bring an epistemology to bear on the world of flux. Nietzsche would agree that the world of flux is not (epistemologically) knowable; it is to be experienced, felt, lived in. As long as the world of being interprets the world of becoming, Platonism and its legacy can be affirmative. The internal rot in its conception is that by postulating the world of being, the will may be deflected to the exploration and defense of this fictional surrogate, and, in coming to regard this as the world that is real, produces an attitude to the actual world of flux that is negative and reactive. Nietzsche is simply willing to give up the pretense that certain knowledge is obtainable.

Chapter 6. Morality

1. Histories of value theories often note that philosophers made valuations as early as the Greeks, often valuing the permanent over the transitory, and so forth. Greek philosophers valued the good and attempted to explain the nature of what is good, and Aristotle even intimates a notion of economic exchange value, but none of this adds up to a general theory of value. By Nietzsche's time, and partly because of a tradition in economics that develops theories of value in the hope of explaining all possible exchange transactions, philosophers began to speak of general theories of value, theories that would include aesthetic, moral, economic, and other values, in a general theory of preference. Exactly how and when such general theories arose is not at all clear, but it is clear that the theories were meant to locate objective values, especially those with economic roots. Nietzsche seems aware of this, but it seems not to be known at present what the history of general value theories is, or what specific contributions Nietzsche may have made to this history. In the economic and philosophical literature, general theories of value seem to have waned with the general consensus that interpersonal comparisons of utility are impossible.

2. Gadamer's *Truth and Method,* an approach to hermeneutics heavily dependent on Heidegger and, in turn, on Nietzsche, insists that we must go out from our current understanding in order to assimilate texts from other historical locations in a meaningful way and suggests that we can find more and more sophisticated readings of important texts over time, without ever locating provably correct readings. When we approach a text, our existence already in the world causes meanings to appear that we can refine and relate over time. We always start from the perspective that we happen to have, but interaction with the text can force us to higher perspectives. The emphasis on language as defining the hermeneutical project has Nietzschean roots. Current struggles to find an objectivity that is not provably true, but also not merely an expression of personal bias, a struggle carefully and coherently undertaken by Gadamer, is indebted to Nietzsche's perspectivism as mediated through Heidegger. It is the possibility of self-transcendence in front of texts that yields the possibility

of such a hermeneutics and avoids an empty relativism. This idea appears elsewhere without mention of Nietzsche. For example, in the philosophy of science, Kuhn's effort in the 1969 postscript to the second edition of *The Structure of Scientific Revolutions* (pp. 174–210) to argue that there isn't a standpoint outside of science for measuring scientific progress, so that progress is simply what happens when criticism, new ideas, and new instruments change things, relies on a thoroughly Nietzschean notion of objectivity.

3. Nietzsche at times attacks various anti-Semites and forms of anti-Semitism in his writings, but interpretation must also confront his blanket and unnuanced condemnation of the role of Jews in the religious development of the table of good and evil in passages such as this one. There is no intention in paraphrasing Nietzsche here to suggest that his views can be defended or that his genealogies are acceptable as they stand. It is also obvious that Nietzsche assumes, rather than proves, a deep identity between Socratic and priestly morality. For a recent discussion of Nietzsche's attitudes, see Heller, "Nietzsche and the Jews." A tracing of shifts in Nietzsche's attitudes against the expected background of prejudice and an incorporation of the influence of his Jewish friends can be found in Bergmann, *Nietzsche, "The Last Antipolitical German."*

4. Nietzsche notes the horror of the German barbarian exhibited by late Roman civilization, so the question of reference is complicated. See Brennecke, "Die blonde Bestie. Vom Mißverständnis eines Schlagworts," and Pütz, "Das Problem der Gewalt bei Nietzsche und seinen Rezipienten."

5. Differences of opinion among early theologians are not considered by Nietzsche who selects Tertullian, his best case, rather than someone like Origen.

6. Scheler, *Ressentiment*, p. 82. Nietzsche attacks Christianity explicitly, and Scheler is defending it. A similar defense of Judaism to the implied Nietzschean attack is also possible. For a discussion of Scheler and Nietzsche, see Gans, "The Culture of Resentment." Girard, "Dionysus versus the Crucified," argues that ressentiment can only flourish where primitive vengeance (a more powerful force) has sufficiently weakened. In a curious argument from a sensitive philosopher, Foot argues that Nietzsche must be an immoralist because he separates justice and morality although they are inevitably conceptually linked. See Foot, "Nietzsche: The Revaluation of Values," p. 166.

7. Nietzsche's reduction of Christianity to a single value table is crude scholarship, indicating an emotional attitude that was never completely overcome in the projected new value table.

8. This idea was taken up again by Critical Theory, and can be found in such sources as Horkheimer, "The End of Reason." Many critics of Critical Theory have argued that part of the practice of everyday life consists in a recognition and distancing from social control, no matter how conformist behavior is, so that revolutionary potential is uniformly higher than the pessimism of Horkheimer and Adorno (and Nietzsche) could grant.

9. The basic argument of Girard, *Violence and the Sacred,* is quite consistent with Nietzsche's intuitions. Girard argues that cycles of revenge threatened to cause chaos in primitive societies, since the two sides involved would probably not agree that equal payments had been made by both sides at any point.

The penal code defines a social notion of equal payment, backed by societal sanctions, so that the full force of social constraint can be brought to bear if the cycle isn't terminated after a legal judgment.

10. An example of Nietzsche's contemporary influence is his well-known appropriation by Foucault. The interpretation of Nietzsche by contemporary French philosophers has taken on a life of its own—and it is not always related carefully to the full range of Nietzsche's texts. Foucault works, early in his writings, especially, with two important notions: that of *archaeology* and that of *genealogy*. Although much in these notions is traced to Nietzsche, it is in fact the case that Foucault's notion of *archaeology* seems closer to what Nietzsche meant by genealogy than does Foucault's notion of *genealogy*. This point is easily obscured by the apparent identity of the term *genealogy* in the two contexts and by the fact that Foucault invokes Nietzsche more directly on those occasions when he is discussing his term *genealogy*, particularly in the essay "Nietzsche, Genealogy, History." (This is translated on pp. 139–64 of Foucault, *Language, Counter-Memory, Practice*.) Foucault's use of the terms *archaeology* and *genealogy* is not based on a rigid conceptual distinction. Insofar as Foucault is looking for a new methodology to study the complicated relationship of knowledge and power in modern society and is tracing the history of these complicated relationships, he *tends* to use the term *archaeology* when analyzing knowledge and the term *genealogy* when analyzing power. *Archaeology* turns up primarily in connection with documents, with discourses, whose meaning is not in any way to be assumed known. The word connotes digging up physical objects with no known meanings. These objects are to be best interpreted on the surface, by direct comparison, rather than through a hypothetical system of meanings, a move reminiscent of certain themes in Nietzsche's hermeneutics. The meaning of such objects shift over time in such a complex pattern that their origins are of little significance. Objects have histories of use surrounded by wildly different fields of meaning. Genealogy traces the confused and shifting spaces within which archaeological texts are always situated—recognizing that these texts are always situated with respect to complicated power relationships involving power centers eager to interpret texts to their own ends, or to create new texts. Let's look for a moment at the essay "Nietzsche, Genealogy, History." It opens:

Genealogy is gray, meticulous, and patiently documentary. It operates on a field of entangled and confused parchments, or documents that have been scratched over many times. (P. 139)

The field of documents seems to be what archaeology attempts to provide. To say that genealogy is gray seems to say that it results in no clear (black and white) discoveries of meanings. It can find no origins that yield concepts or institutions interpretable as directed toward final ends. Beginnings are obscure and slow and are subject to shocks of change before what exists can take on a significant contemporary meaning. We can talk about the sudden appearance (*Entstehung*) of something and its descent to the present without the presumption that we are going back to absolute beginnings. What is the relationship of genealogy to history? The genealogist is always "at the surface" and does not and cannot assume a suprahistorical perspective. In recording the eruptions and shifts of power and knowledge, genealogy writes "effective history"—a history that recognizes no absolutes, no eternal truths, no immortal souls, no continuing consciousness, no goals in history, and even more important—no constant human body with a natural stock of sensations and feelings. In spite of the verbal agreement between Nietzsche and Foucault on many points, it seems clear on reading Foucault's historical studies that they differ remarkably from Nietzsche's. Nietzsche's three essays in *Genealogy* have little to do with historical detail of the kind that abounds in Foucault's studies. Is it that Nietzsche's enormous erudition is carried more lightly than Foucault's and that Nietzsche's perspective is therefore "higher"? Nietzsche confronts us with breaks in history, transvaluations, before and after which there is less homogeneity than there seems to be in Foucault's history. Every age contains the capacity for a return to the past. The great moral systems of good/bad, good/evil confront one another as workable essences in Nietzsche's useful history, although their detailed instantiations are confused. Nietzsche didn't cheat: he acknowledged that his histories were also will to power. Foucault wants to say that there are no essences, not even useful "ideal types" for consideration, thus smoothing Nietzsche into a metaphysical straitjacket, but he also believes that he can write a history without theory. Foucault believes that he can "see" how things are, and that a monumental piling up of texts and observations will make it clear what he sees. Derrida has provided an apparently incisive critique of Foucault's attempt to write a history of madness, a history that always falters on the point that history must be written in the language of reason. Even if one consciously writes a history of silences and not a history of psychiatric discourse, the problem remains. The silences are the negations of spaces of reasons assumed in the master's language, but they can't truly be represented in that language. (See Derrida, "Cogito and the History of Madness," and the reply by Foucault appended to the second French edition of *Madness and Civilization*.) Foucault never leaves the house of scholarship. He tries to find a unique and superior place within it by locating a new method and a new form of discourse, but his appeal is precisely to Nietzsche's scientists. A glance at his referential apparatus will make that plain. Nietzsche is lighter because he leaves the house of scholarship by his own admission and by his own practice. He writes for all but, more important in this respect, for none. Only a free spirit could dispense with evidence, knowing that it wouldn't prove the truth of any narrative account. Ultimately, that's why it's possible to summarize most of Foucault's books, in spite of their wealth of detail, whereas Nietzsche's work resists compression.

Chapter 7. Society

1. This is a bit summary in judgment, since we're rushing toward Nietzsche. The problem with industry and technology from an anarchist point of view is that the permanence of equipment over time produces a hysteresis in reaction that inevitably connotes planning if the equipment is to be used in some optimal way. This is, of course, not a logical certainty, since luck can always defeat careful planning—with a little luck.

2. It's hardly ever noticed that models of capitalism are in a sense holistic. A slight change in the price of a commodity, for example, causes instantaneous shock waves throughout the system. Many of the theorems cannot be worked through unless there is a body of entrepreneurs in struggle with one another (perfect competition). It is misleading that exposition often starts with individuals in competition, because that is both a mathematical convenience and part of the ideology. Students of these models are encouraged to imagine themselves winners.

3. Nietzsche's critique of surrounding society and emergent socialism, coupled with the aesthetic aspects of his writings, can be urged to fit (unconsciously, perhaps) into a negative bourgeois reaction to progressive historical movements that threatened the position of the bourgeoisie, or at least of certain bourgeois elements. If some have seen Nietzsche as sharing romantic nausea over an emerging industrialization and economization of life in Europe, Marxists have seen him frequently as a figure of bourgeois reaction against an emerging proletariat, especially interesting because his sensitivity was not mediated by conscious apologetics. Such an approach makes irrationalism a general philosophical posture in the face of a world no longer comprehensible and makes Nietzsche an important figure within the irrationalism associated with a world turning opaque to bourgeois sensibility. Lukács provides perhaps the most straightforward and interesting example of this strategy in a long study designed to trace philosophical irrationalism as the bourgeois philosophical reaction to the emerging triumph of dialectical materialism. (See Lukács, *The Destruction of Reason*.) Although natural sciences continued to develop after Hegel, bourgeois philosophy seemed to enter a crisis phase in Europe. The conservative polemics of bourgeois philosophy are at first directed toward attacking materialism (a surrogate for science) or dialectics (a surrogate for socialism). Schelling and Schopenhauer belong to this phase. As the increasing strength of the proletariat leads to a more convincing socialism, bourgeois apologetics must attack it directly, rather than attacking its philosophical representatives. The major problem with singling out Nietzsche as a philosopher whose life work was a polemic against Marxist socialism would seem to be that Nietzsche appears not to have read Marx, and mentions socialism explicitly only on limited occasions. Lukács's charming answer to this problem is a dose of the dialectic: all content in philosophy is determined by the situation in class struggle, and Nietzsche's content, even if not consciously worked out in terms of class struggle, is no exception. Nietzsche felt the emergent outlines of imperialism and recognized the significance of a brutal capitalist economic struggle for the mandarin privileges of philosophy and its associated intelligentsia. Nietzsche's combination of subtle feelings and outbursts of brutality are taken by Lukács as typical signs of decadence. (See Lukács, *Destruction*, pp. 309–99.) Nietzsche's philosophy is designed to rescue and redeem bourgeois intellectual self-understanding. A revolution is projected that will save the intelligentsia first and foremost. In fact, it is precisely from the decadence of the intelligentsia that a renewal of humankind could be projected. Culture was the center of the problem; politics and economics always appear on a remote, abstract horizon. Even some

"progressive" socialist intellectuals were seduced by the apparent center of culture. Nietzsche expresses precisely the lasting features of reactionary attitudes to the imperialist period. Nietzsche's aphorisms could be shunted about more cleverly than pieces of a system (such as Hegel's) in order to mobilize philosophical resources for this fight. Nietzsche was no "innocent" thinker; there are none. Nietzsche's antisystem was a splendid political weapon, since the great idealist systems had to crash in view of the critique provided by dialectical materialism. But Nietzsche's aphorisms can be fit (contrary to his intention!) into a systematic coherence. Nietzsche's early influence was Prussian patriotism—stressing discipline. Nietzsche went back to Greece—emphasizing that slavery is essential to any real civilization. He found parallels between Greek and Prussian discipline. This mixture of ideas is flatly opposed to the social views of apologists for the French Revolution. Nietzsche wishes to contrast a great bygone era with the present and dares to suggest that Germany (Prussia) could recover the past. The young Nietzsche makes the contest (*agon*) central to a healthy society, in this case mythicizing capitalist competition. The contest created superior types, thus fueling the welfare of the whole. This is contrasted with flabby and forgiving modern democracy and its rampant civility—the need to avoid aggressively putting oneself forward in real tests of strength. Wagner, Schopenhauer, and others gradually have been moved by social pressure into the circle of democratic decadents. Nietzsche took the outlines of his superior type from the decadent intellectual. This is why a morality appears in the collapse of Christianity into nihilism, and why Nietzsche is no simple decadent. The insertion of Dionysus as the god in this system allows Nietzsche's social and political consequences to appear in a kind of haze. Nietzsche's atheism is an attempt to combat socialism, which he sees as arising from this sequence:

Christianity→French Revolution→Democracy→Socialism.

New kinds of domination produced by transcendence inside the species are required to prevent this dreary spectacle. (Couldn't socialists agree?) Nietzsche thought that his (contemporary) surrounding "democratic leaders" were too politically conservative and accommodating to be anything but a disaster. The Eternal Return (in terms of its ideological significance) amounts to the denial that history could produce anything that was new in principle. (The Third Reich could itself be seen as a renewal of ancient racial energies.) A correct coupling of being and becoming, freedom and necessity, required the materialist linkage of Marxism:

The epistemological appeal to adopt the most extreme irrationalism, to deny completely all knowability of the world and all reason, coupled with a moral appeal to all the bestial and barbaric instincts, is an—unconscious—admission of this position. Nietzsche's uncommon gift is manifest in his ability to project, on the threshold of the imperialist period, a counter-myth that could exert such influence for decades. Viewed in this light, his aphoristic mode of expression appears the form adequate to the socio-historical situation. (Lukács, *Destruction*, p. 395)

But if Nietzsche is to be accused of ideology, Lukács can only avoid the same fate on the improbable defense that he has located absolute truth. Lukács gives a reason not to read Nietzsche that is determined by his own polemical purposes, in spite of the shrewd interpretive thrusts that occur in his exploration. The selection of textual material is as sporadic as that provided by Nazi editors, however, and Lukacs's treatment provides very little detailed discussion of specific passages from Nietzsche. An interesting effort to provide a sophisticated development from Lukács's point of view can be found in Mattenklott, "Nietzsches 'Geburt der Tragödie' als Konzept einer bürgerlichen Kulturrevolution." Recent east European views concerning Nietzsche are summarized in Behler, "Nietzsche in der marxistischen Kritik Osteuropas."

A sophisticated Marxist positioning of Nietzsche, coupled with textual sensitivity, can be found in Nietzsche's utilization by Critical Theory. Adorno, in particular, was subtly influenced by Nietzsche even if there is little sustained explicit discussion of Nietzsche in Adorno. (See Rose, *The Melancholy Science*, pp. 17–25, for a discussion, and also Miller, "Some Implications of Nietzsche's Thought for Marxism," esp. p. 36.) Adorno's description of *Minima Moralia* as "the melancholy science," for example, is a play on the title *The Gay Science,* and Adorno's aphorisms are obviously indebted to Nietzsche. The affirmative side of Nietzsche is rejected by Adorno, who considered it inappropriate in the Nazi era. (Both he and Horkheimer recognized that Nietzsche's Nazi appropriation was ridiculous, but they were concerned with possibly misleading appearances.) Adorno and Horkheimer were fascinated with the aphoristic repudiation of systematic truth and the use of aphorisms to open quick insights through apparent paradox. Adorno and Horkheimer were concerned to attack systematic Marxism. Nietzsche provides an important theoretical purchase point for a critique of socialist rigidity. Critical Theory wrestled with the problem of whether fascism, unanticipated as a social formation by early Marxist theoreticians, was a desperate form of late capitalism or a distorted form of early socialism. Their theoretical relationship to fascism was more complex than Lukács's, a fact allowing Critical Theory to fit Nietzsche into a more interesting location than that of an irrationalist. Horkheimer and Adorno trace three lines of philosophical development from Kant, whose critical theory is an important pivot point in all three lines. (See Adorno and Horkheimer, *Dialectic of Enlightenment,* pp. 101–3.) The three lines of development they discuss are:

1) Kant→Fichte→Schelling→Hegel→Later Philosophy (including Schopenhauer and Nietzsche)

This line of development is what is emphasized in purely philosophical history, Nietzsche representing an existential reaction to Hegel's system. Heidegger's study would also belong to the development of this sequence, as Nietzsche is considered by Heidegger to be a philosopher arguing within the Western metaphysical tradition.

2) Kant→Hegel→Marx

This line of development is a critique of the first line, a critique that is oriented toward socialist practice, and argues that the standard history of philosophy tends inevitably toward pure theorizing without consideration of practice. Perhaps inevitably, this critique contains the danger of also falling back into a rigid theoretical structure. Lukács, who also belongs here, shows this in his treatment of Nietzsche, in spite of his own philosophical flexibility with respect to other Marxist philosophical ideologues. Emphasis on this line of development requires positioning Nietzsche as a cranky right-wing reactionary figure who is seen as a fascist precursor, fascism itself being regarded without ambiguity as a last, desperate form of the capitalist social formation.

3) Kant→Sade→Nietzsche

This line of development provides a self-critique of the "rationality" central to the first and second lines. This line also contains the danger of a terminating rigidity, a justification of fascism, but it provides at the same time in its antisystematic thrust the most powerful critique of positivist, systematic, mechanical Marxism. Kant's contradictions allow a vision of utopia, but its full recognition is blurred by an irrational component. Science, which is analyzed by Kant's epistemology, is ultimately controlled by irrationally postulated religious impulses. Sade abandons the control of religious impulses, allowing scientific inquiry to be directed to any postulated end and to be used to overtly plan and coordinate any human grouping. With the irrationality of religious control frankly confronted, the full potential of instrumental rationality comes into view. The coordination required by an orgy, maximizing the joint use of the bodies involved, fades into the coordination of the factory assembly line. Control is steered rationally, and the full repressive horror of total rationality is laid out in a consistent philosophical metaphysics. Sade, however, only (ultimately) negates Christianity, in showing its values to be arbitrarily selected, thus staying within the boundaries of the same discourse. Nietzsche, in attempting to break these boundaries and justify an alternative, adopts a biologism legitimating the rule of the strongest. Science may be called in to assist the strong, even if (as in fascism) the overt ideology happens to be egalitarian, that is, egalitarian with the führer removed from the structure. Nietzsche's critique cuts deeper than Sade's, but ambiguities resulting from the looseness of the meaning of *strength* mean that he can't avoid fascist appropriation. Nietzsche is a valuable pivot point for correcting the positivism latent in the second line of development. In particular, Nietzsche anticipates the use of the culture industry (making an appearance as journalism in his time) for political domination, and he anticipates the flattening of evaluation entailed by economism. This enormously suggestive idea, that various lines of development can be traced from Kant and articulated against one another, wasn't developed in detail by Adorno and Horkheimer. (Chances are that the idea of taking Sade seriously as a philosopher has dulled the enthusiasm of even the deviant for working on this project.) With respect to the relationship of Critical Theory to Nietzsche, this is surely the high point of sophistication. Later, Habermas also took up Nietzsche, but with the judgment that Nietzsche had been guilty of a crippling self-misunderstanding. Habermas relies in critique on a privileged notion of disembodied discursive rationality that is so obviously at odds with Nietzschean perspectivism that Nietzsche must give way. It would be interesting to add Habermas to the second line of development mentioned above, as providing a rational system within which all the pieces of society can be fit, and then working out a continuation of the third line of development as a critique of Habermas's rationality. There are signs that this is happening in a critical confrontation between Habermas and recent French writers influenced by Nietzsche, but a consideration of the tea leaves in this cup would lose firm touch with the Nietzsche scholarship that is our focus.

4. This may explain why Plato comes into such sharp focus as an object of attack in *Birth* and remains a special object of criticism throughout Nietzsche's career. Platonic metaphysics requires Nietzsche's attack, but a special edge to the criticism may lie in the fact that Plato is the one previous social and political philosopher of prominence that Nietzsche most needed to displace from the conceptual location that he had discovered.

5. Weber was obviously deeply influenced by Nietzschean critiques of liberalism. See Eden's study, *Political Leadership and Nihilism*, esp. pp. 72–97. Eden's Nietzschean political vision calls for a revision in society led by philosophers at the cutting edge of scientific inquiry, but Eden (and Weber) tempers this into a reformism that is somewhat at odds with the more apocalyptic vision offered here. The impact of Nietzsche on Weber is also discussed in William Shapiro, "The Nietzschean Roots of Max Weber's Social Science," and Nietzsche's impact on sociology is studied in Baier, "Die Gesellschaft—ein langer Schatten des toten Gottes." The relationship between Nietzsche and modern political philosophy is studied in articles by Eden and Waite in *Nietzsche heute*, ed. Bauschinger, Cocalis, and Lennox.

Bergmann's *Nietzsche, "the Last Antipolitical German"* discusses Nietzsche's attack on the political, an attack based on fear that the enlargement of politics would be at the expense of culture when the state became strong enough to regulate culture. Bergmann relates Nietzsche's biography to surrounding political events. Mitchell, "Grounds and Foundations of a Social Theory in Nietzsche's Philosophy," is an attempt to locate a Nietzschean social and political philosophy from textual fragments.

Chapter 8. Women

1. Schulte, *"Ich impfe euch mit dem Wahnsinn."*
2. See, for example, Schutte, *Beyond Nihilism: Nietzsche without Masks*. Schutte's charges are often muted, but see p. xi and numerous other passages through the book. For a discussion, see Eden's review. For a quite different approach, reminiscent of earlier feminist attempts to enlist Nietzsche in a revolutionary transvaluation of current relationships, see Parsons, "Nietzsche and Moral Change."
3. From the last paragraph of Schopenhauer's essay "On Women," quoted here from the Modern Library translation, included in *Studies in Pessimism*.
4. See the discussion in Argyros, "Daughters of the Desert," p. 32.
5. The absence of complexity in expository literature is sufficiently indicated by the following passage in Garland and Garland, *The Oxford Companion to German Literature*, p. 639. After describing Nietzsche as a schizophrenic whose public gentleness was compensated for by a fantasy life of brutality, the text continues: "Other of the less attractive features [of Nietzsche] (his attitude to women and particularly the fantasies of taking a whip to them) are

attempts to compensate for his own inadequacy in his personal relations."
The possible ambiguities in the phrase "taking a whip to them" pretty well
disappears on this reading. (The phrase in square brackets has been added to
make the quotation readable out of context.) Such a reading also glosses over
Nietzsche's intellectual relationships with various women, notably Lou Salomé.

6. See aphorism 131 of *Beyond Good and Evil*.
7. Oliver, "Woman as Truth in Nietzsche's Writing," discusses three kinds of
women noted in Nietzsche, an approach taken over from Derrida's in *Spurs*.
8. There is a suggestion of a pun here, since *truth* (*Wahrheit*) is a feminine noun
in German, but this can't be rendered in English.
9. Those who do not read German should know that Übermensch connotes a
transcendent human being, and not a transcendent male human being, as far
as grammar is concerned. One problem is that the solitude of the Übermensch
does not permit a companion, male or female, an aspect of the vague description of this creature.
10. Heidegger's reading of self-control or self-overcoming stresses that if you
don't control yourself, you will experience external control. Whether Heidegger can interpret something called *the* will to power in Nietzsche, or whether
this doctrine is pluralistic, as is supposed here, is discussed by Müller-Lauter
in *Nietzsche,* as well as in his article "Das Willenswesen und der Übermensch.
Ein Beitrag zu Heidegger's Nietzsche-Interpretationen." See also the comments by Weischedel in "Der Wille und die Willen." No summary of this
length can do justice to the complexity of Heidegger's discussion, but we can
highlight a few of its features. One of Heidegger's achievements, quite independent of one's valuation of other aspects of his treatment of Nietzsche, is to
argue that the Eternal Return and the drive to the Übermensch (buttressed by
the will to power) are compatible doctrines. Before Heidegger, it had seemed
to many commentators that if the Eternal Return meant that there was never
anything new under the sun, it was silly and inconsequential to issue a call for
precisely what was to be something new, the Übermensch. Heidegger's exposition resolves this problem, showing that the Eternal Return can only be
grasped from the point of view of will to power. From that point of view, the
Eternal Return is the fictional belief that can be used to work out or effect the
transvaluation of all values requisite to the appearance of the Übermensch.
Heidegger's critique of the supposed opposition between these doctrines is
based on the idea that those seeing an opposition are employing a notion of
Eternal Return based on a point of view transcending time, which is an
impossibility for Nietzsche (as it is for Heidegger). The Eternal Return teaches
that there is no time between moments; there is only the moment of experience. With the disappearance of the viewpoint of abstract scientific intel-
ligence, all linear measures of time become incomprehensible.

A more controversial question is whether Heidegger is right that Nietzsche
was the last of the metaphysicians, a view implying a serious error of self-
evaluation on Nietzsche's part, or whether Nietzsche, as he thought, escaped
the snares of metaphysics as it had existed before him. It is suspiciously self-
serving that Heidegger's placement of Nietzsche as the last metaphysician

permits Heidegger to announce himself as the first nonmetaphysician, to give himself this privilege of placement. Further, it is not clear that Heidegger himself isn't in some sense a metaphysician with the doctrine of Being. Heidegger accepted that Nietzsche had shown that a Hegelian synoptic approach was fatally crippled. But Nietzsche stays within metaphysics for Heidegger because he provides only an account of existents, not an account of Being. Nietzsche places man among existents, and this is a metaphysical placement for Heidegger. Will to power is the description of the totality of existents, and the Eternal Return describes how that totality appears to one who becomes aware of it. The two doctrines thus bring together the two metaphysical ways of seeing existents—as fixed (Parmenides—Eternal Return) and as becoming (Heraclitus—will to power)—two ways of seeing existents whose dialectic has animated all metaphysics. Heidegger's reference point is directly to a philosophical dialectics, not to a suspension of Apollo and Dionysus that gradually takes on a philosophical form.

11. Derrida has had a kind of double career. In his early works, especially those on Husserl, Derrida reveals himself to be a powerful philosopher who provides a trenchant attack on the notion of phenomenological presence and who finds a way of suggesting that all dyadic and triadic logics of meaning, and all philosophical systems based on them, are in error. The effort to express these insights, however, runs into the difficulty that the language we use has itself been captured in terms of its structure by these logics of meaning. Hegel's impact here is enormous, since the Hegelian system seems capable of absorbing whatever can be expressed in words. The project of decentering authoritarian semantics must thus take place in the margins or folds of systematic discourse, by a prolix kind of double reading in which it is seen how the apparent securities and hierarchies of discourse are undermined by the power of what is repressed when they are established. In one sense, this is a strategy quite the opposite of the arrow or the aphorism; one keeps on talking until the system is led into unguarded observations. It is a mistake to suppose that Derrida is intending to propose a different system; that he privileges writing over speech, for example, in order to grasp linguistic meaning. Rather, Derrida establishes that speech is already a form of writing. Instead of writing representing absent speech, speech in the present allowing us to refer to what is present during the act of speech, speech itself contains inevitable reference to what is *not* present and is hence itself a form of writing—or even better, the elaboration of the distinction between speech and writing undermines that distinction. This is not Hegelian. The distinction is not synthesized; it is exposed as the consequence of an originary metaphor that has no ultimate defense. Derrida's second career relates to his writing and to his experimentalism in writing. His texts are often attempts to instance a nonsystematic style by unusual typographical displays (different columns being printed adjacent to one another), nongrammatical sentences, and so on. This side of Derrida has had a measurable influence on literary criticism. When Derrida's texts are adapted to purposes of literary criticism, they suggest that there is no ultimate distinction between philosophical and literary texts and that any text can be given an unlimited number of different readings, due to the instability of

reference. These straightforward assertions imply that there is a radical ambiguity and fissure in all texts.

For an incisive introduction to Derrida's relationship to Nietzsche (and Heidegger), see Behler, *Derrida-Nietzsche: Nietzsche-Derrida*, and "Apokalyptische Nietzsche-Interpretationen: Heidegger und Derrida."

12. Derrida, "The time of a thesis: punctuations," p. 46.

13. Derrida, *Spurs*, p. 37.

14. Nietzsche, in his essay on Strauss, objected that good style is always *translatable*. Can Derrida and Heidegger be successfully translated, and if not, does Nietzsche's opinion have to give way, or should we decide that Derrida and Heidegger write texts to which Nietzschean hermeneutics do not apply?

15. Derrida, *Spurs*, pp. 63–101. See also Oliver, "Woman as Truth," for a discussion.

16. This may rest on the dubious assumption that a self-perception of love appropriately excludes hate.

17. The umbrella fragment is not completely isolate when one remembers that Nietzsche received an umbrella as a present from his mother, who urged him not to forget it in the rain. See Kofman, "Baubô," p. 200 of the translation in *Nietzsche's New Seas*, ed. Gillespie and Strong.

Chapter 9. Power

1. The Übermensch is a prophetic fiction, possibly not a creature that could exist in the Dionysian flux, but an ideal type toward which humans can attempt to move. Life is breathed into the Übermensch in order to simplify discussion, so as not to have to say constantly that will to power suggests certain idealized strategies as asymptotic guides.

2. The textual basis is sufficiently and thoroughly discussed in Müller-Lauter, *Nietzsche*, and in Müller-Lauter, "Nietzsches Lehre vom Willen zur Macht."

3. See Müller-Lauter, *Nietzsche*. For some of the central texts, see *The Will to Power*, aphorisms 331, 556, 567, 634, 639, 656, 675, 678, 688, 692, 702, 711, and 1067. Müller-Lauter responds in "Nietzsches Lehre vom Willen zur Macht" to criticisms by Köster, "Die Problematik wissenschaftlicher Nietzsche-Interpretation," and by Weischedel, "Der Wille und die Willen."

4. There was no unified physics at the time for Nietzsche to refer to, and even today a lack of unified theories makes Nietzsche's intuition relevant to a consideration of the structure of science.

5. Nietzsche claims, in *Ecce Homo*, to have been more whole and unified than his contemporaries, but he merely *asserts* this; he could not explain or prove it. At best, he can suggest that his works *show* that fact.

6. It is worth remarking that Deleuze, who has wider explanatory ambitions in the discursive mode than Nietzsche had, must here introduce some special formulations and some special terminology, no matter how minimal. Deleuze attempts a complex interworking of Marx and Freud, heavily influenced by Nietzsche, in which capitalism appears as the great destroyer of the past and as a system in which altered and contracted time frames approach the outlook attributed by some commentaries to the Übermensch. Capitalism must be

affirmed, if everything is to be affirmed. The topic is bizarre and fascinating, but it loses touch with Deleuze's stricter attempts to read Nietzsche.

7. As noted elsewhere, Nietzsche's views of an inflexible science piling up settled facts is ensconced in a (correct) nineteenth-century conception of science. The current picture, allowing revolutions in science, permits a form of flexible scientific knowledge that assists a conceptual rapprochement between art and science, although the permanent mix of clashing scientific opinion still doesn't underwrite a Nietzschean unified strategy.

8. I owe this point, and many others, to perceptive comments by my longtime editor at the University of Massachusetts Press, Richard Martin. His constant enthusiasm for new ideas will be missed close to home.

9. See the elaboration of this point in Taureck, "Macht, und nicht Gewalt."

Chapter 10. Return

1. No proof of the Eternal Return as a cosmological fact could have explained its emotional power, or why rewilling was required whenever the thought occurred. Perhaps Nietzsche was only out to establish that the Eternal Return was compatible with what could be known by scientists; that's all he really required.

2. Danto, "The Eternal Recurrence."

3. See the discussion in Simmel, *Schopenhauer and Nietzsche*, pp. 170–79.

4. See Sterling, "Recent Discussions of Eternal Recurrence: Some Critical Comments."

5. Soll, "Reflections on Recurrence."

6. Zuboff, "Nietzsche and Eternal Recurrence."

7. Magnus, "Eternal Recurrence," discusses Sterling, "Recent Discussions," but relies on the discussion in his book, *Nietzsche's Existential Imperative*.

8. Humor collectors won't want to miss the opening quotation from Bertrand Russell (who sounds a lot like the Übermensch) at the start of Magnus's book.

9. Schacht, *Nietzsche*, pp. 253–66.

10. See Nietzsche's remarks on Heraclitus in his *Philosophy in the Tragic Age of the Greeks,* and also his remarks on Anaxagoras there, to which Schacht does not refer.

11. This central dichotomy is attached to all the considerations of the Eternal Return in Nietzsche. See, for example, the last few lines of the discussion in aphorism 341 of *The Gay Science.*

12. The other path from the failure of any cosmological proof is to return Nietzsche to metaphysics, a move that takes Nietzsche's Greek roots seriously, but must convict him of a fundamental failure to understand his own work. This path is nicely illustrated by Heidegger and his students. Heidegger felt that Nietzsche had not understood himself at all. For Heidegger, the doctrine of the Eternal Return is not provable—it just burst in on Nietzsche. This was not properly a subjective, existential turn; it is actually the revelation of Being in a thought that can be endlessly developed. On Heidegger's interpretation of Nietzsche, the sum total of the world, in all epochs, is chaos. (See aphorism 109 of *The Gay Science.*) The impact of this doctrine must either be

skepticism or its "forgetting," along with the adoption of a perspective or a worldview. What man is, is then forgotten as well. But Dionysian chaos is chaos only in terms of our everyday descriptive resources.

Nietzsche's conjectural proof is not scientific, as Heidegger observes. Heidegger thinks that the categories of the proof are metaphysical (equality, becoming, space, time, chaos, . . .). Science can measure these things, but cannot say what they are. This last, ontological task, is attempted by Nietzsche, but he remains crippled by a link to science. Nietzsche's development of the Eternal Return is actually a development of the human perspective, which includes the moment. It is a realization of the place of humans in the world, their temporal and spatial location, but not a full realization that this is the human perspective. But this is why the Eternal Return focuses inevitably on this world; that's all that can be found in the moment. What happens to freedom? Freedom is measured against causality as a temporal sequence with certain properties, but there is no temporal sequence in the Eternal Return; there is just the new (the same) appearance. The conceptual apparatus necessary to define "freedom" drops out. There is no time between moments. Thus the Eternal Return turns out itself to be a form of nihilism.

Stambaugh, a student of Heidegger's, interprets Nietzsche as remaining in the metaphysical tradition because he doesn't reject the notion of eternity. (See Stambaugh, *Nietzsche's Thought of Eternal Return*.) No thing is permanent in Nietzsche, but time is eternal. What does it mean to say that the same returns? Two shirts can be the same, i.e., two shirts can have all the same properties (size, style, etc.) but be numerically distinct. Nietzsche must have meant by *same* that each moment contains past, present, and future all together. The exact moment recurs, but not at different times; it just recurs. This is why "old" experiences (in the ordinary sense) can be reexperienced as totally new. (See *Zarathustra*, "The Convalescent," where this happens.) The disgust caused by the doctrine is that everything is alike, nothing is different, new, more worthwhile. The Eternal Return (nihilism) is forced on us by thinking through the inadequacies of the Platonic tradition in a way that cannot escape metaphysical presuppositions.

13. See Nehamas, "The Eternal Recurrence," or chapter 5 of *Nietzsche: Life as Literature*. For a discussion of Nehamas's book, see Ackermann, "Current American Thought on Nietzsche."

14. Strong, *Nietzsche and the Politics of Transfiguration*. A discussion between Nehamas and Strong on pages 473–94 of *Nietzsche-Studien* 12 (1983) is also relevant.

15. Various readers have been much more taken by Strong's analogy than this author. Apparently the author, who seems to fall harder while skiing than other philosophers, was wrong not to have laughed at his last concussion.

16. Klossowski's book on Nietzsche has not been translated, but a relevant section of it appears on pages 107–20 of Allison, *The New Nietzsche,* and on pages 138–49 of *Semiotexte*, "Nietzsche's Return." That these translations are quite different in places suggests the difficulty of the original.

17. For a discussion, see Descombes, *Modern French Philosophy,* pp. 182–84.

18. See aphorism 56 of *Beyond Good and Evil* for a text that explicitly avoids

mention of a future that has already occurred. For a text suggesting that the return is conscious for Nietzsche, but was conceptually latent for the Greeks, see *Kritische Gesamtausgabe,* ed. Colli and Montinari, IV₁, p. 119.

19. See Deleuze, *Nietzsche and Philosophy,* esp. pp. 39–72. The Würzbach selection from *Nachlass,* titled *Umwertung aller Werte,* is not the same as the selection translated as *The Will to Power* by Kaufmann and Hollingdale. Deleuze relies on some aphorisms (312, 322, 323, 324, 329, 330) in the Würzbach selection that are not available in the English translation.

20. It is a Hellenic notion that doubles should multiply in times of crisis. See the discussion of doubles in Girard, *Violence and the Sacred.*

Bibliography

Nietzsche's Works

German Editions

Werke: Kritische Gesamtausgabe. Edited by Giorgio Colli and Mazzino Montinari. 30 vols. Berlin: Walter de Gruyter, 1967–78. This replaces all earlier German language editions for completeness and accuracy. *Kritische Studienausgabe in 15 Bänden* (1980) is a somewhat shortened version of the same texts.

English Translations Cited in the Text

The Antichrist. Translated by Walter Kaufmann. In *The Portable Nietzsche*, edited by Walter Kaufmann, pp. 565–656. Harmondsworth: Penguin Books, 1983.

Beyond Good and Evil. Translated by Walter Kaufmann. In *Basic Writings of Nietzsche*, edited by Walter Kaufmann, pp. 179–435. New York: Random House, 1968.

The Birth of Tragedy. Translated by Walter Kaufmann. In *Basic Writings of Nietzsche*, pp. 1–144. See *Beyond Good and Evil.*

Daybreak. Translated by R. J. Hollingdale. Cambridge: Cambridge University Press, 1982.

Ecce Homo. Translated by Walter Kaufmann. In *Basic Writings of Nietzsche*, pp. 655–791. See *Beyond Good and Evil.*

The Gay Science. Translated by Walter Kaufmann. New York: Vintage Books, 1968.

Human, All Too Human. Translated by Marion Faber and Stephen Lehmann. Lincoln: University of Nebraska Press, 1984.

On the Genealogy of Morals. Translated by Walter Kaufmann. In *Basic Writings of Nietzsche*, pp. 437–599. See *Beyond Good and Evil.*

Philosophy in the Tragic Age of the Greeks. Translated by Marianne Cowan. South Bend, Ind.: Gateway, 1962.

Thus Spoke Zarathustra. Translated by Walter Kaufmann. In *The Portable Nietzsche,* pp. 103–439. See *The Antichrist.*

Twilight of the Idols. Translated by Walter Kaufmann. In *The Portable Nietzsche,* pp. 463–563. See *The Antichrist.*

Untimely Meditations. Translated by R. J. Hollingdale. Cambridge: Cambridge University Press, 1983.

The Will to Power. Translated by Walter Kaufmann and R. J. Hollingdale. New York: Vintage Books, 1968.

Other Works Cited in the Text

Ackermann, Robert. "Current American Thought on Nietzsche." In *Nietzsche heute,* edited by Sigrid Bauschinger, Susan Cocalis, and Sara Lennox, pp. 129–36. Bern: Francke, 1988.

———. *The Philosophy of Karl Popper.* Amherst: University of Massachusetts Press, 1976.

———. *Religion as Critique.* Amherst: University of Massachusetts Press, 1985.

Adorno, Theodor. *The Jargon of Authenticity.* Translated by Knut Tarnowski and Frederic Will. Evanston: Northwestern University Press, 1973. (German original, 1964)

———. *Minima Moralia.* Translated by E. F. N. Jephcott. London: New Left Books, 1974. (German original, 1951)

Adorno, Theodor, and Max Horkheimer. *Dialectic of Enlightenment.* Translated by J. Cumming. New York: Herder and Herder, 1969. (German original, 1944)

Allison, David, ed. *The New Nietzsche.* New York: Dell Publishing, 1977.

Andreas-Salomé, Lou. *Friedrich Nietzsche in seinen Werken.* Frankfurt am Main: Insel, 1983. (German original, 1894)

Argyros, Alexander. "Daughters of the Desert." *Diacritics* 10 (1980): 27–36.

Baeumer, Max. "Das moderne Phänomen des Dionysischen und seine 'Entdeckung' durch Nietzsche." *Nietzsche-Studien* 6 (1977): 123–53.

Baier, Horst. "Die Gesellschaft—ein langer Schatten des toten Gottes. Friedrich Nietzsche und die Entstehung der Soziologie aus dem Geist der Decadence." *Nietzsche-Studien* 10/11 (1981/1982): 6–22.

Behler, Ernst. "Apokalyptische Nietzsche-Interpretationen: Heidegger und Derrida." In *Nietzsche heute,* pp. 105–28. *See* Ackermann, "Current American Thought."

———. *Derrida-Nietzsche: Nietzsche-Derrida.* München: Ferdinand Schöningh, 1988.

———. "Nietzsche in der marxistische Kritik Osteuropas." *Nietzsche-Studien* 10/11 (1981/1982): 80–96.

Bellone, Enrico. *A World on Paper.* Translated by Mirella Giacconi and Riccardo Giacconi. Cambridge: MIT Press, 1980. (Italian original, 1976)

Bergmann, Peter. *Nietzsche, "the Last Antipolitical German."* Bloomington: Indiana University Press, 1987.

Birus, Hendrik. "Nietzsche's Hermeneutical Considerations." In *Nietzsche: Literature and Values,* edited by Volker Dürr, Reinhold Grimm, and Kathy Harms, pp. 66–80. Madison: University of Wisconsin Press, 1988.

Bowker, John. *Problems of Suffering in Religions of the World*. Cambridge: Cambridge University Press, 1970.

Breazeale, Daniel. "The Hegel-Nietzsche Problem." *Nietzsche-Studien* 4 (1975): 146–64.

Brennecke, Detlef. "Die blonde Bestie. Vom Mißverständnis eines Schlagworts." *Nietzsche-Studien* 5 (1976): 113–45.

Butler, Eliza. *The Tyranny of Greece Over Germany*. Boston: Beacon Press, 1958. (Original edition, 1935)

Cooper, David. *Authenticity and Learning: Nietzsche's Educational Philosophy*. London: Routledge and Kegan Paul, 1983.

Dannhauser, Werner. *Nietzsche's View of Socrates*. Ithaca: Cornell University Press, 1974.

———. "The Trivialization of Friedrich Nietzsche." *The American Spectator* 15 (May 1982): 7–13.

Danto, Arthur. "The Eternal Recurrence." In *Nietzsche*, pp. 316–21. *See* Solomon.

———. *Nietzsche as Philosopher*. New York: Macmillan, 1965.

Darnoi, Dennis. *The Unconscious and Eduard von Hartmann*. The Hague: Martinus Nijhoff, 1967.

Deleuze, Gilles. *Nietzsche and Philosophy*. Translated by Hugh Tomlinson. New York: Columbia University Press, 1983. (French original, 1962)

Derrida, Jacques. "Cogito and the History of Madness." In Derrida, *Writing and Difference*, pp. 31–63. Chicago: University of Chicago Press, 1978. (French original, 1967)

———. *Spurs: Nietzsche's Styles*. Translated by Barbara Harlow. Chicago: University of Chicago Press, 1978. (French original, 1972)

———. "The time of a thesis: punctuations." In *Philosophy in France Today*, edited by Alan Montefiore, pp. 34–50. Cambridge: Cambridge University Press, 1983. (French original, 1980)

Descombes, Vincent. *Modern French Philosophy*. Translated by L. Scott-Fox and J. M. Harding. Cambridge: Cambridge University Press, 1980. (French original, 1979)

Dodds, Eric. *The Greeks and the Irrational*. Boston: Beacon Press, 1957. (Original edition, 1951)

Eden, Robert. *Political Leadership and Nihilism*. Tampa: University of South Florida Press, 1984.

———. Review of *Beyond Nihilism*, by Ofelia Schutte. *Political Theory* 12 (1984): 611–15.

———. "To What Extent Has the World of Concern to Contemporary Man Been Created by Nietzschean Politics?" In *Nietzsche heute*, pp. 211–26. *See* Ackermann, "Current American Thought."

Ehrlich, Edith. "Suffering in Nietzsche: Motive and Mask." Ph.D. diss., University of Massachusetts, Amherst, 1975.

Fischer, Kurt. Review of *Nietzsche as Philosopher*, by Arthur Danto. *Journal of Philosophy* 64 (1967): 564–69.

Flashar, Helmut, Karlfried Gründer, and Axel Horstmann, eds., *Philologie und Hermeneutik im 19. Jahrhundert*. Göttingen: Vandenhoeck and Ruprecht, 1979.

Foot, Philippa. "Nietzsche: The Revaluation of Values." In *Nietzsche,* pp. 156–68. *See* Solomon.

Foucault, Michel. *I, Pierre Rivière, having slaughtered my mother, my sister, and my brother . . . : A Case of Parricide in the Nineteenth Century.* Translated by Frank Jellinek. New York: Pantheon, 1975. (French original, technically a collaborative effort, 1973)

———. *Language, Counter-Memory, Practice: Selected Essays and Interviews.* Edited by Donald F. Bouchard. Translated by Donald F. Bouchard and Sherry Simon. Ithaca: Cornell University Press, 1977.

———. *Madness and Civilization.* Translated by Richard Howard. New York: Vintage Books, 1973. (Foucault's reply to Derrida's "Cogito and the History of Madness" appears as an appendix to the Gallimard edition of 1972. It is not translated here, but can be found as "My Body, This Paper, This Fire," translated by Geoff Bennington, in *Oxford Literary Review* 4 (1979): 9–28.)

———. "Nietzsche, Genealogy, History." In Foucault, *Language, Counter-Memory, Practice: Selected Essays and Interviews,* pp. 139–64 (see above).

———. *The Order of Things: An Archaeology of the Human Sciences.* Translated by Alan Sheridan-Smith. New York: Random House, 1970. (French original, 1966)

Gadamer, Hans-Georg. "The Drama of Zarathustra." Translated by Thomas Heilke. In *Nietzsche's New Seas,* edited by Michael Gillespie and Tracy Strong, pp. 220–31. Chicago: University of Chicago Press, 1988. (German original in *Nietzsche-Studien* 15 (1986): 1–15)

———. *Truth and Method.* No translator given. New York: Continuum, 1975. (German original, 1960)

Gans, Eric. "The Culture of Resentment." *Philosophy and Literature* 8 (1984): 55–66.

Garland, Henry, and Mary Garland. *The Oxford Companion to German Literature.* Oxford: Clarendon Press, 1976.

Girard, René. "Dionysus versus the Crucified." *MLN* 99 (1984): pp. 816–35.

———. *Violence and the Sacred.* Translated by Patrick Gregory. Baltimore: The Johns Hopkins University Press, 1977. (French original, 1972)

Goedert, Georges. "Nietzsche und Schopenhauer." *Nietzsche-Studien* 7 (1977): 1–15.

Grau, Gerd-Günther. "Nietzsche und Kierkegaard: Wiederholung einer unzeitgemässen Betrachtung." *Nietzsche-Studien* 1 (1972): 297–333.

Grundlehner, Philip. *The Poetry of Friedrich Nietzsche.* Oxford: Oxford University Press, 1986.

Habermas, Jürgen. *Knowledge and Human Interests.* Translated by Jeremy J. Shapiro. Boston: Beacon Press, 1971. (German original, 1968)

———. *The Philosophical Discourse of Modernity.* Translated by Frederick Lawrence. Cambridge: MIT Press, 1987. (German original, 1985)

Hartmann, Eduard von. *Philosophy of the Unconscious.* 3 vols. New York: Macmillan, 1884. (German original, 1867)

———. *The Sexes Compared.* Essays translated by A. Kenner. (No first name given; the name might be a joke.) London: Swan Sonnenschein, 1895.

Heidegger, Martin. *Being and Time.* Translated by John Macquarrie and Edward Robinson. New York: Harper and Row, 1962. (German original, 1927)

———. *Nietzsche.* 4 vols. Translated by David Krell. New York: Harper and Row, 1979–1987. (This translates most of the German original of 1961. See notes in the translation for the location of other translated essays from the original.)

Heller, Peter. "Nietzsche and the Jews." In *Nietzsche heute,* pp. 149–60. *See* Ackermann, "Current American Thought."

Higgins, Kathleen. *Nietzsche's Zarathustra.* Philadelphia: Temple University Press, 1987.

Horkheimer, Max. "The End of Reason." In *The Essential Frankfurt School Reader,* edited by Andrew Arato and Eike Gebhardt, pp. 26–48. New York: Urizen Books, 1978. (Originally in *Studies in Philosophy and Social Sciences* 4 (1941): 366–88)

Houlgate, Stephen. *Hegel, Nietzsche, and the Criticism of Metaphysics.* Cambridge: Cambridge University Press, 1986.

Ijsseling, Samuel. *Rhetoric and Philosophy in Conflict: An Historical Survey.* The Hague: Martinus Nijhoff, 1976.

Jaynes, Julian. *The Origin of Consciousness in the Breakdown of the Bicameral Mind.* Boston: Houghton Mifflin Co., 1977.

Kaulbach, Friedrich. "Nietzsche und der monadologische Gedanke." *Nietzsche-Studien* 8 (1979): 127–56.

———. *Nietzsches Idee einer Experimentalphilosophie.* Köln: Böhlau, 1980.

Kierkegaard, Søren. *The Concept of Irony.* Translated by Lee M. Capel. Bloomington: Indiana University Press, 1965. (Danish original, 1841)

Klossowski, Pierre. *Nietzsche et le cercle vicieux.* Paris: Mercure, 1969. (One section is translated in *The New Nietzsche,* pp. 107–20 [*see* Allison] and in *Semiotexte* 3, no. 1 [1978]: 138–49, "Nietzsche's Return.")

Köster, Peter. "Die Problematik wissenschaftlicher Nietzsche-Interpretation: Kritische Überlegungen zu Wolfgang Müller-Lauters Nietzschebuch." *Nietzsche-Studien* 2 (1973): 31–60.

Kofman, Sarah. "Baubô: Theological Perversion and Fetishism." Translated by Tracy Strong. In *Nietzsche's New Seas,* pp. 175–202. *See* Gadamer. (French original, 1979)

Koigen, David. *Die Kulturanschauung des Sozialismus.* Berlin, 1903. (See review by Ferdinand Tönnies in his *Soziologische Studien und Kritiken,* Jena: G. Fischer, 1925–1929, vol. 3, pp. 410–13.)

Krüger, Heinz. *Studien über den Aphorismus als philosophische Form.* Frankfurt am Main: Nest, 1957.

Kuhn, Thomas. *The Structure of Scientific Revolutions.* Chicago: University of Chicago Press, 1970.

Lacan, Jacques. *Speech and Language in Psychoanalysis.* Translated, with notes and commentary, by Anthony Wilden. Baltimore: The Johns Hopkins University Press, 1968.

Lampert, Laurence. *Nietzsche's Teaching: An Interpretation of "Thus Spoke Zarathustra."* New Haven: Yale University Press, 1986.

Löwith, Karl. *Nietzsches Philosophie der ewigen Wiederkehr des Gleichen.* Stuttgart: Kohlhammer, 1956. (Original edition, 1935)

Luckmann, Thomas. *The Invisible Religion.* New York: Macmillan, 1967. (German original, 1963)

Luft, Eric von der. "Sources of Nietzsche's 'God is Dead!' and Its Meaning for Heidegger." *Journal of the History of Ideas* 45 (1984): 263–76.

Lukács, Georg. *The Destruction of Reason.* Translated by Peter Palmer. Atlantic Highlands, N.J.: Humanities Press, 1981. (Hungarian original, 1953)

MacIntyre, Alasdair. "Nietzsche's Titanism." *Encounter* 32 (April 1969): 79–82. (A discussion follows in subsequent issues.)

Magnus, Bernd. "Eternal Recurrence." *Nietzsche-Studien* 8 (1979): 362–77.

———. *Nietzsche's Existential Imperative.* Bloomington: Indiana University Press, 1978.

Mattenklott, Gert. "Nietzsches 'Geburt der Tragödie' als Konzept einer bürgerlichen Kulturrevolution." In *Positionen der literarischen Intelligenz zwischen Reaktion und Imperialismus,* edited by Gert Mattenklott and Klaus Scherpe, pp. 103–22. Kronberg: Scriptor, 1973.

Miller, James. "Some Implications of Nietzsche's Thought for Marxism." *Telos,* no. 37 (Fall 1978): 22–41.

Mitchell, John. "Grounds and Foundations of a Social Theory in Nietzsche's Philosophy." Ph.D. diss., University of Montreal, 1978.

Müller-Lauter, Wolfgang. "Das Willenswesen und der Übermensch: Ein Beitrag zu Heideggers Nietzsche-Interpretationen." *Nietzsche-Studien* 10/11 (1981/1982): 132–77.

———. *Nietzsche: Seine Philosophie der Gegensätze und die Gegensätze seiner Philosophie.* Berlin: Walter de Gruyter, 1971.

———. "Nietzsches Lehre vom Willen zur Macht." *Nietzsche-Studien* 3 (1974): 1–60.

Nehamas, Alexander. "The Eternal Recurrence." *Philosophical Review* 84 (1980): 331–56.

———. "Immanent and Transcendent Perspectivism in Nietzsche." *Nietzsche-Studien* 12 (1983): 473–90.

———. *Nietzsche: Life as Literature.* Cambridge: Harvard University Press, 1985.

Nelson, Donald. "Nietzsche, Zarathustra, and *Jesus Redivivus:* The Unholy Trinity." *Germanic Review* 48 (1973): 175–88.

Nordau, Max. *Degeneration.* 4th edition. New York: Appleton, 1895.

O'Flaherty, James, Timothy Sellner, and Robert Helm, eds. *Studies in Nietzsche and the Classical Tradition.* Chapel Hill: University of North Carolina Press, 1976.

Oliver, Kelly. "Woman as Truth in Nietzsche's Writing." *Social Theory and Practice* 10 (1984): 185–99.

Parsons, Kathryn. "Nietzsche and Moral Change." In *Nietzsche,* pp. 169–93. *See* Solomon.

Pütz, Peter. "The Problem of Force in Nietzsche and His Critics." In *Nietzsche: Literature and Values,* pp. 14–28. *See* Birus.

Rahden, Wolfert von. "Eduard von Hartmann und Nietzsche. Zur Strategie der verzögerten Konterkritik Hartmanns an Nietzsche." *Nietzsche-Studien* 13 (1984): 481–502.

Rée, Paul. *Der Ursprung der moralischen Empfindungen.* Chemnitz, 1877.

———. *Die Entstehung des Gewissens.* Berlin: Carl Duncker, 1885.

Reinhardt, Karl. *Vermächtnis der Antike.* Essays, collected by Carl Becker. Gottingen: Vandenhoeck and Ruprecht, 1966.

Rose, Gillian. *The Melancholy Science.* New York: Columbia University Press, 1978.

Salomé, Lou. *Friedrich Nietzsche: The Man in His Works.* Redding Ridge, Conn.: Black Swan Books, 1988. An edited translation by Siegfried Mandel of Lou Andreas-Salomé's *Friedrich Nietzsche in seinen Werken.*

Schacht, Richard. *Nietzsche.* Boston: Routledge and Kegan Paul, 1983.

Scheler, Max. *Ressentiment.* Translated by William Holdheim. New York: Schocken Books, 1972. (German original, 1915)

Schlecta, Karl. *Nietzsches Grosser Mittag.* Frankfurt am Main: Klostermann, 1954.

Schopenhauer, Arthur. *Studies in Pessimism.* No translator given. New York: Boni and Liveright, Modern Library Edition, n.d. [early 1920s].

Schulte, Gunter. *"Ich impfe euch mit dem Wahnsinn."* Frankfurt am Main: Qumran, 1982.

Schutte, Ofelia. *Beyond Nihilism: Nietzsche without Masks.* Chicago: University of Chicago Press, 1984.

Shapiro, Gary. "The Rhetoric of Nietzsche's *Zarathustra.*" *Boundary* 2 8 (1980): 165–89.

Shapiro, William. "The Nietzschean Roots of Max Weber's Social Science." Ph.D. diss., Cornell University, 1978.

Simmel, Georg. *Schopenhauer and Nietzsche.* Translated by Helmut Loiskandl, Deena Weinstein, and Michael Weinstein. Amherst: University of Massachusetts Press, 1986. (German original, 1907)

Soll, Ivan. "Reflections on Recurrence: A Re-examination of Nietzsche's Doctrine, *Die ewige Wiederkehr des Gleichen.*" In *Nietzsche,* pp. 323–42. *See* Solomon.

Solomon, Robert, ed. *Nietzsche: A Collection of Critical Essays.* Garden City, N.Y.: Doubleday, 1973.

Stambaugh, Joan. *Nietzsche's Thought of Eternal Return.* Baltimore: The Johns Hopkins University Press, 1972.

Sterling, Marvin. "Recent Discussions of Eternal Recurrence: Some Critical Comments." *Nietzsche-Studien* 6 (1977): 261–91

Strauss, David. *The Life of Jesus.* St. Clair Shores, Mich.: Scholarly Press, 1970. (German original, 1835/1836; many subsequent editions)

Strong, Tracy. "Comment." (On Nehamas.) *Nietzsche-Studien* 12 (1983): 491–94.

———. *Friedrich Nietzsche and the Politics of Transfiguration.* Berkeley: University of California Press, 1975.

Taureck, Bernhard. "Macht, und nicht Gewalt. Ein anderer Weg zum Verständnis Nietzsches." *Nietzsche-Studien* 5 (1976): 29–54.

Thomas, Richard. *Nietzsche in German Politics and Society 1890–1918*. Manchester: Manchester University Press, 1983.

Tönnies, Ferdinand. *Soziologische Studien und Kritiken*. 3 vols. Jena: G. Fischer, 1925–1929.

Vogel, Martin *Apollinisch und Dionysisch*. Regensburg: Gustav Bosse, 1966.

Waite, Geoffrey. "Zarathustra or the Modern Prince: The Problem of Nietzschean Political Philosophy." In *Nietzsche heute*, pp. 227–50. *See* Ackermann, "Current American Thought."

Weischedel, Wilhelm. "Der Wille und die Willen." *Zeitschrift für philosophische Forshung* 27 (1973): 71–76.

Wilamowitz-Moellendorff, Ulrich von. *History of Classical Scholarship*. Translated by Alan Harris. Baltimore: The Johns Hopkins University Press, 1982. (German original, 1921)

Wilde, Oscar. *The Artist as Critic*. Edited by Richard Ellman. Chicago: University of Chicago Press, 1982.

Würzbach, Friedrich. *Umwertung aller Werte*. München: DTV, 1977.

Zuboff, Arnold. "Nietzsche and Eternal Recurrence." In *Nietzsche*, pp. 343–57. *See* Solomon.

Index